JENNIFER SERRAVALLO

New York Times best-selling author of *The Reading Strategies Book*

Understanding Texts & Readers

Responsive Comprehension Instruction with Leveled Texts

HEINEMANN
Portsmouth, NH

Heinemann
361 Hanover Street
Portsmouth, NH 03801–3912
www.heinemann.com

Offices and agents throughout the world

© 2018 by Jennifer Serravallo

A Note About Text Levels Assigned to Childrens Books

This book includes discussion of a variety of quantitative and qualitative text leveling systems (i.e., DRA, Fountas and Pinnell Text Level Gradient™, Reading Recovery, Lexile, and more). For the purposes of consistency, all children's books I write about in *Understanding Texts & Readers* were checked through www.fountasandpinnellleveledbooks.com. Their leveling system is used by others across other leveling sites and apps, but the website is the only official source. Some books mentioned in *Understanding Texts & Readers* did not appear in the database at all, and in those cases I approximated the levels based on the text characteristics identified by Fountas and Pinnell in their many publications, including *The Literacy Continuum*. If you use another leveling source, or rely on a different leveling system without an official source, you may find discrepancies across different sites and apps.

As you read the book, you'll learn that leveling is not a perfect science. The level assigned to a specific book can sometimes change based on new thinking by experts. It's crucial to build your knowledge about texts and become comfortable forming your own judgments about the books you offer your readers. I hope *Understanding Texts & Readers* helps you do just that.

The author and publisher wish to thank those who have generously given permission to reprint borrowed material:

Hierarchy of Reading Goals from *The Reading Strategies Book* by Jennifer Serravallo. Copyright © 2015 by Jennifer Serravallo. Published by Heinemann, Portsmouth, NH. All rights reserved.

Credits continue on page x.

Cataloging-in-Publication Data is on file at the Library of Congress.
ISBN: 978-0-325-10892-6

Editor: Zoë Ryder White
Production: Victoria Merecki
Cover and text designs: Suzanne Heiser
Front cover art: © Maxchered / Getty Images
Photography: Nicholas Christoff and Michelle Baker
Typesetter: Gina Poirier, Gina Poirier Design
Manufacturing: Steve Bernier

Printed in the United States of America on acid-free paper
22 21 20 19 18 VP 1 2 3 4 5

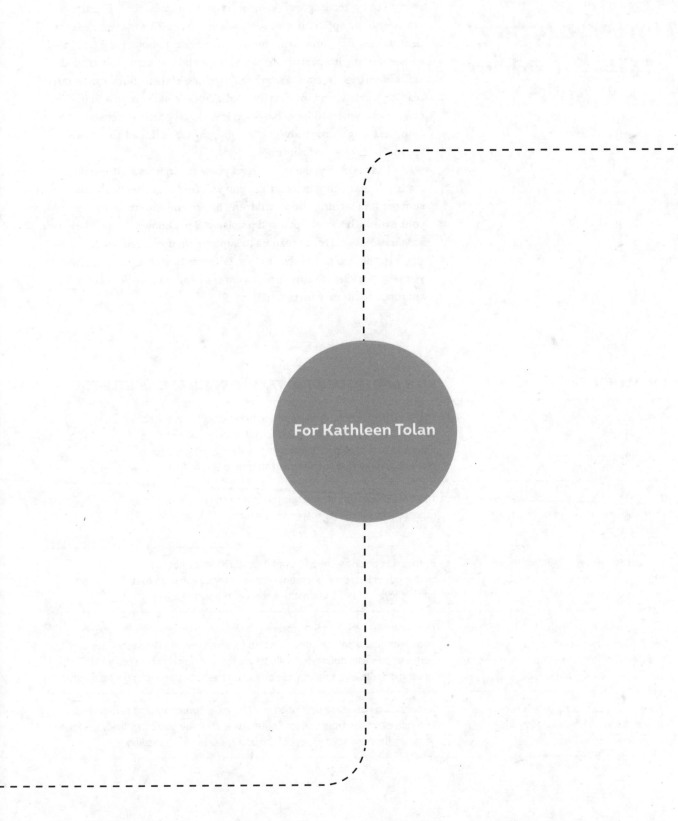

For Kathleen Tolan

How Understanding Texts & Readers Can Help

My preferred framework for reading instruction is balanced literacy, with a strong reading workshop at its core. In classrooms like these, teachers offer opportunities for students to practice reading independently every day; some time for kids to work collaboratively and in conversation with partnerships and book clubs; instruction around skills identified in standards through whole-class minilessons, shared reading lessons, and interactive read-alouds; small-group and one-on-one lessons with students based on individual goals; and instruction using a strong word study/phonics program. You'll read about this approach throughout this book.

That said, if you or the school you work in uses a different approach to reading instruction, you will find that this book offers you support for learning about children's books and the students under your care with more depth and precision. This knowledge will help you as you assess and teach readers to support their comprehension.

In the two tables that follow, I discuss how this book can help you with various reading instruction challenges regardless of your approach to literacy instruction.

CHALLENGE	HOW *UNDERSTANDING TEXTS & READERS* CAN HELP YOU
Leveled texts are misunderstood.	This book helps position levels where they belong: as a teacher's tool, not as a label for kids. This book will show you *how* to use them as a tool to help with assessment, identifying goals for readers, and figuring out which strategies to teach.
It can be hard to confer with readers when you haven't read the book the student is reading.	This book shows you how to use text characteristics and expectations for reader response to inform your instruction.
If you use guided reading, for it to be most effective, it needs to be about teaching the *reader*, not just the *book*.	By focusing on characteristics of texts, you'll learn what to focus on during guided reading lessons, what strategies will work best for that level of text, and what to expect of reader response.
Comprehension can feel nebulous. It's one thing to identify that kids aren't "getting it" but harder for you to put your finger on what skills, exactly, you should teach.	This book relies on the same goals as *The Reading Strategies Book* which so many have found help to clarify what to focus on and where to start. Student work samples with annotated callouts clearly and quickly show you what "getting it" looks like, even if you don't know the book the student is reading.
Other guides to text complexity are filled with hard-to-understand terminology, and can make it all feel just . . . complex.	Text characteristics are described in short, easy-to-understand paragraphs with rich examples from children's literature. This way, you can quickly get a handle on what to expect of the books students are reading.

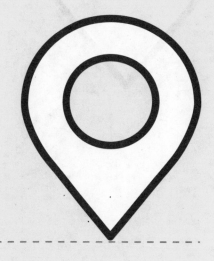

LITERACY FRAMEWORK	HOW *UNDERSTANDING TEXTS & READERS* CAN HELP YOU
Guided Reading	Guided reading is most effective when instruction focuses on what readers need and when you provide help for students as they navigate texts at their instructional level. This book will help you better understand how to identify comprehension skills that students need and how to make strategies transferrable.
Basal Reader/Anthology	Most reading textbooks include reading passages from a wide range of text levels although the book is purported to be for a single grade level. In addition, it's not always the case that texts increase in complexity as the year progresses. In this book, you can learn about text complexity and use that to better understand the level, and therefore the characteristics, of the texts that the students are reading. This will help you anticipate the kinds of challenges that will need to be scaffolded for readers and the strategies to teach.
Reading Workshop *or* Independent Reading *or* Daily 5™/CAFE	The heart of the reading workshop is independent reading with conferring and small-group instruction. This teaching is most powerful when it is responsive and goal-focused. This book will help you to find the right comprehension goals for readers, by using one of the various comprehension assessments described in the book and/or by using the skill progressions to identify student strengths and needs in the books they are reading. When students are reading books that you haven't read, especially at higher elementary and middle school levels, you can feel uncertain that you are choosing the right things to teach. The skill progressions and sample student work, with generalizable "look-fors," offered in this book will help you feel more sure-footed in conversations with readers, even when you haven't read the book they are reading.

Contents

Acknowledgments

I am endlessly grateful to my thought community at the Teachers College Reading and Writing Project. Even though I haven't worked closely with this community for about six years, the eight years I spent at the Project learning alongside the brilliant minds there will stay with me for my whole life, and my community will be with me with every word I write and speak. Lucy Calkins' mentorship and encouragement made me into the author and teacher I am today. The late Kathleen Tolan, who led the upper-grade reading work at the Project, was a true innovator who challenged all of us to outgrow ourselves, improve our teaching, and always advocate for children. Her words and wisdom live with me every day, and I miss her terribly.

A fraction of this book's raw material was culled from two previous publications—*Independent Reading Assessment: Fiction* and *Independent Reading Assessment: Nonfiction*—where I first described my thinking around comprehension skill progressions and text complexity. Deep thanks to the Scholastic editorial team who worked with me on that project from 2011 to 2013: Sarah Longhi, Wendy Murray, and Lynne Wilson.

This work would not be in your hands today were it not for the vision and tenacity of Vicki Boyd at Heinemann. Double rainbows to you, my friend. The great care my wonderful editor Zoë White showed to the manuscript in its final months before publication fulfilled my hopes and dreams. This book wouldn't be half as good without her critical edits and suggestions. Thanks also to the rest of the Heinemann team for the breathtaking design, amazing editorial coordination, and whip-smart marketing: Suzanne Heiser; Victoria Merecki; Catrina Marshall; Eric Chalek, Elizabeth Silvis, and team; Sherry Day, Michael Grover, and Dennis Doyle; and Brett Whitmarsh and team.

Thank you to my talented colleagues who read early versions of part or all of the book and provided me with invaluable feedback, which informed dramatic revisions: Berit Gordon, Mary Howard, Adria Klein, Clare Landrigan, Tammy Mulligan, and Franki Sibberson.

Thank you to Mercy Chang; the North Brunswick, New Jersey, School District; and teachers Nicole Stewart, Cassandra Maneri, and Emily (Szczerba) Angeles for allowing photographers and me into your classrooms. We are lucky to have images of your engaged, thoughtful students fill the pages of this book. Thank you to Kelly Boyle, Merridy Gnagey, Barb Golub, and Lauren Knoke for donating classroom charts featured in this book.

Finally, and perhaps most importantly, thanks to my family.

Understanding
Texts & Readers

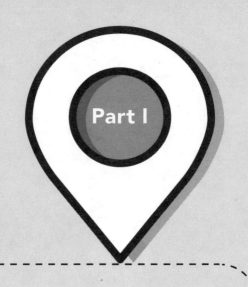

Part I

Readers, Texts, and Levels—and What It All Means for Comprehension

I met Vanessa in her fourth-grade classroom. Press-on nails. Rainbow-striped hoodie. Glasses. A glowing smile. The first time I talked with her about a book, she was halfway through *Rules* by Cynthia Lord. I wasn't her teacher; I was a visiting staff developer, fortunate to work with the dedicated teachers in her South Bronx school. The focus of our professional learning was to improve our understanding of the readers in the class and, from there, offer them targeted, specific goals and strategies to support their comprehension growth. Vanessa came up during our prelab site meeting as a student who puzzled her teacher, a student she wanted me to work with in the classroom as an audience of teachers observed.

Vanessa's background was challenging: this wasn't her first time in fourth grade. In fact, she'd been retained for two years in a row for not being able to pass the state test (the New York State ELA exam). That's heartbreaking enough, but what concerned her teacher even more was that she wasn't quite sure what she should be doing to help Vanessa grow as a reader. Her teacher had administered their school-sanctioned running records, and according to that assessment, Vanessa could read texts at Level R with fluency, accuracy, and comprehension.

For the running record, Vanessa read a 200-word excerpt from a novel and did well: 100 percent accuracy, strong fluency, correct responses to the comprehension questions. Level R texts, incidentally, are typically what fourth graders read between November and March. So, according to that measure, she was "on grade level." The running record, intended to be a formative assessment, offered her teacher little direction because Vanessa did so well. Yet, her teacher reasoned, she must need *some* support because she was not passing her state tests: tests that were written on a fourth-grade level, tests that asked her to demonstrate comprehension.

What is going on? we all wondered.

Around the same time I met Vanessa, I was involved in a professional learning group at the Teachers College Reading and Writing Project. We were studying how to track student comprehension across whole, continuous chapter books. With these collegial conversations fresh in my mind, I wondered if the short-passage assessment Vanessa's teacher had used wasn't giving us all the information we needed to match Vanessa to texts and to appropriate goals. To test my theory, I created whole-book assessments for Vanessa and her peers.

I decided these whole-book assessments would be most helpful beginning with books at Level J, because that was the level at which students were

Vanessa
Book: Rules, p. 1–2

✓✓✓/✓✓✓✓✓/✓✓✓
✓/✓✓✓/✓✓✓✓✓/
✓✓✓✓✓✓✓/✓✓✓
✓✓✓✓✓✓/ ← changed voice for dialogue.
✓✓✓✓✓/✓✓/✓✓✓✓
✓✓✓✓✓/✓✓✓
✓✓✓✓✓✓✓/
✓✓ ✓✓/✓–✓✓✓✓/
✓✓✓✓✓✓✓/
✓/✓✓ ✓✓✓✓✓
✓✓/ ← used expression
✓✓✓/✓✓/✓✓✓✓✓/
✓✓✓
✓✓✓✓✓

Retelling:
The narrator is trying to get David to get ready to go somewhere. It's the start of vacation. It's not raining but for some reason David wants his umbrella. David is her brother

Q.1 – where are they going?
– A clinic
Q.2 – Why does D like the video store?
– previews, reading all the boxes
Q.3 – How does she feel about David?
– embarrassed?
Q.4 – Ideas about her?
– mother-like.

Vanessa's teacher used a running record to learn how Vanessa reads 200 words aloud. As she read, her teacher took notes on her accuracy and fluency. After reading, Vanessa retold the text and answered four questions—two literal and two inferential.

being asked to read excerpts, rather than whole books, during their running record assessments. With the books getting longer beginning at Level J, I was curious how the length impacted student comprehension. I read a few books at the level, selected two that I thought represented the sorts of challenges readers are likely to encounter at that level, then repeated the process at Levels K, L, M, N . . . all the way up to W. I stopped at W (well into the sixth-grade benchmark) because I feel that children who are reading at Level W with depth can often work with more challenging levels flexibly. I wove about a dozen open-ended prompts into two books at each level and planned to offer the student a choice of texts. The prompts were designed to help me understand how the reader made sense of plot, setting, characters, vocabulary, figurative language, themes, and ideas.

I asked Vanessa to select between the two book choices at Level R because that was the level she had been reading. She did. I told her that as she read the book independently, she would come upon ten-or-so sticky notes with prompts, and that when she did, she should stop and jot a response. It took her a couple of days to finish the book and turn in her responses. I promptly read them with the teacher team at the school. Unfortunately, we discovered, none of Vanessa's responses were correct.

How was it, we started to wonder, *that a student could appear to comprehend a certain level of text when presented with a 200-word excerpt, and yet, when she tried to read an entire book at that same level, she struggled with comprehension?*

We repeated this procedure (gave her a choice of two texts, asked her to read the book independently and respond to the prompts) with texts at Level Q. Then P. Then O. Then N. Vanessa read the whole book independently, answered questions, and responded to prompts. We looked at her responses and found she was barely getting the gist. It wasn't until we saw her responses to a text at Level M, *Stuart Goes to School* by Sara Pennypacker, that we found what we thought was a level of text that she could read with comprehension during independent reading. For this book, she answered two-thirds of the questions in a way that demonstrated comprehension. A few questions were still tricky for her—questions that asked her to retell important events, put things in sequence, and connect causes and effects. All of the questions that challenged her were related to Plot and Setting, so that became her goal. Going forward, she'd practice strategies for helping her with retelling, sequencing, and synthesizing as she read many books at or around Level M. (More on this later, but for now it is important to note that we didn't limit Vanessa's choice to just one level.)

Just to recap: Vanessa was a fourth-grade student reading at a second-grade level whose age would have put her in a sixth-grade class.

We started to wonder about the discrepancy between the level on which Vanessa demonstrated comprehension on a running record and the level she showed understanding in a whole text. Was this wide gap—the difference between M and R—a fluke? Or were many kids attempting to read books that they weren't actually comprehending?

I asked all the children in the class to select one of the books with prompts on sticky notes to read, asking them to select between those books that were at or around the level at which they'd demonstrated independence on the running record. After looking at their responses and repeating the assessment at lower levels as necessary, I found that, on average, students could read the short running records with accuracy, fluency, and comprehension at about two reading levels more complex than what they showed they could comprehend with this assessment. Why this discrepancy between comprehension on short texts or excerpts, and long texts? One possible explanation is that when students read chapter books, they need to track the plot over dozens of pages (possibly over days), infer about characters and notice how they change over many pages, and interpret a theme from a whole book. This thinking that readers do across many pages and days can be assessed only when students are reading whole books, and the current short-text assessments used widely in today's classrooms offer a limited view of what readers are able to do.

I was curious to see if what we found with Vanessa and her classmates would be true in other schools, so I sent chapter books with embedded questions and prompts to dozens of schools across the country. Hundreds and hundreds of student responses were mailed back to me, and I pored over them one summer with a volunteer group of educators from the tri-state area. Our findings were consistent with what we had seen in most of that South Bronx fourth-grade class: when looking at whole-book comprehension, students typically demonstrated strong comprehension in books about two levels lower than a short-passage running record indicated. There were some exceptions (about a quarter of students) where the short-text and whole-text assessments matched. And there were some exceptions where, like Vanessa, the text levels between long- and short-text reading were multiple levels apart.

Am I saying that running records are invalid? No, not at all. Vanessa could read that 200-word excerpt of a Level R text with comprehension, accuracy, and fluency. The assessment didn't lie, and her teacher didn't administer it incorrectly. But when she read a whole text, the longer text pushed her beyond her current skill level when it came to memory, sequencing, and synthesizing and suddenly interfered with her ability to completely comprehend. The running record was evaluating a different reading task than the one required by a whole book.

After learning so much about Vanessa, her teacher and I decided that we'd help her select books that were shorter and less complex than what

> *"If we teach a child the skill of reading without encouraging the love of reading, we will have created a literate illiterate."*
>
> —KYLENE BEERS (2017)

she'd been reading. We offered her strategies over time in conferences and small groups that helped support her with the goal of Plot and Setting: strategies focused on supporting her ability to remember, sequence, retell, and synthesize important events. After she'd read several books at and around Level M, we supported her practice in texts at and around Level N, then at and around Level O, then at and around Level P, and so on throughout the year, always checking back in on her comprehension and how she was making sense of plot, setting, character, vocabulary, and themes. With practice, she got comfortable with retelling and summarizing, and as she moved into more challenging texts she started working on strategies for new goals that matched what she needed at the time.

This story has a happy ending: Vanessa passed her fourth-grade test that year with flying colors. More importantly, though, she became a reader. She was engaged, excited about books, and chose to read outside of "reading time" in school. She pulled me aside later in the year and said, "Ms. Jen! I get it now! When you say 'make a movie in your mind,' you mean that you can actually see it in your mind like a movie! I see it now!"

Vanessa's story can teach us a number of important lessons about reading instruction, each of which will be explored in this book.

- Comprehension is not fixed; it's fluid, based on a number of factors.
- The level of text that a student can read depends on multiple variables.
- Text leveling isn't a perfect science.
- Matching books and readers is not as simple as it may seem.
- One single assessment often doesn't give us the entire picture.
- Responsive instruction is crucial to the development of readers.

A Note About This Book

Comprehension and leveled texts are topics that are heavily researched and can become deep and complex. What I aim to do in this book is to honor the extensive research on these topics but make the understandings about texts and readers that I believe to be essential for reading teachers more accessible and doable. Let's all learn from Vanessa's story and approach our readers with a deeper knowledge about them and the texts they read to match them with books they can read with independence and engagement, goals they can work toward that are meaningful and matched to their needs, and strategies that will help them work on those goals so they become strong, confident, engaged lifelong readers.

Comprehension Goals and Considerations

Reading is a complex process. Teaching children to read is challenging in part because comprehension is largely invisible. Although miscue analysis provides a window into the student's processing and use of strategies as they read (Goodman, Watson, and Burke, 1987; Clay 2000; Wilde 2000), and although we can tap into student thinking through the use of questions and prompts, we can't be completely sure about what is happening inside the mind of a reader. In addition, different scholars and researchers offer a range of perspectives on what it means to "comprehend" a text, which can cause confusion about where to begin, what to focus on, and how to best support learners.

Rosenblatt (1978), for example, argues that a text's meaning is created as a reader transacts with the text. In this way, the reader is a "co-author" of the text, constructing meaning alongside the author's words. The same text, with different readers, would yield different meanings. For example, I recently read DiCamillo's incredible *The Miraculous Journey of Edward Tulane* to my seven-year-old. I cried through the last two chapters as I read to her, and she looked at me

Understanding as you're reading helps you to engage with the text, read accurately, read with fluency, understand what the author is saying, and think beyond the text. In essence, comprehension is everything.

wondering why I was so sad. Edward was reunited with Abeline. That's a happy ending! She didn't comprehend it less than I did; we simply had different interpretations.

At the other end of the debate, Coleman and Pimental (2012) have argued for teaching children to read "within the four corners of the text," closely examining the work in a way that leaves the reader out of the text and instead asks the child to engage with text-dependent analysis.

With such differing advice, what's a teacher to do?

Research That Informs My Thinking

The roots of my thinking about reading comprehension were most shaped by the comprehension research published in journals in the 1980s and popularized in professional books during the 1990s and early 2000s. Often referred to as the "proficient reader research" and informed by cognitive psychology, it focused on what proficient readers do to make meaning from a text. Important works include Gordon and Pearson (1983), Hansen (1981), Duffy et al. (1987), Paris, Cross, and Lipson (1984), and Afflerbach and Johnston (1986), to name a few, along with those by researchers at the Center for Study of Reading (CSR) at the University of Illinois. They outline the characteristics of skilled readers and define reading as a constructive process. At CSR, under the leadership of learning theorist and cognitive psychologist Richard C. Andersen, literacy specialists, cognitive psychologists, learning theorists, linguists, and other scholars produced research over two decades that provided educators with instructional frameworks that are used in elementary classrooms today to support the teaching of reading (Hammond and Nessel 2011).

Comprehension Goals, Skills, and Strategies

One of the characteristics of skilled readers most central to my thinking in this book is that skilled readers are strategic. This speaks to the metacognitive aspect of the comprehension process—that is, skilled readers think about their thinking and apply their skills as they read to reach deeper levels of comprehension (Afflerbach, Pearson, and Paris 2008). Translated by practitioners into classroom practice and popularized by books such as *Mosaic of Thought* (Keene and Zimmermann 1997), *Reading with Meaning: Teaching Comprehension in the Primary Grades* (D. Miller 2002), and *Strategies That Work* (Harvey and Goudvis 2000), this idea of strategic reading in turn led to the identification of a handful of thinking skills that all proficient readers use.

These seven areas (or "keys") to comprehension provided educators with a needed frame for their reading instruction (Zimmermann and Hutchins 2003). For me, the beauty of framing instruction around these areas is that they apply to both narrative and informational texts. It is really about the mind work that readers do as they approach a text; the application changes slightly because the text structure and composition change. In the table below you can see some of the ways in which these seven areas can be applied to reading fiction and nonfiction texts. This list is not exhaustive but rather offers examples to help define them in light of different text types.

READING COMPREHENSION SKILL	EXAMPLES OF HOW THIS SKILL IS USED WHEN READING FICTION TEXTS	EXAMPLES OF HOW THIS SKILL IS USED WHEN READING NONFICTION TEXTS
Determining Importance	• Determining the most important events in a plot • Determining theme(s)	• Determining main idea(s) of a section or whole text • Determining important facts or details that support a main idea
Inferring/Interpreting	• Developing ideas, thoughts, and insights about characters • Interpreting the meaning of a symbol • Determining the meaning of an unfamiliar word using context	• Figuring out an author's purpose or main idea when it is not explicitly mentioned • Determining the meaning of an unfamiliar word using context
Synthesizing/Retelling	• Putting together causes and effects or problems and solutions • Retelling the most important plot events in order	• Putting together all the details within a section to determine a main idea
Questioning	• Asking questions about character motivation • Questioning author's craft (e.g., why the author used a certain symbol, chose a particular setting, or made a particular plot decision)	• Approaching a text with curiosity—asking questions about the content and reading on to discover answers • Questioning the author's authority to write about the topic, and the author's possible bias
Visualizing	• Creating multisensory images about setting • Picturing the character's physical traits as well as emotions based on body language or facial expressions	• Developing a moving picture ("movie in the mind") based on the photographs or visuals provided and the descriptions an author gives about the topic in question
Activating Prior Knowledge	• Activating relevant prior knowledge about a time period, a type of person, or a place • Activating knowledge about the author, series, or genre	• Activating relevant prior knowledge about a topic; comparing what the reader knows (or thinks they know) with what the author teaches
Utilizing Fix-Up Strategies	• Monitoring for understanding and using a strategy to determine the meaning of an unfamiliar word	• Monitoring for understanding and using a strategy to determine the meaning of an unfamiliar word

A Hierarchy of Reading Goals

Understanding as you're reading helps you to engage with the text, read the words accurately, read with fluency, understand what the author is saying, and think beyond the text. In essence, comprehension is everything.

But saying "comprehension is everything" can make the job of teaching reading feel nebulous. With a child who needs support, where do I start? In an effort to organize myself, and to support teachers who are working with student readers, I created a hierarchy of reading goals (page 11). My intention is not to say one goal is more or less important than another; they are all equally important and part of a whole. The reason for organizing reading into goals is to help teachers know where to start when a child would benefit from support in more than one area and to be more targeted and focused with the skills and strategies we introduce to students, based on a goal. It's also a way to guide teachers to help students make book choices; if students seem to need instruction in many of the goals, then the level of text they've selected is too challenging. Each goal encompasses a few skills, and all of them rely on comprehension in various ways.

At the top of the hierarchy is a goal called **Emergent Reading**. Emergent Reading is really a stage of reading development, when children first start becoming aware of how books—and eventually, print—work. As part of this goal, very young children rely on pictures to read: connecting pages in a storybook, learning information from informational texts. As they read from pictures, they are solidifying an understanding that reading is about making meaning: understanding what characters do and say; understanding how one event in the story leads to another; having their own ideas and reactions to the text; learning information and connecting information between parts and pages and to their own lives.

Goals, Skills, and Strategies Defined

These three terms—*goals*, *skills*, *strategies*—are used in a variety of ways by a variety of reading researchers and practitioners. In this text, and in my other works, I use them consistently with both the way my former thought community at the Teachers College Reading and Writing Project uses the terms and Afflerbach, Pearson, and Paris' explanation (2008). Here are some brief definitions.

Goals: A large category. Something that readers can work toward for several weeks, more or less. Goals include multiple skills. Examples of goals include Fluency (which includes multiple skills, such as improving prosody, expression, and phrasing); Character (which includes inferring about character feelings, traits, changes, and relationships); and Conversation (which includes improving speaking and listening skills while in partnerships and book clubs).

Skills: A proficiency, something a reader is able to do. For comprehension, I refer to the seven areas—determining importance, retelling and synthesizing, activating prior knowledge, and so on—as "skills."

Strategies: A strategy is a step-by-step how-to to help a reader work toward a skill and/or a goal. A strategy is not a single word or phrase; rather it is a series of steps, like a recipe. After the reader is skilled, the need to apply conscious attention to the strategy fades away.

A Hierarchy of Reading Goals

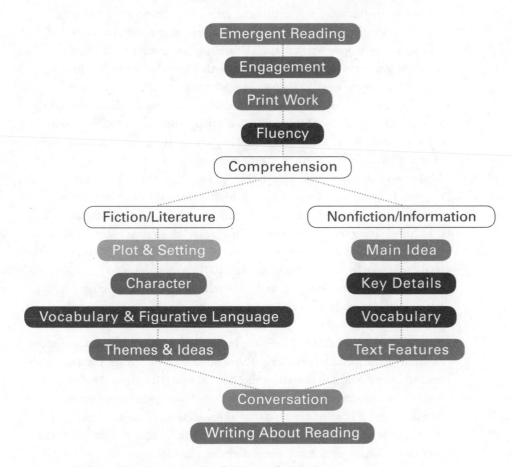

From *The Reading Strategies Book* (Serravallo 2015)

Next on the hierarchy is **Engagement**. This goal includes skills like choosing books that will be interesting and being able to enter a state of "flow" or "the reading zone," enabling the reader to read for long stretches of time and with attentional focus (Csikszentmihalyi 1991; Atwell 2007). While it's possible to teach children strategies to be aware of their own attention, find better books, or read for longer stretches by breaking up their work into smaller page or time chunks, to really achieve engaged reading means to really comprehend. When they enter the state of flow during reading, many readers describe it as "making a movie in your mind," "slipping into the world of the story," and "walking in a character's shoes." This means engaged readers are strategic: they visualize, infer, synthesize events in the story, and more (Guthrie, McGough, Bennett, and Rice 1996). Therefore, sometimes what appears as a lack of *engagement* with reading actually has its roots in a *comprehension* difficulty; after all, it's boring to read something you aren't understanding.

Print Work is the next goal on the hierarchy, and it includes being able to read accurately, monitor one's own reading, use decoding and other word-solving strategies at a point of difficulty, and self-correct after a miscue. Some may incorrectly assume this goal is all about reading the words, but none of it can happen without understanding. As children read, they are constantly constructing meaning and use that together with their knowledge of how words work to figure out what the text says. In other words, proficient readers don't just "sound it out"—they think about the sounds the letters make while also thinking, "What's happening in the text right now? What word would make sense here?" They are also using their knowledge of language and the structure of sentences, or syntax, and thinking, "What kind of word would sound right in this spot in the sentence?" Researchers and theorists who have studied children's reading by taking running records refer to this juggling act using different terms. Clay (2000) describes it as "integrating sources of information," with the sources being meaning, syntax, and visual information. Goodman, Watson, and Burke (2005) use the terminology of "cueing systems" to refer to the same processes.

Fluency is the next goal, and it too relies on meaning-making. For example, fluent readers are able to read with proper phrasing, pausing in places in a sentence that maintain the author's meaning. Anyone who has read Truss' *Eats, Shoots & Leaves* (2006) knows that where you place a pause in a sentence can change the meaning of it. Or as the popular meme suggests, commas (and pauses) can save lives in sentences such as "Let's eat, Grandma." Fluent readers also read with intonation, expression, and emphasis. Again, meaning comes into play here. If I can understand that a character is sad, then when I read the dialogue (aloud or in my head) I can communicate the emotion. If I read a sentence in a happy voice, my misreading can impede my understanding. So, a reciprocal relationship exists between a reader's ability to communicate the meaning of the text through the way they read it, and the way they read it is informed by how well they understand (Rasinski 2003; Kuhn 2007).

For comprehension, I organize my thinking around goals that help me to prioritize ways to support readers with goals within a genre. This way of thinking about a reader orchestrating multiple skills for an overarching reading goal is influenced by the work of Lucy Calkins and the Teachers College Reading and Writing Project. For fiction, I use the goals of **Plot and Setting**, **Character**, **Vocabulary and Figurative Language**, and **Themes and Ideas**. For nonfiction, my goals are **Main Idea**, **Key Details**, **Vocabulary**, and **Text Features**. For each of the comprehension goals, the skills from the previously discussed proficient reader research (inferring, retelling, determining importance, and so on) are folded into the goals. See the tables on page 13 for details on which skills support readers with each goal. It is important to note that although these eight categories are under the "comprehension" heading, it is true that *all* of the thirteen goals relate to comprehension. These are headed as "comprehension" goals because they are focused on helping readers to go deeper within the text.

A HIERARCHY OF COMPREHENSION GOALS: FICTION

GOAL	SKILLS
Plot and Setting	• Retell important events • Synthesize cause and effect • Identify problems • Visualize setting
Character	• Infer about, interpret, and analyze main character(s) • Synthesize character change • Infer about, interpret, and analyze secondary character(s)
Vocabulary and Figurative Language	• Monitor for meaning and use context
Themes and Ideas	• Interpret a story by naming life lesson(s) or theme(s) • Identify and interpret social issues • Identify and interpret symbols

A HIERARCHY OF COMPREHENSION GOALS: NONFICTION

GOAL	SKILLS
Main Idea	• Synthesize and infer to determine the main idea(s) of a page, section, or chapter • Synthesize and infer to determine the main idea(s) of a whole book
Key Details	• Determine importance to support a main idea with key details from the text • Compare and contrast key details
Vocabulary	• Monitor for meaning and use context
Text Features	• Derive meaning from a text feature by synthesizing information from that feature, the text, and, if present, other text features

Next on the thirteen-goal hierarchy is **Conversation**. Included within Conversation are several speaking and listening skills, including actively listening; staying on-topic; using respectful language; questioning; using flexible thinking; debating; and more. For conversations to go well, though, readers need to do more than use conversational skills; they also need to understand the text deeply and bring conversation-worthy topics to the discussion table. At the same time, the opportunity to have conversation about texts can bring about deeper understanding (Keene 2012; Nichols 2006). It is important, therefore, to ensure that children both understand the texts they are reading and have regular, ample time for conversations about texts with pairs, groups, and the whole class to deepen those understandings and clarify misunderstandings.

Writing About Reading, the final goal on the hierarchy, includes a variety of types of informal, quick writing readers may do before, during, or after reading to help them prepare to read, hold on to ideas as they read, or explore ideas after reading. I think of formal, longer-form writing about reading, such as literary essays and book reviews, as something I'd likely teach during writing workshop; the writing here is meant to be a small part (proportionally) of students' reading time. As with conversation, it helps if children comprehend the text they are reading before they start to write about it (otherwise, kids are prone to just copy things from the text without understanding what they are writing down), and the act of writing in and of itself can help readers to clarify and deepen their thinking about texts.

No matter how you slice it—by skill or by goal—categories can be useful for examining the whole reader. We can use each part like a checklist to help develop a complete picture of what it means to comprehend a text and as a way to help us identify goals for students. Of course, any attempt at fitting something as complex and nuanced as the reading process into neat-and-tidy boxes and categories is likely to be flawed. Natural overlaps occur. For example, it is impossible to offer a strong retelling of a text without determining which events are most important. It's hard to use a fix-up strategy to determine the meaning of an unfamiliar word without activating prior knowledge about the topic. These goals are not offered as be-all-and-end-alls but rather as a way to help explain and manage a cognitive process that by its very nature is hard to codify.

Reader and Text Variables That Impact Comprehension

Educators have relied on levels as a valuable tool to help them match students to texts they can read independently with fluency, accuracy, and comprehension. After all, it's well established that independent reading time is most effective when children are engaged in reading that they can read truly independently (Allington 2000, 2005, 2011a; Allington and Gabriel 2012). However, the truth is that leveling books and using levels as a tool to match students to texts isn't as straightforward as we might hope (Glasswell and Ford 2010; Dzaldov and Peterson 2005; Sibberson and Szymusiak 2008). We can evaluate books based on a variety of characteristics, but because qualitative leveling is done by humans and is, therefore, subjective, different people examining the same book may draw slightly different conclusions about what level is the best designation. We can

Overemphasis on levels diminishes student agency and negatively impacts the development of a reading identity.

use assessments to learn about what text a reader can read with accuracy, fluency, and comprehension—but based on a number of reader and text variables, what may be just right in one text on one day may differ from another text on another day.

You Can't Level a Reader

The way levels are used in many classrooms has strayed far from their original intent. Kids are walking around self-identifying by a level ("I'm a P!" "I'm a 38 . . .") and are pigeonholed into choosing books out of the single basket in the classroom library marked with the same letter or number. No matter what leveling system is used, kids nationwide have become aware of something that many would argue they shouldn't be aware of at all (Fountas and Pinnell 2016; D. Miller 2017; Schwanenflugel and Flanagan 2017; Ripp 2017). This "leveling mania," a term coined by Sibberson and Szymusiak (2008), has had a negative impact on students' beliefs about themselves as readers, causing some students to compete, race through levels, and experience shame. The truth is, the practice of using levels so stringently, although well intentioned, actually reveals gross misunderstandings.

The truth is, *you can't "level" a reader.*

A number of variables impact what students are able to comprehend from a text, and based on them, one individual child is likely to be able to read a range of levels and text types with independence. Some of these variables are related to the text itself (Fiction or nonfiction? Long or short?), and some are factors that the reader brings to the text (Prior knowledge? Motivation?). (See page 17 for more on reader and text variables that impact a reader's comprehension of a text.) Start combining the variables and it soon becomes clear that matching readers and texts requires more than a single assessment to determine *a* level and instead requires a knowledgeable teacher who is in regular conversation with readers.

There are so many variables, and yet the one many tend to pay the most attention to is the level of the text, and some have been using that one variable in a very fixed way. As Glasswell and Ford (2010) have written, it's important not to take a "simplistic approach to a complex phenomenon" (57) by labeling books with levels, using those labels inflexibly, and losing sight of reader or teacher expertise.

Read the two case studies on page 18. They illustrate how challenging it is to box a reader in to just one level, because a variety of factors come into play when considering whether the text is just right for them.

Reader and Text Variables Besides Level That Impact Comprehension

 Memory, stamina, and attention. Reading a several-hundred-word excerpt or passage is not the same task as reading an entire chapter book. Students with memory challenges will find it harder to read longer works.

 The receptive modality. For some readers, listening to a text read aloud makes it easier to comprehend than reading it independently, while the opposite may be true for others (Wu and Samuels 2004; Carretti, Caldarola, Tencati, and Cornoldi 2014).

 The productive modality. For some readers, responding to comprehension questions orally or engaging in a discussion about the text may yield seemingly deeper comprehension than responding in writing. For some students, the opportunity to write about reading could improve their comprehension (Graham and Hebert 2010).

 The instructional support. Some assessments ask students initial questions followed by prompting. With additional prompting, support, and scaffolding, students may be able to demonstrate stronger comprehension than if the questions or prompts are more open-ended. Students who discuss their reading with peers can improve comprehension (Cazden 1988; Fall, Webb, and Chudowsky 2000).

 The reader's prior knowledge. The role of background knowledge or schema that the reader brings to the text impacts comprehension. Two texts at the same level—one on a topic the reader knows a lot about and a second on an unfamiliar topic—will not be equally challenging (Anderson and Pearson 1984; Kintsch 2004).

 A reader's command of English. Emerging bilingual students are improving their English skills while also improving reading skills. Vocabulary, syntax, dialect, and language variances in texts may pose challenges to readers, while reading can also support language growth and development (Gibbons 1993, 2014).

 A reader's age and maturity level. The age of characters in fiction books typically matches the age of the book's intended reader, to allow readers to relate to characters. When a reader's ability exceeds or falls short of others of that same age, they may not relate to characters and themes in books and/or may be unfamiliar with content in nonfiction (DeFord and Klein 2008). Older readers who struggle may need hi/lo books to have content that appeals to them in texts that are easier to read; advanced readers may need help finding material that has appropriate themes, ideas, and content.

 The cultural relevance of the text. Related to the point about prior knowledge is the fact that children learn best when the classroom environment is respectful of their linguistic, social, and cultural heritage. When the books children read are culturally appropriate and relevant, they tap into students' background knowledge and experiences, increasing students' engagement and comprehension (Tatum 2009; Hunter 2012; Ebe 2011; Souto-Manning and Martell 2016).

 The reader's choice and engagement. Engagement with the text plays a role in a child's motivation to read it. When texts are self-selected rather than assigned, children are typically more engaged, can comprehend more challenging texts, and will even choose to read more (Kragler and Nolley 1996; Guthrie, Wigfield, Barbosa, et al. 2004).

 The social context of the reading experience. When children participate in a book club, reading partnership, or whole-class reading experience, they may be able to comprehend with more depth than they would independently because of the collaborative social support.

 The text genre. Some children prefer nonfiction, others fiction. Familiarity with a genre or text type—and engagement with a particular text type—influences comprehension.

"In most cases, teachers are left with insufficient knowledge about details of the determinants of leveling, and they follow the levels with relatively little adjustment for their students' interests experiences, cultural perspectives, and competencies"

—MARGARET E. MOONEY (2004)

Case Study 1: A third grader spends every weekend at the Museum of Natural History. It seems as though she knows almost as much about dinosaurs as the museum's resident paleontologist and is motivated to learn more. She's just initiated a dinosaur book club with a few of her third-grade friends who are as obsessed with the topic as she is. When she independently reads fiction texts, she chooses books at or around a Level O. What level texts about dinosaurs could she read with comprehension? We'd have to check in as she tried a book or two, but I'd say she might be able to read books that are more challenging than her go-to reads for fiction—maybe Q or even R. Why? She's got a high level of background knowledge/schema, a high level of motivation, and the support of peers to discuss the book with her.

Case Study 2: A fourth grader who loves mystery books gravitates toward the ten-minute mysteries—a collection of short stories within one book. However, her tutor tells her that she has to read Katherine Paterson's *Bridge to Terabithia*, which she's dreading because she's heard it's sad. She prefers happy and exciting! Her tutor asks her to write her ideas about *Terabithia* on sticky notes as she reads, explaining that he will evaluate her response when they meet in two weeks. If this student typically reads other books at the same level as *Bridge to Terabithia*, do we expect she's going to comprehend this book deeply? Let's review the facts: she prefers (and likely has more experience with) short texts, and this is a longer novel; she didn't select the text herself, and she's not particularly interested in it; she's not familiar with its genre, realistic fiction; she's reading it alone without support; and her tutor expects her to write her responses independently. I suspect that *Terabithia* might be a more challenging read for her than mystery short stories at the same level, possibly compromising her comprehension.

All of the reader and text variables in the chart on page 17 matter, and yet, when teachers administer a single assessment—typically a running record or a computer-based short-passage multiple-choice assessment—and use it as a summative assessment, a student is assigned a fixed independent and instructional level. Teachers are asked to report this fixed level as if it is the student's "score" and use it to guide much of what happens in the reading classroom after that. The child uses the independent level to select independent reading books, and the teacher frames their guided reading teaching around the instructional level. These levels are often reported to the administration, studied in school or district data meetings, used to set student growth targets, used to identify students for intervention, or even used to evaluate teacher effectiveness. These practices abound with problems.

- A single assessment measure is woefully inadequate.

- A formative assessment (meant to inform instruction) should not be used as a summative "pass or fail" test.

- Pressure to move kids through levels emphasizes breadth rather than depth—students are expected to read increasingly more challenging texts with accuracy, fluency, and some comprehension rather than working for deep comprehension of texts.

- Book leveling, though well-informed and conducted by literature experts, is nevertheless subjective and not as scientific as some would like to believe (Hiebert and Pearson 2014).

- When taking both quantitative and qualitative factors into consideration and combining those with all of the other factors influencing a reader's ability to access a text we see that the reader-text match is always evolving.

Reader, Text, and Task Variables at Play: A Demonstration of Why a Reader Doesn't "Have" One Level

READER	TEXT	TASK	WILL THE STUDENT COMPREHEND?
Highly motivated, high level of background knowledge on the topic.	At a lower reading level than what she typically reads, on a topic she knows a lot about.	Read and discuss with a peer.	Likely, comprehension will be strong.
Didn't select the text. Doesn't know much about the topic. Isn't motivated to read it. Tends to avoid written assignments.	At a level that the student typically reads. The book has unfamiliar formatting.	Read it and answer several comprehension questions in writing to demonstrate analytical thinking.	Likely, the comprehension will be shaky.
Highly motivated to read the text. All of his friends are reading it, and he wants to read and talk about it with them.	At a higher level than what he typically reads.	Read for fun and discuss with peers at recess.	Comprehension will likely be okay and strengthened through the conversations with peers.

Book Leveling Is Not a Perfect Science

Now, don't get me wrong. I'm not saying to stop using levels. I'm just saying that we should understand the larger context in which levels are determined, and be thoughtful about how they are used.

As a reading teacher, understanding text characteristics and how books become increasingly more challenging is crucial and extremely helpful. In fact, as I visit classrooms and confer with students I've never met, who are reading books I've never read, my knowledge of children's literature and text-level characteristics is invaluable. Even after a quick, one- or two-minute discussion with a reader, I'm usually able to determine their

strengths and the sorts of instructional support they need. The responsive reading teacher who understands text leveling can anticipate what sorts of things the reader will encounter in each book and how to ascertain the skills and behaviors the reader needs to successfully tackle the text challenges (Fountas and Pinnell 2017b; Hiebert and Pearson 2014; Calkins 2017a, 2017b; Calkins and Ehrenworth 2017).

For example, if a student has chosen to read the Level R book *Because of Winn-Dixie,* and her goal is to better understand characters, then I would approach a conference or small-group lesson with the expectation that she's thinking about the complexity of the characters, the impact of secondary characters on main characters, and the relationships between characters. This is my expectation because I know (based on my own study of many texts at Level R and what is written about characters at that level by Calkins [2017b] and Fountas and Pinnell [2017b]) that a key trait of Level R texts is that main and secondary characters are well developed and the relationships between them are important to driving the story. If I ask her, "Tell me a little bit about the main character," and she responds, "India Opal is really caring. She cares a lot about Winn-Dixie," I could then compare her response against what I know to expect of character responses at Level R. Her response—*even if I haven't read the book*—informs me that she could benefit from strategies that would help her to understand characters with more depth, teaching her how to think about a character's multiple traits.

As students' reading skills and background knowledge develop and they are able to read more and more challenging texts, moving from simple chapter books like the beloved Lobel series Frog and Toad, to character-driven chapter books such as those in the Amber Brown series by Paula Danziger, to longer novels such as Christopher Paul Curtis' *The Watsons Go to Birmingham—1963*, they encounter more and different text challenges. They discover various plot structures and characters with varying levels of depth; the themes and ideas in the texts become more varied, deeper, and require more maturity to understand. Additionally, students encounter a wider variety of words, learning their meanings from the context of the story. The same is true for nonfiction—texts at lower levels offer lots of supports for readers, such as challenging vocabulary being defined on the page; high levels of text cohesion, where all the facts on a page are about one topic; and text features that provide meaning support. In higher levels, students must infer main ideas, details are plentiful, and vocabulary words require more synthesis to determine their meaning.

Understanding subtle shifts and increases in demands from level to level is helpful for a teacher to know what readers are encountering in texts, especially when the teacher is working with a student reading a text that the teacher hasn't read. This knowledge can guide what a teacher asks the student, what a teacher expects of the student, and what the teacher therefore teaches the student. Knowing text level characteristics and the work readers need to take on at each level can and should be an important consideration when planning your whole-class, small-group, and one-on-one teaching decisions.

The idea of leveling texts and using leveled texts in classroom instruction has a long history, which I've provided highlights of in the timeline on pages 22–23. It's important to understand this history to see how we've arrived where we are today and to better conceptualize some of the initial intentions behind leveled books.

Entire books and countless scholarly articles, chapters, and websites are dedicated to the topics of text complexity and text leveling (e.g., Fisher, Frey, and Lapp 2012; Fountas and Pinnell 2017a, 2017b; https://bit.ly/2LDsqfT). Although a deep understanding of text leveling and readability formulas is unnecessary for most teachers, you may find it helpful to understand how to evaluate the complexity of text to better match your students with those texts and to be able to anticipate, in general, the sorts of challenges readers are likely to encounter in the books they choose to read.

Quantitative Leveling

To arrive at a quantitative level, a computer program counts aspects such as word length, numbers of syllables, sentence length, and text length and does a calculation based on word frequency and text cohesion (see box to right). Websites and computer programs that analyze quantitative dimensions often arrive at a readability score, which may be one—but shouldn't be the only—consideration in helping teachers to match readers to appropriate texts (Fisher, Frey, and Lapp 2012). Still, these aspects can directly impact the reader. Longer sentences mean the reader has more to synthesize within each sentence as well as from sentence to sentence. A high degree of cohesion means the passage may be easier to comprehend.

Quantitative Dimensions of Complexity

Quantitative dimensions of complexity are those aspects that are best measured by computer. Depending on the formula being used (Fry Readability Formula, Flesch–Kinkaid, Dale-Chall, ATOS Readability Formula, Lexile, etc.), what's measured may include:

- **Word length and syllable count.** The number of letters in the words on average, and the range of lengths of words in the text, used as a proxy for semantic complexity.

- **Word frequency.** The amount of repetition and how much the same word appears.

- **Sentence length.** The number of words in a sentence, used as a proxy for syntactic complexity.

- **Text length.** How many words are in an entire text.

- **Text cohesion.** The extent to which words within the selection relate to each other (i.e., cup, plate, bowl).

Historical Highlights of Text Leveling in the United States

1800s–early 1900s. Texts were grouped by grade levels. Each year, students received one book that included a year's worth of stories deemed grade-level appropriate for that year (Smith 2002).

1946. Betts describes three levels of readability: instructional, independent, frustration.

1948. Edgar Dale of Ohio State University and Jeanne Chall of Harvard University published a readability formula in an attempt to more precisely determine a text's grade level for instruction. This readability formula was based on the semantic frequency of the words and the length of the sentences.

1950s. and 1960s. Dick and Jane and similar texts were created for instructional purposes using readability formulas. The end result? Short, choppy texts that were devoid of natural language and, instead, featured a controlled vocabulary and short sentences, which often bored or even confused young readers (Cullinan and Fitzgerald 1984–1985).

1958. Science Research Associates, a small Chicago-based publishing company, begins publishing SRA Reading Laboratory kits, an attempt at managing independent, multilevel reading in the classroom.

1968. Fry develops the Fry Graph Readability Formula, which uses a graph to calculate grade-level readability by correlating the number of sentences (y-axis) and syllables (x-axis) per hundred words.

1970s. Marie Clay's Reading Recovery program in New Zealand, aimed at supporting first-grade children in need of extra reading support, relied on the use of "little books," which were organized into twenty numeric reading levels (1–20), with Level 20 typically correlating to an end-of-first-grade reading level. (Pinnell, DeFord, and Lyons 1988). A teacher was to take the child's background experience into consideration when deciding on each child's text progression.

1970s–1980s. Researchers studied the needs of first graders, looking at not only reading of the controlled texts but also reading of familiar story-books. They concluded that children were often able to read and comprehend authentic literature better than the controlled stories for a range of reasons, including the richness of language; sentence structure matching the children's own speech patterns; the story structure of the authentic texts and the children's knowledge of how texts unfold and should sound; and the ways in which illustrations support meaning-making (Rhodes 1979; Gourley 1984). Based on readability formulas, literature-based anthologies start replacing grade-level books.

1990s. For years, literature-based anthologies dominated the educational publishing market. Criticisms that they were not meeting the needs of struggling readers and teachers' desires to match kids to books they can read with independence increased the market for little books in the United States (DeFord and Klein 2008).

1991. Barbara Peterson of Ohio State University published *Literary Pathways*, which offered advice for teachers about organizing books along a gradient of difficulty by considering a multitude of qualitative factors.

1996. Fountas and Pinnell published their first edition of *Guided Reading*, which described ten features and characteristics of texts to consider when leveling books along thirteen levels (A–M).

2000. Allington's *What Really Matters for Struggling Readers*, first edition, was published. In it, he reviewed research that showed how students need a high volume of books that they can read with fluency, accuracy, and comprehension to grow. Future editions of this book in 2005 and 2011 reviewed up-to-date research and asserted the same need for matching students to books they can read accurately, fluently, and with comprehension.

2000. In *The Art of Teaching Reading,* Calkins suggested leveling books in a classroom library to support students' text selection during an instructionalized independent reading time, otherwise known as a reading workshop.

2001. *Beyond Leveled Books* cautioned against the "leveled book mania" that was sweeping the country and advised teachers to take a more balanced approach (Szymusiak and Sibberson 2001).

2002. Pearson published Joetta Beaver's *Developmental Reading Assessment* (DRA), a leveled reading assessment.

2005. In *Leveled Books, K–8,* Fountas and Pinnell advised against leveling or labeling books in the classroom library; they intended their book-leveling framework to be used for guided reading instruction only.

2007. Fountas and Pinnell published the *Continuum of Literacy Learning, Grades 3–8,* which expanded their leveling system through Z, and the *Benchmark Assessment System*—a running record system for assessing students' instructional reading level and determining goals to be taught during guided reading.

2010-2012. Common Core State Standards provided a backward-mapped staircase of text complexity, working from the expectations of college and the workplace down through the grades. The standards drew on the three criteria—quantitative, qualitative, and reader and task—to determine the complexity of each text. However, a table in Appendix A of the standards document recommended new Lexile ranges for each grade level in grades 2 and above that resulted in schools' increasing the complexity of texts that students are asked to read and in some cases using only the Lexile leveling system.

Limitations of Quantitative Leveling

Although some educators, eager for reliability and accuracy, are reassured by the calculations that computers can do, they erroneously assume that the numbers and calculations around text complexity are foolproof and exact. The truth is that computerized calculations of complexity miss important aspects of texts, such as layers of meaning, that only people can evaluate. Computers are missing a lot. A mathematical calculation does not guarantee that an emerging bilingual student can comprehend a book whose text may be poetic rather than literal. It does not predict whether a child will be able to handle the content-specific vocabulary of an unfamiliar informational topic. When leveling books in the absence of themes, ideas, vocabulary, plot structure, and character development, it becomes easier to see how a book that is studied by college students ends up with almost the same Lexile score as another book recommended for a second grader, as is the case with Steinbeck's *The Grapes of Wrath* (Lexile 680) and Kline's *Horrible Harry and the Birthday Girl* (Lexile 660).

Computers miss the layers of meaning in *Grapes* and see only the short sentences and seemingly simple language as an indication that the book is "easy." As text complexity expert Elfrieda Hiebert (2011) puts it, quantitative data can get you only "within the ballpark" (2). This is why, when it comes to using a leveling system to help match children to books that they'll be able to comprehend, it's not a good idea to rely solely on quantitative leveling.

Lexiles offer only a partial picture . . . Do these side-by-side texts seem equally complex to you?

Horrible Harry and the Birthday Girl by Suzy Kline (Lexile 660)	*The Grapes of Wrath* by John Steinbeck (Lexile 680)
Ivy and Bean by Annie Barrows (Lexile 580)	*The War That Saved My Life* by Kimberly Brubaker Bradley (Lexile 580)
Hatchet by Gary Paulsen (Lexile 1020)	*1984* by George Orwell (Lexile 1080)
Trixie the Halloween Fairy from the Rainbow Magic Series by Daisy Meadows (Lexile 700)	*The Running Man* by Stephen King (Lexile 700)

Lexile levels as found at www.lexile.com

Qualitative Leveling

Qualitative leveling considers dimensions such as levels of meaning, structure, language, and knowledge demands of the reader (see box below). One such tool is the Fountas and Pinnell Text Level Gradient™. Rooted in the work of Clay, Peterson, and others (see the timeline on pages 22–23), their framework for understanding how texts increase in complexity is extremely helpful (Fountas and Pinnell 2017b). The leveling system uses letters from A–Z, and books are evaluated based on ten characteristics (genre, text structure, content, themes and ideas, language and literary features, sentence complexity, vocabulary, illustrations, book and print features). As I've already mentioned, when you see letter levels mentioned in this book I am referring to their leveling system. With the acknowledgment that some readers may use a different leveling system, or may be new to leveling systems at all, I offer the correlation chart on the following page. It is important to note that these suggested correlations draw from a variety of sources, including but not limited to: The Teachers College Reading and Writing Project's website,

Qualitative Measures of Complexity

Qualitative measures of complexity refer to aspects of the text best measured by a human reader. Depending on the formula (Fountas and Pinnell Text Level Gradient™, DRA Levels, Reading Recovery), what's measured may include:

- **Levels of meaning or purpose.** A novel's themes and ideas; the main ideas a nonfiction author is communicating and whether those ideas are straightforward or need to be inferred; traits that create well-rounded, full characters; a subtle slant the author assumes to share information.

- **Structure.** How a book is organized, the layout of the information along with the text features, whether there are flashbacks or foreshadowing, or if the plot is sequential.

- **Language conventionality and clarity.** Consider how often a reader encounters a key vocabulary word that may be unfamiliar, or phrases that are not meant to be taken literally requiring context and background knowledge to understand.

- **Knowledge demands.** The topics and issues that are central to the text, how many of those topics and issues are included, and the sorts of background knowledge a reader would need to comprehend.

Common Core State Standards Appendix A, and Fountas and Pinnell's *Leveled Literacy Intervention* materials. There were slight variations in each of these sources, and an internet search for "level correlation chart" easily yields a dozen more variations! What follows is a synthesis of all the information I collected and is simply a guide, and **should not be interpreted as an endorsement of these correlations.**

GRADE LEVEL	FOUNTAS AND PINNELL TEXT LEVEL GRADIENT™	READING RECOVERY LEVEL	DRA2 LEVEL	LEXILE LEVEL
K	A–D	1–5/6	A–6	Up to 450
1	D–J	5/6–17	6–18	80–500
2	J–M	17–20	18–28	450–650
3	M–P	20–38	28–38	550–770
4	P–S	38–40	38–40	770–860
5	S–V	40–N/A	40–50	830–980
6	V–X	N/A	60	980–1030
7	X–Y	N/A	70	1030–1070
8	Y–Z+	N/A	80	1070–1155

> "A book about rain or the seashore may need a higher level for children living in a desert climate than for those residing in a coastal state."
>
> —GAY SU PINNELL, DIANE DEFORD, AND CAROL LYONS (1988)

The Process of Qualitatively Leveling a Book

It would be incorrect to claim that books fit into hard and fast level categories. Books don't perfectly meet all the characteristics of any single level, partly because children's trade authors don't sit down intending to write within the confines of a particular level (could you imagine E. B. White working on *Charlotte's Web* thinking . . . "How can I make this an R?"). In most cases, there isn't a drastic difference between one level and the next, just subtle shifts here and there. Comparing a Level K book with a P is easy; comparing an O and a P is much harder.

When well-trained leveling experts sit down to determine a level for a book, two people might arrive at a slightly different level. To determine a level, the expert needs to weigh a variety of text characteristics and may assign a different weight to each one. This informed but nevertheless subjective process explains why you may find that a book that was previously leveled N is suddenly an O on your favorite go-to leveling website or app. You may also find a text listed at Level J on one website, while on another it is listed as K or L. Different sites may use different criteria even though they use letters to name the levels, certain apps or sites may have different teams of people deciding on levels, and still others allow for "crowd-sourced" level assignment, where any user can upload the level they think best matches a text.

Level variability can be frustrating for a teacher who is working hard to match children to books, organize a classroom library, and/or to select books for instruction. In fact, some of my colleagues have moved away from single levels (J, K, L) for fiction and instead work with level "bands" where several levels are grouped together (Calkins and Tolan 2010). While I question drawing three specific levels into one fixed band because that may over-emphasize a break between two bands, I do agree that a text that is leveled K, for example, could possibly slide down to J or up to L, depending on the evaluator. It's helpful to have a somewhat flexible view.

Considerations When Qualitatively Leveling Nonfiction

- **Main Idea.** How explicit is/are the main idea(s)? Is it clear what the part is about or does it need to be inferred? Inferring makes it harder. Is the selection of text focused on one main idea or multiple ideas? Multiple makes it harder.

- **Key Details.** How much information is on the page? Does the information seem to all go together clearly and obviously, or is there a lot of information that feels tangential? More information, and information that is less cohesive, makes the book harder.

- **Vocabulary.** How many content-specific vocabulary words appear on the page? More usually means harder, unless the words are clearly defined and supported by context (within-sentence definitions, a text feature such as a photograph that shows the meaning of the word, a glossary). What sorts of information and concepts are explored in the book? More complex topics make the book more challenging.

- **Text Features.** How challenging are the features? Do they require reading or specific skills to figure out the meaning they convey? I usually consider features like photographs and illustrations to be "easier" than sidebars, timelines, and maps because the latter require more reading and studying, almost like their own section. Also, look to see how many features a reader would need to synthesize within a spread. When a reader encounters many features on a spread, they need to synthesize them, making the text more challenging. Also, consider whether the features add extra information or reiterate the information in the main text. When the features are very close to the text on the page, they offer the reader an extra chance to learn the information and are supportive (easier); when the features add extra information, it's more challenging because it means that the child needs to do more thinking to put the information together.

Qualitative Leveling: A Nonfiction Example

The task of leveling books precisely is challenging, perhaps even more so with nonfiction texts than fiction texts. When I search for a fiction title on a variety of different leveling websites and apps, I find minor occasional variability. For nonfiction, though, major discrepancies seem to be more common.

Nonfiction, it seems, is particularly tricky to level because of the "weight" individual people assign to each of the considerations. For example, some would say that a book about whales is automatically easier than a book about the Civil War. The topic and reader's prior knowledge are important considerations, so some leveling experts assume that topics that primary-grade students would know about are automatically easier than topics that typically appear in upper-grade curricula. Another evaluator might look at vocabulary and heavily weight its importance. Yet another person may consider books with a number of text features on a single page that require reader synthesis more challenging than those with a simple photo and a few sentences of text. Still other readers may consider the density of information (how many facts on a page) or the explicitness of the main idea(s) (Is it clear what the authors' main points are or do they need to be inferred?) to be a primary factor in considering text difficulty. And then there's the issue that not every page spread in a nonfiction book looks the same: one page spread may seem like it fits with books generally leveled at M, but another looks more like P, and still another presents as a K . . . *so what level is right?*

Let's look at one book as an example to illustrate this point. On the left you'll find a page from *The Moon Book* by Gail Gibbons (1997). Take a close look and jot in the margin or on a sticky note what level you would assign the book. As you evaluate the book, be sure to think about the different considerations that appear in the box on page 27.

Look closely at the first page (to the left) and see what you think.

I notice that there are illustrations on the page that very closely match the words. The word *astronomers* is illustrated with a picture of two scientists in lab coats engaged in some work. The definition appears right next to the word. Same with the term *orbit*—a definition and illustration support the reader's understanding of the concept. In the text at the bottom, there is support for the term *collided* in the far-left-hand picture. The three sentences are all about the same main idea—how astronomers believe the moon was formed. There is not a lot of information—just three facts plus definitions of key terms. The only term that doesn't have an explicit definition

ASTRONOMERS study the planets, rheir moons, and the stars.

An ORBIT is the path of one object around another.

Most astronomers and other scientists think our moon formed about 4.5 billion years ago. Some believe something collided with Earth that tossed out a cloud of rock and debris. While orbiting around Earth, the rock and debris came together to form the moon.

is *debris* but it's used twice with "rock and . . ." and
its meaning may be easily inferred by a reader.
Overall, looking just at this page, I'd say this book
should be leveled as somewhere in the neighborhood of L or M.

Now study a second page from the same
book (to the right). Take a look at it and again
consider main idea, key details, vocabulary, and
text features (see box on page 27). What level
does it seem to you?

Visually, this second page feels very different from the other. Whereas on the previous
page we noticed just a few sentences and a few
illustrations, on this page we encounter twelve
illustrations and a timeline with information
next to each date. The amount of information on
this page, and the way it is represented, is already
making me think it's much more challenging
than the L/M estimate I made looking at the last
page. Now, as we look closely at the information, we can see that there are a lot of concepts

and terms that may pose a challenge to the reader: *lunar eclipses, philosopher,
astronomer, the effect the moon has on tides, telescope, moon mapping,* and more.
Alongside almost every new date, a new term and/or proper noun is introduced. In the left column alone we learn about Mesopotamia, Anaxagoras,
Aristarchus, Posidonius, Syria, Galileo, and Hevelius. Not only is the quantity
of terms and names challenging, but there is also very little support for many
of them. If I didn't already know what *Syrian* means, could I find it out from
this page? No. All of the facts on the page do relate to the moon, milestones,
and important events. With this page in mind, I'm thinking that this book
might be better leveled at P or Q.

Analyzing a few page spreads and listening to me think aloud about
finding the level demonstrates the subjectivity of the process. Perhaps
you're a fourth-grade teacher who just finished an astronomy unit with your
class, so your students are familiar with the words *astronomer* and *telescope*—which makes the text easier. Or maybe you thought that the sentence
structure and syntax felt challenging for your emerging bilingual students,
leading you to judge the book more challenging.

When attempting to determine a book's level, it's important to read
the whole book, study all the pages, and evaluate its complexity holistically.
Different pages may present different challenges. If several of the pages seem
harder, that usually means the whole book should be tagged more challenging. Some quantitative formulas (and even some qualitative) sample the book
and don't go page by page in making leveling decisions, and this can account
for some inconsistency in what level the book is considered to be.

If we looked "behind the leveling curtain" and listened in on the conversations evaluators have when deciding which level to assign to each book, what would we see? Typically, multiple readers examine the book, consider the characteristics, and discuss their level judgments with other evaluators. They may disagree or decide to compromise. The level listed online in the leveling database is their best estimate based on their expertise—but in some cases they could have chosen a level lower or higher because certain aspects of the text may have felt on the "leveling cusp."

As unscientific as this all may feel, I still believe that qualitative leveling of texts, alongside a knowledge of the child, is our best tool when trying to match children to books of appropriate complexity. The meaning-based considerations (Which words might be tricky? What synthesis is required? How much is on a page? Is the main idea clear?) are more sensitive to a child's comprehension development than levels based only on a computer count of the numbers of words in a sentence or the average number of letters in words.

I also hope that this exercise shows you that with some practice and a deeper knowledge of leveling (which is explored in Parts II and III of this book), you, too, can develop more comfort and expertise around it. Understanding what books ask of readers at Level N, or O, or Q will help you better facilitate your students' choices, plan thoughtful instruction, and guide their reading. Indeed, this was one of Clay, Peterson, and Fountas and Pinnell's original intents: that teachers would learn to level books themselves and gain an insider's knowledge of demands placed on readers at each level that would inform their teaching (1994, 1991, 1996).

Developing Your Own Expertise Around Leveled Books

When I lead professional development about understanding texts and readers, I often begin by engaging teachers in an exploration of texts.

1. First, I ask teachers to bring a bunch of books from their own collections that they've read and are familiar with to explore with colleagues.

2. Second, I introduce teachers to the text characteristics I use to evaluate complexity, as you will read more about on pages 54–81 for fiction and 126–153 for nonfiction.

3. Then, I share with them a "touchstone" text—a text that squarely meets the characteristics of the level. To learn about the characteristics of that level, we work together to create tables, like the samples that begin on page 32.

4. Next, teachers sort through their stack to find books that look like the touchstone and then explain how these meet the characteristics of the level. As they work, I remind teachers that authors don't write books to fit into these categories (thank goodness!) so they're not looking for a perfect matchup but more of an overall alignment.

Devoting attention to learning about text characteristics and text levels can help you become a more thoughtful and thorough reading teacher. You'll be able to better understand what to highlight in texts as you think aloud, what to look for when assessing readers, and what strategies to offer to support comprehension. It will also help you to match students to texts so that they can understand what they're reading, increasing enjoyment and motivation.

Text Characteristics Charts: Fiction Example

As you study texts with colleagues, you may want to create tables like the ones beginning on page 32 to help you articulate the ways in which particular texts align to text-level characteristics. More on the text characteristics I use to evaluate texts that will fill the left-hand column is in Part II of this book, on pages 54–81. For now, know that these characteristics come from my own study of children's literature as well as my interpretation of Fountas and Pinnell's leveling system as described in their various publications (1999, 2005, 2010, 2017a, 2017b) and Calkins' interpretation of these same levels (2017b). These charts examine the way that *Taking Sides* by Gary Soto exemplifies characteristics of fiction books at Level S. Other sample charts for fiction books at levels J–W can be found at http://hein.pub/UTR (click on Companion Resources).

Taking Sides by Gary Soto—Level S

GOAL: PLOT AND SETTING

Text Characteristics	Examples from *Taking Sides*
Books are longer, with many chapters. Each chapter is long (~10 pages), with small print and no pictures.	135 pages 13 chapters
Plotlines are more complex. They are often driven by what the character wants. The internal journey of the character is as important as the external plot. The main character faces multiple conflicts and/or obstacles, both internal and external.	Linc's struggle is one of finding his place with new friends, in a new neighborhood, on a team he doesn't feel a part of. To understand the significance of moments in the story, the reader needs to understand the struggles of the main character.
Unfamiliar settings should be expected and must be understood. The setting(s) may be distant in time or place. Setting has an impact on the plot and characters.	The story is set on both "sides of the tracks"—a hard-knocks barrio and a safer, mostly white suburban neighborhood. The contrasts between these two places and Lincoln's struggles to fit in are important to understanding the story. This book is also set in California in the 1980s or 1990s and some references may be unfamiliar to readers today—like the rapper Ice-T or cassette players.
Specific descriptions of setting require the reader to visualize. Setting may help communicate the mood or tone of a scene.	The contrasts between Linc's old and new neighborhoods are important. See, for example, the description on the first couple of pages of Chapter 6. The setting communicates a change in mood and affects the characters.
There are some challenging plot-structure elements, such as flashbacks, foreshadowing, and subplots/multiple plotlines.	The title, *Taking Sides*, relates to multiple subplots of side-taking in this book: Linc takes sides between friends, teammates, and neighborhoods.
Stretches of narration help give the reader backstory and information on the character, and/or move the story through time.	This book has a third-person narrator. The narration gives a great deal of Linc's internal thinking, provides setting details, and compares his present life to his past life. See, for example, pages 11–13. Movement through time is slow at the start of the chapter as he approaches the school, then it moves quickly through several periods of the day.

Taking Sides by Gary Soto—Level S

GOAL: CHARACTER

Text Characteristics	Examples from *Taking Sides*
Main characters are complex. They demonstrate different aspects of their personality and have traits, thoughts, and/or feelings that conflict. A reader can develop an interpretation of a main character by synthesizing multiple traits and characters' perspectives.	The main character, Linc, is complex in his thoughts and feelings. He's an eighth grader who is concerned with fitting in in an unfamiliar neighborhood; has romantic feelings for a girl; tries to be a good son to his single, working mother; and is grappling with friendships from his old school and his new one.
Main characters change and learn lessons.	Lincoln mostly learns about how to fit in and be at peace despite his new environment. He realizes he can relax and settle in with the knowledge that he doesn't have to take sides—he can maintain who he is even in a different place.
Secondary characters may be more complex. To understand the secondary characters, the reader needs to see them from multiple perspectives. The main character's view of the secondary characters may change across the course of the story.	Lincoln's view of Roy, his mother's boyfriend, changes throughout the story. He sees him as an outsider at first. He gets to know him, though, through the stories of his basketball days and conflicts with Linc's coach when he was a player on an opposing team. This is part of the beginning of Lincoln's ability to be at peace in the new place.
Secondary characters affect the main characters. Relationships between main characters and various secondary characters are important.	Lincoln's relationships with his mom, Tony, and James each have an impact on him and his growth across the story. With Tony, it seems as if he's with family. With James, he seems all proper. His mom causes him to act differently than he does at school around his friends and Monica. To gain insight into Lincoln, it's important to track his different behaviors around the variety of secondary characters.

Taking Sides by Gary Soto — Level S

GOAL: VOCABULARY AND FIGURATIVE LANGUAGE

Text Characteristics	Examples from *Taking Sides*
New vocabulary is often unexplained and is critical to comprehension of the text. There is a heavy load of complex vocabulary. The vocabulary may relate to unfamiliar settings or topics.	For example: *homeboy* (p. 1) On page 2: Spanish words like *ese* (*dude*), *hombre* (*man*), *menso* (*fool*), and *vatos* (*guys*) are all undefined in the book but available in the glossary in the back of the book. *asphalt* (p. 2) *hovering* (p. 3) *dank* (p. 3) *ransacked* (p. 3)
Metaphors and similes, and words and phrases that are used figuratively and/or have connotative meanings, are pervasive, and are essential to understanding characters, plot, and setting.	For example: "The rising sun hurled a spear of light through Lincoln's kitchen window." (p. 1) "His face was brown, like coffee laced with cream." (p. 2) ". . . Ford Torinos bleeding black oil." (p. 2)

GOAL: THEMES AND IDEAS

Text Characteristics	Examples from *Taking Sides*
Some themes are easily accessible to middle-grade readers.	Fitting in.
Some themes and ideas require emotional maturity on the part of the reader. They might deal with important human problems, social issues, and/or cultural diversity.	Feeling like an outsider because of your race and/or cultural background; racism and name-calling relating to Coach Yesutis.
Symbolism may be used and, when understood, can offer insights into the story's characters and/or themes.	Flaco, Lincoln's dog, seems to be symbolic. His injury and healing seem to foreshadow and parallel Linc's injury and healing. The stolen television with Linc's crayon scrawls that is recovered at the end of the story could be symbolic of his childhood and the last place he lived merging with his new life and environment.

Text Characteristics Charts: Nonfiction Example

As you study texts with colleagues, you may want to create tables like the ones that follow to help you articulate the ways in which particular texts align to text-level characteristics. More on the text characteristics I use to evaluate texts that will fill the left-hand column is in Part III of this book, on pages 126–153. These charts examine the way that *Germs Make Me Sick!* by Melvin Berger exemplifies characteristics of nonfiction books at Level O. Other sample charts for nonfiction books at Levels J–W can be found at http://hein.pub/UTR.

Germs Make Me Sick! by Melvin Berger—Level O

GOAL: MAIN IDEA

Text Characteristics	Examples from *Germs Make Me Sick!*
The entire book is focused on one overarching, complex main idea. Each chapter may address a subtopic or sub-main idea that relates back to the overarching main idea.	This book is about germs. One main idea is, "Germs make you sick, but you can be healthy if you know how to avoid them," but within that concept there are subtopics. Readers of this book will learn about viruses and bacteria and the illnesses they cause and how to stay healthy.
The book is usually divided into sections or chapters, which may have a title or section heading. A main idea of each chapter or section may be more implicit than it is at prior levels. Sometimes chapter titles or section headings hint at the main idea of that part.	There are no official section breaks, but the entire book is about three main subtopics: viruses, bacteria, and staying healthy. The main idea of the whole book is clear from the first page. A main idea about each subtopic is less explicit.
A concluding page or section, or an introductory page or section, may summarize a main idea of the whole book.	The final page addresses the reader: "Germs do make you sick—sometimes. But you can help yourself be fit as a fiddle all the rest of the time!"

Germs Make Me Sick! by Melvin Berger—Level O

GOAL: KEY DETAILS

Text Characteristics	Examples from *Germs Make Me Sick!*
There are around ten to fifteen sentences or details per page. A main idea is often carried across more than one page.	The main text includes about seven to ten facts or sentences per two-page spread. However, a lot of the content is presented in the other text features, bringing the total number of details within a page closer to ten to fifteen.
Within-sentence complexity, including linking words and phrases such as *unlike, also, instead*; pronouns with antecedents such as *they* and *these*; and temporal words or phrases such as *later, about 10,000 years ago,* and *today* challenge readers to understand the relationship between key details.	On page 16 alone, the sentences are linked with words *they, each, then,* and *in a few hours*. This section of text explains a sequence: a reader would have to follow that to understand the details the author presents. Consider the sequence of sentences on pages 10–11: "Germs often get stuck there. *They* don't go any farther. *Yet* some germs do slip in every once in a while." [italics added]
Photographs and other illustrations show isolated facts on the page. Many important details are explained in the text alone.	On page 7, a series of illustrations helps to show the virus and bacteria types being described in the text. On pages 14–15, for example, some of the text is supported by pictures, but some is not illustrated—e.g., "Some germs stay in the body and make you sick."
Additional key details may be found in other text features, for example, in captions, labels, sidebars, and maps.	This book relies heavily on illustrations and diagrams. Many have labels. Some labels or speech bubbles are written in a playful way, and a reader needs to work to learn the information. For example, page 10 shows some children hanging a poster of a girl's head, seen in cross section, to highlight the flow of oxygen into her nose and mouth, and the hairs that filter out the germs. A boy is sawing, a dog says, "Be careful," and another girl below answers, "Looks OK." These types of comic illustration could distract a reader.

Germs Make Me Sick! by Melvin Berger—Level O

GOAL: VOCABULARY

Text Characteristics	Examples from *Germs Make Me Sick!*
The author assumes some prior knowledge on the part of the reader. The reader can expect to encounter several content-specific vocabulary words on each page. Those that are important to learning key details and main ideas are often supported by context.	Not only the words, but also the concepts, are challenging in this book. A reader needs to understand the concept of microscopic organisms. Some words that the author likely expects the reader to know are: *germs, sick, living,* and *thousands.* Words that are explained, supported by context, or defined are: *virus, bacteria, harmful, proteins,* and *antibodies.*

GOAL: TEXT FEATURES

Text Characteristics	Examples from *Germs Make Me Sick!*
Photographs and other illustrations support some facts within the main text. Some of these features offer information beyond that in the main text.	Illustrations are used on every page. Many show a scene that enacts the concept being explained. For example, on page 11 the author describes how a sneeze can spread germs, making you sick. The illustration is of a class on a field trip to a museum, with one of the children sneezing and another shielding himself from the spray.
More challenging features such as tables, maps, sidebars, and procedure pages may appear at times. Tables of contents, glossaries, and indexes are common.	Some diagrams, like those on pages 14 and 15, are used to support key information in the text. The cartoonlike illustrations may challenge some readers, adding to the difficulty of understanding abstract concepts. There is no table of contents, index, or glossary in this book.

Merging Levels and Comprehension

What to Expect in the Parts Ahead

Parts II and III are set up to help you develop expertise around text characteristics of children's literature from Levels J–W and to help you see what strong comprehension may look and sound like, goal by goal and skill by skill. I am choosing to focus on this level range because although comprehension assessment and instruction is something that is important for teachers to consider at all levels, around Levels J/K is where there is increased demand on readers to synthesize and accumulate many events and details to understand plot, setting, character, figurative language, and themes in fiction; and to understand main ideas, key details, vocabulary, and text features in nonfiction. Levels J/K is also around where many children begin to read with more accuracy and fluency and where teachers need to devote more attention to comprehension skill development. There are exceptions to this, of course, but it is true for many. For teachers who work with

> *Matching readers and texts requires more than a single assessment A knowledgeable teacher in regular conversation with readers is key.*

38

students who are reading independently below Level J, the information in these sections will still be incredibly helpful as you plan other balanced literacy components where they will be listening to or reading texts above their independent reading level (i.e., shared reading, guided reading, read-aloud, and so on). I chose to end at level W because most students who are able to read and deeply understand Level W texts will likely also be sure-footed in X–Z, and the added challenges they encounter will tend to be more about the content in the book and how much knowledge the reader brings to the text. Again, there are some exceptions but this is generally true. Overall, I hope what's included in Parts II and III helps you consider readers' comprehension development within and across text levels and understand what to expect of the texts they are choosing to read.

Part II focuses on *fiction* texts and readers, and Part III focuses on *nonfiction* texts and readers. In the first section of each part, I explain what I understand about text levels from my study of qualitative text leveling and from my own immersion in children's literature, reading dozens of children's books at each level. I use the four comprehension goals of each genre as a way to organize the discussion of texts. (See page 11 for goals.) While the first half of each part is organized by levels, the second half of each part is organized by goals (e.g., Plot and Setting) and skills (e.g., retelling important events) across the levels, to allow you to see how readers' comprehension develops. I provide samples of student writing about reading to show what strong comprehension sounds like within each goal, as students move to increasingly challenging texts.

Part IV will offer advice for applying all of this knowledge of texts, readers, levels, and comprehension to the classroom: from establishing class-room libraries and matching students to books, to creating whole-book and short-passage comprehension assessments, to using the information from Parts II and III in your evaluation of student responses to reading and selection of comprehension strategies and methods of teaching.

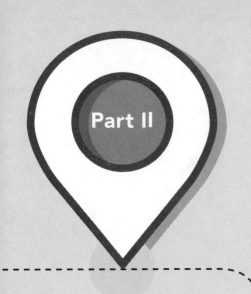

Part II

Fiction

TEXTS, READERS, AND COMPREHENSION

Fiction refers to stories, or narratives, that are created from an author's imagination. They have plots (a series of events), settings (places where the story happens), characters (people or animals who act in the story), and themes (ideas that can be inferred). Fiction can be rooted in truth—the author can choose to base a character on someone real, write about problems and issues that exist in the world, or set a story in a real historical period, for example—but overall the story is invented. Written works of fiction can be short (short stories, picture books), long (novels), or told with pictures (graphic novels).

There are many types of children's fiction. In Part II of this book, you'll be seeing examples of and reading descriptions about realistic and genre fiction, with an emphasis on whole books/novels.

Realistic fiction tells stories of characters to whom young readers can relate and whose adventures contain no magical elements. *Tales of a Fourth Grade Nothing* by Judy Blume (1972) and *Save Me a Seat* by Sarah Weeks and Gita Varadarajan (2016) are both examples of realistic fiction.

Genre fiction includes mysteries (in which there is often a detective who attempts to crack a case, as in the Cam Jansen series by David Adler), historical fiction (stories set in the past, with made-up characters, such as *Sadako and the Thousand Paper Cranes* by Eleanor Coerr [2004]), and fantasy (including magical fantasy books, such as books in the Harry Potter series and science fiction titles such as *The Giver* by Lois Lowry [1993]).

A Partial List of Fiction Text Types

Fiction

Genre Fiction   Realistic Fiction

Fantasy   Mystery   Historical Fiction   Traditional Literature

Science Fiction   High Fantasy   Folk Tales   Fables   Legends

Listed below are the four goals for fiction comprehension that form the framework for the fiction section of this book.

Plot and Setting

Character

Vocabulary and Figurative Language

Themes and Ideas

Studying Fiction and Supporting Readers

A Framework for Comprehension

Beginning on page 54, I describe characteristics of texts, level by level, from J to W. Note that although I use Fountas and Pinnell's Text Gradient™ levels in this book, I have chosen to organize my thinking about each level and associated teaching guidance around the four comprehension goals for fiction that I have written about in *The Reading Strategies Book* (Plot and Setting, Character, Vocabulary and Figurative Language, Themes and Ideas), rather than their ten characteristics (Fountas and Pinnell 2017b; Serravallo 2015). My hope is that these sections will help you understand text levels in a way that will help you support your readers' comprehension.

Beginning on page 88, I provide an overview of how expectations for reading response need to shift and grow as readers move through increasingly complex texts. Each spread is dedicated to a skill that is part of each goal. On these pages, you'll see sample written responses with callouts to explain how children demonstrate increased sophistication based on complexity in the books they read.

Before getting to the level-by-level descriptions and the goal-by-goal student samples, an overview follows that describes each of the four main comprehension goals, the skills that are a part of them, and how these goals and skills are important to understanding fiction texts and readers of fiction.

A Crash Course on Plot and Setting

Skills That Enhance Understanding of Plot and Setting

- Retelling important events

- Synthesizing cause and effect

- Identifying problems

- Visualizing setting

Many teachers and researchers have likened the act of reading to filmmaking. When we read, we create the world of the story by making a "movie in our mind" (e.g., Wilhelm 2001; Harvey and Goudvis 2000; Calkins and Tolan 2010). It's a useful analogy to have in our heads as we teach students to understand the plot and setting of the books they read. A reader whose mental movie is clear and accurate is likely a reader who will be able to retell the important moments in the story, will be able to track changes in settings and/or scenes, and will be able to synthesize details and events to determine problems and solutions and causes and effects in the story. When the mental movie breaks down, then it's time for some strategic interventions.

Retelling and synthesizing have long been an important part of any elementary school reading curriculum. Kylene Beers (2002) defines retelling as "an oral summary of a text based on a set of story elements, such as setting, main characters, and conflicts" (152). Beers goes on to explain that "students use retellings to help them be more specific in their summarizing, to get more organized, discover main ideas and supporting details" (152). In her book *When Kids Can't Read: What Teachers Can Do*, she declares retelling to be an after-reading strategy to help students make sense of what they've read.

What makes for a good retelling isn't always the same. It depends on the amount of text that's being retold and on the complexities of the plot within the story.

A plot is the sequence of events in the story, the "who did and said what to whom." In lower-level books, events are told in the order in which they happened (chronological order). As books get more complex, the author may also tell the story through flashbacks or foreshadowing to introduce past memories or future predictions. It's extremely important to remember the facts of the plot accurately.

Many of us are familiar with Freytag's pyramid, shown at left. Although it may not be important for our students to understand plot in precisely this way, it is a helpful tool for understanding where in the story you currently are and for figuring out how much farther you have to go.

Climax

Rise **Fall**

Introduction **Resolution**

Think about watching a *Law and Order* episode. You've no doubt had the experience of watching the detectives interview a suspect in their house, and you catch yourself thinking, "This person just has to be the one who kidnapped the victim." You're sure of it. Then you glance at the clock and realize you're only twenty minutes into the episode. "Nope, can't be her," you think. That's because you know how the episodes tend to go. This innate sense of plot structure helps you to make good predictions, sure, but it also helps you synthesize and retell the events that have come before.

To understand plot and teach it well, consider what educator Janet Burroway (2006) says: "The features of the story form are fewer than those of a face. They are *conflict*, *crisis*, and *resolution*. Conflict is the first encountered and the fundamental element of fiction, fundamental because only trouble is interesting" (31). Examples abound in the books students read, from Lilly's being in trouble with her teacher in *Lilly's Purple Plastic Purse* to Harry Potter's quest to overcome the evil Lord Voldemort, whose aim is to subjugate all nonmagical people, conquer the wizarding world, and destroy all those who stand in his way, including Harry.

Plot and setting are at times intermixed. When retelling plot, it's important to include details of setting. Flashbacks and foreshadowing, as in the case of *Jake Drake, Bully Buster* (2007), or time travel, as in the Time Warp Trio series, can be confused if readers aren't visualizing the changes in time and place.

Setting, the time and place in which the story happens, can be evoked using relatively few details. Unlike in a technical report from a scientist, writers select specific elements of a place for associations they predict we will imagine when we see them on the page. Imagine what is conjured up for you when I mention a saloon with dusty wooden floors and the clomp of cowboy boots. Or the Atlantic City boardwalk in the 1920s. Likely your mental picture is way more complete than just the few words I used to describe the setting. In a story, the author might mention just the elements of the landscape (plants, animals, buildings, and people), but they can also include the time of day, year, or era.

In lower levels, the settings are often very familiar to the reader and serve well as an almost unnoticed backdrop. By around Level R, the setting plays an increasingly important role in the story. *Sadako and the Thousand Paper Cranes* (2004) could not have been set at any other time or place than post–World War II Japan. The setting may be important to understanding deeper meaning in the story.

A Crash Course on Character

Janet Burroway says, "Conflict is at the core of character as it is of plot. If plot begins with trouble, then character begins with a person in trouble; and trouble most dramatically occurs because we all have traits, tendencies, and desires that are at war, not simply with the world and other people, but with other of our own traits, tendencies, and desires" (2006, 106).

Writers of fiction develop their characters in various ways, and it's helpful to make these elements clear to readers to help them uncover the meanings in their stories. Some means of character development that students should be looking for in texts follow:

- Wants and desires: What does the character want? What is driving the character into action?

- Trouble brewing: Who is creating problems and obstacles and why?

- Moments of contentment: What or who is causing them? Why?

- Moments of discomfort: What or who is causing them? Why?

- Turning points: What discovery or decision is the main character making?

Just as a writer might mention a setting and expect us as readers to conjure up a more complete image, literary characters are constructed out of bits of information that readers are expected to use, like detectives, to fill out the missing parts. Readers can learn to be attuned to evocative details that will help them infer about characters' traits, feelings, and changes. These details include

- Appearance, physical characteristics, clothing, favorite possessions, and so on

- What is said, habits of speech, vocabulary, and tone of speech

- What is unsaid—details that surround the dialogue

- Thoughts

- Mood and emotion

- Basic persona—e.g., funny, serious, shy, outgoing, smart, goofy

- What is done—the character's actions

- Response to the actions and revelations of others

- Attitudes, background, beliefs, social class

- Opinions of other characters about them

Characters can be "round" or "flat," as novelist E. M. Forster suggests (1927). Round characters are more fully represented and seem as complex as real people, a mixture of good and bad traits. They can grow, learn, and even mature from childhood into adulthood during the course of the story, and they also can feel pain or joy, which the audience tends to empathize with.

Main, and sometimes even secondary, characters tend to be "round" at Level N and above. Occasionally a book or series at a level below N has a main character that is more complex, as in the Judy Moody series or Ivy and Bean series where the title characters experience a variety of emotions and work through challenges with relationships to other characters.

Flat characters usually are suggested to us with less information. Flat characters don't grow, change, or mature. Cartoons, like the Road Runner and Coyote series, are composed entirely of flat characters who behave in the same way from episode to episode. Flat characters are often those in the more plot-driven series books up to and including those at Level M, such as Cam Jansen, Horrible Harry, and many of the Magic Tree House books.

When teaching children about characters in their books, we can think about the following dimensions:

- One is the difference between *characterization* and *character development* (Lynch-Brown and Tomlinson 1993). *Characterization* refers to the way an author helps the reader know a character—through the character's physical appearance and traits, revealing thoughts or actions, interactions with other characters, or the narrator's descriptions. *Character development* refers to any changes—good or bad—that the character may experience during the events of the story.

- Another dimension of character is what Calkins and Tolan (2010) suggest: we can "help children approach their study of character *aesthetically* (walking in the shoes of characters, seeing through characters' eyes, empathizing and predicting) and . . . *efferently* (pulling back to develop a bird's-eye view of a text, gleaning facts and insights about characters that they can carry away from the text, synthesizing this information into evidence-based theories, and talking about these theories with others)" (ix).

What is important is that young readers have a sense of the significance of characters. You should therefore help readers understand how character development is often intertwined with plot development. This will help readers to connect to the story, stay engaged while reading, and also learn about lives outside of their own. Students should also consider how characters interact with and impact one another. You should guide them to understand relationships between characters and how characters learn and grow as a result of those relationships. The goal of understanding character lays an important foundation for readers' thinking about lessons, big ideas, or messages that the characters learn or internalize; readers can learn valuable lessons along with the characters. (See Themes and Ideas, page 49.)

Skills That Enhance Understanding of Vocabulary and Figurative Language

○ Monitoring for meaning and using context

A Crash Course on Vocabulary and Figurative Language

As part of their craft, writers play with words, and readers can learn to watch for and enjoy the way an author uses words in surprising ways to paint images, make us chuckle or gasp, or reveal a clever observation. Scan any of your favorite chapter books or picture books, and you're likely to find the following:

- Puns
- Words with multiple meanings
- Invented words
- Allusions
- Expressions and idioms
- Metaphors and similes

- Hyperbole
- Onomatopoeia
- Personification
- Alliteration
- Dialect
- And so on . . .

Although understanding vocabulary and figurative language is important to comprehension, I want to make the point that we should not have our students overly fixated on naming the types of words and phrases they encounter but instead encourage them to relish language, to enjoy the ways that authors surprise us and paint pictures in our minds with words, and to be sure that, as readers, they are making sense of the overall story.

A reader's ability to understand vocabulary and language in a text has been empirically linked to reading comprehension (Baumann and Kame'enui 1991; Becker 1977; Stanovich 1986; Beck, McKeown, and Kucan 2002). Research shows that if students are truly to understand what they read, they must grasp upward of 95 percent of the words (Betts 1946; Carver 1994; Hu and Nation 2000; Laufer 1988). Vocabulary and figurative language in texts is also an important consideration for emerging bilinguals, who may develop conversational English skills in two to three years but may continue to work on their academic English skills for five to eight (Cummins 2008). As they learn to read in a second language, they draw on their own cultural, linguistic, and cognitive development (Freeman, Freeman, Soto, and Ebe 2016).

To this end, one aim is to help children to accomplish "lexile dexterity"—that is, a useful sense of what a given word means in its specific context.

Interestingly enough, research has also shown that while it is helpful to explicitly teach readers words and phrases, most word learning occurs unconsciously and through regular reading, writing, speaking, and listening (G. A. Miller 1999; Nagy, Anderson, and Herman 1987). Therefore, creating a classroom culture where children love language, notice it in their reading, use it in their speech, and try it in their writing will go a long way toward achieving your vocabulary and language instruction goals.

A Crash Course on Themes and Ideas

Theme is what the story is about—the main idea or ideas a reader can take away. Determining theme can pose a challenge to some readers because it can be abstract and is rarely stated outright in the text. Nevertheless, with instruction, modeling, examples, and strategies, students can learn to tune into the bigger ideas in the texts they read.

Stephanie Harvey and Anne Goudvis (2000) explain, "Themes in books are the underlying ideas, morals, or lessons that give the story its texture, depth, and meaning. . . . We infer themes. Themes often make us feel angry, sad, guilty, joyful, frightened. We tell kids that we are likely to feel themes in our gut" (109).

Now, I am going out on a limb in that I do think there are a great many feelings, attitudes, and ideas that an author purposefully puts in a story and hopes readers will pick up on. But I don't mean to imply that a novel has a single set of meanings that are correct or that, in the case of theme, the author deliberately weaves in all the themes we may find. In that curious way, the author doesn't fully own all of the ideas—and is not entirely responsible for them.

And so the "truth" of a novel's characters and ideas belong to the author and the reader. Along with literary theorist Louise Rosenblatt (1978), I think that interpretation of theme (or character, or setting, and so forth) is in part the result of the way the reader transacts with the text. That means instead of finding the "right" answer, the reader should experience something from reading the text and infer a truth that resonates from using their own prior experience, together with the experiences of the characters in the text, to come up with a deeper meaning. It's easy for students to rush toward a neat and tidy truth (love heals, war is bad, friends are important, and so on), but it's good to remind them that the themes we take away can be as multidimensional, contradictory, and messy as the characters.

Skills That Enhance Understanding of Themes and Ideas

- Interpreting a story by naming life lesson(s) or theme(s)

- Identifying and interpreting social issues

- Identifying and interpreting symbols

"We might start to understand theme if we ask the question, 'What about what it's about?' What does the story have to say about the idea or the abstraction that seems to be contained within it? What attitudes or judgments does it imply?"

—JANET BURROWAY (2006)

Inferring the meaning of symbols belong to the realm of themes and ideas because they are abstract and often used by authors to "show, not tell" a theme. Symbols are people, places, or objects that represent something beyond their physical description. They can succinctly communicate complex ideas. The notion that something real and/or concrete can stand for something conceptual is challenging for the youngest readers but becomes more possible for sophisticated readers by around Level P. For instance, in the book *Koya DeLaney and the Good Girl Blues* by Eloise Greenfield (1995), the main character has a dream about a dragon, which serves as a symbol for the anger she's feeling in a previous scene. Because this level is among the first when students might encounter symbolism, Greenfield makes the abstract meaning pretty clear, and its meaning is somewhat unpacked by the narrator. By around Level T, the reader will need to do more inferring to determine the significance of a theme with less support from the text.

Some readers may be taught to be on the lookout for details and to figure out what the author intended when he or she kept mentioning the clock over and over again, or when the author took two pages to describe the monster a character sees in her dream. Readers can be ready to ask,

What is the author intending by having this repeat? By having it take up all this space in the book? Could this stand for something bigger, something deeper, something more meaningful than what it appears to be? Other readers, though, might learn to try "turning the details of their books—the colors and names and recurring objects or places—into symbols," as Donna Santman suggests in *Shades of Meaning* (2005, 99).

Notice the different approaches—in one instance, readers position themselves to figure out what an author wants them to understand, and in the other, readers explore their own transaction with the text to help them create personal meaning. As you work with your own readers on discovering thematic elements in the stories they read, be aware of the ways you help them find meaning in the text.

Understanding Fiction Texts

A Level-by-Level Guide to Characteristics

By studying the information in this section, you'll learn about the text characteristics of fiction books at Levels J to W. This will help you to know children's literature so that when you are working with students in conferences or small groups, even if you don't know the specific book the child is reading, you'll have a sense of what to generally expect of books at that level. The knowledge will also help you plan when you do know the book the child is reading, because focusing on the text characteristics, rather than on the book itself, will help children to generalize your teaching from book to book.

Each spread focuses on one level. For each level, I offer a description of text characteristics, a "look-fors" checklist for studying student response to reading, and examples of books.

Developing an understanding of text characteristics offers you a crucial context for understanding what to expect of readers.

A "look-fors" checklist that will allow you to apply the text complexity knowledge to student-written responses and conversation about books. This will help you apply what you know about text levels to *any* text at that level, even one you haven't read yourself. A more in-depth look at student development within and across levels begins on page 86. When the look-fors have changed from the previous level, it is indicated with a "shift from" note.

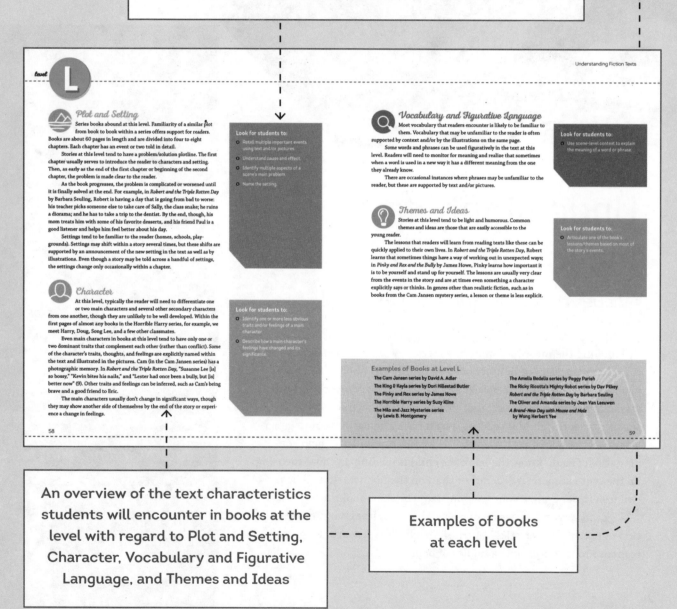

An overview of the text characteristics students will encounter in books at the level with regard to Plot and Setting, Character, Vocabulary and Figurative Language, and Themes and Ideas

Examples of books at each level

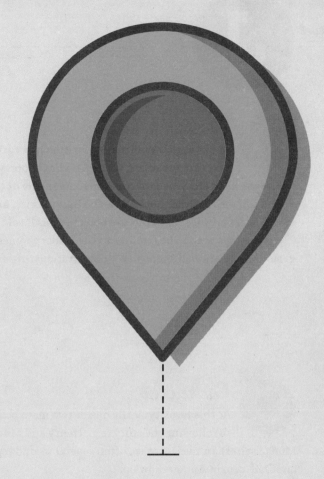

Developing an
understanding of text
characteristics offers
you a crucial context
for understanding what
to expect of readers.
To determine whether
students "get it," we have
to know what "it" is.

Plot and Setting

Books at this level may be written in a variety of ways. Some texts are organized with episodic chapters, where each chapter is its own short story tied together by some theme or time period, as in the Poppleton series. Other books, like the Beezy series, are one continuous story. There are also many picture books at this level.

Settings tend to be familiar to the reader (homes, schools, playgrounds) and are well supported by illustrations, often in full color.

Look for students to:

- Retell multiple important events using text and/or pictures.
- Understand cause and effect.
- Identify multiple aspects of a scene's main problem.
- Name the setting.

Character

At this level, typically one or two main characters are important to following the story (e.g., Henry and Mudge in the Henry and Mudge series). In these stories, often several secondary characters (e.g., Mom and Dad, cousin Annie) show up.

Main characters in books at this level are simple, with one or two traits that generally are similar (e.g., the character of Fox in the Fox series is a troublemaker who is annoyed by his sister). Main characters usually don't change in significant ways, though they may show a change of feelings or opinion. For example, Poppleton might feel frustrated when his neighbor Cherry Sue continually invites him over, but when they talk about it, he realizes he was wrong, apologizes, and feels better.

Look for students to:

- Identify one or more less obvious traits and/or feelings of a main character.
- Describe how a main character's feelings have changed.

Vocabulary and Figurative Language

Vocabulary and language is likely to be familiar and is often repetitive from sentence to sentence. High-frequency words are prevalent. When a reader does encounter an unfamiliar word, there will likely be picture support to help decipher meaning.

Figurative language is very rare. When it does appear, it feels almost as if it were put there to entertain an adult reader. For example, in one Poppleton story where Poppleton goes to the library, the narrator mentions that he brings lip balm for the "dry parts" in the books he reads. This type of language is likely to be lost on the young reader, but this won't negatively impact overall comprehension and enjoyment of the story.

Look for students to:

o Use scens-level context to explain the meaning of a word or phrase.

Themes and Ideas

Stories tend to be light and humorous. Common themes and ideas are easily accessible to the young reader: problems with friends, at school, or at home. The lessons readers learn from texts like these can be quickly applied to their own lives: talk to friends when you have a problem, it feels good to care for a friend, or parents are there to help you.

At times, a theme may be explicitly stated at the end of the story by one of the main characters or easily inferred from a solution to the problem in the story.

Look for students to:

o Articulate one of the book's lessons/themes based on most of the story's events.

Examples of Books at Level J

The Clifford and the Big Red Dog series by Norman Bridwell

Baseball Ballerina by Kathryn Cristaldi

Have You Seen Duck? by Janet A. Holmes

The Katie Woo series by Fran Manushkin

The Fox series by Edward Marshall

The Little Bear series by Else Homelund Minarik

The Henry and Mudge series by Cynthia Rylant

The Mr. Putter and Tabby series by Cynthia Rylant

The Poppleton series by Cynthia Rylant

Fiesta Babies by Carmen Tafolla

Plot and Setting

Chapter books at this level may be written in a variety of ways. Some texts are organized with episodic chapters, where each chapter is its own self-contained story, as in the Frog and Toad series. Other books, like the Andy Shane series, are organized as one story. Still other books at this level may be entire stories that are not broken up by chapter, such as books in the Nate the Great series. Stories often focus around a central problem that gets solved by the end. Plots within a series are predictable, which supports the reader.

Settings tend to be familiar to the reader (homes, schools, playgrounds). Settings may shift within a story several times, but these shifts are supported by text as well as illustrations.

Look for students to:

- Retell multiple important events using text and/or pictures.
- Understand cause and effect.
- Identify multiple aspects of a scene's main problem.
- Name the setting.

Character

At this level, there are typically one or two main characters that are important to following the story, such as Frog and Toad in the Frog and Toad series, Nate in the Nate the Great series, and Andy Shane in the Andy Shane series.

Even main characters in books at this level tend to have just one or two traits that generally are similar (e.g., someone, like Dolores in the Andy Shane series, is bossy and forthright). Main characters usually don't change in significant ways, though they may show another side of themselves by the end of the story or experience a change of feelings or opinion. They often learn a lesson by the end of the story. In the first story of *Days with Frog and Toad* by Arnold Lobel, for example, Toad starts out proclaiming he's "down in the dumps," and there is a picture of him moping in bed (9). By the end of the story, he declares, "Now I feel better . . ." (14). Changes that characters feel are usually explicit at this level.

Secondary characters are usually peripheral and one-dimensional and help to move the plot along but have a minimal effect on the main character.

Look for students to:

- Identify one or more less obvious traits and/or feelings of a main character.
- Describe how a main character's feelings have changed and its significance **(shift from Level J)**.

Vocabulary and Figurative Language

The vocabulary is likely to be familiar. At times language is repetitive from sentence to sentence. High-frequency words are prevalent. Unfamiliar vocabulary words are often supported by context and/or same-page illustrations.

Words and phrases will occasionally be used figuratively. Readers must monitor for sense and realize that when a word is used in a new way, its meaning is sometimes different from one they know. For example, in *Nate the Great and the Snowy Trail* by M. Weinman Sharmat, Nate says, "I was feeling drippy. Snow from the trees was falling on me" (5).

Readers will find text and picture support for the rare instances where phrases are unfamiliar. Understanding phrases helps overall understanding of the plot or character but is usually not essential.

Look for students to:

○ Use scene-level context to explain the meaning of a word or phrase.

Themes and Ideas

Stories tend to be light and humorous. Common themes and ideas are easily accessible to the young reader: friendship, the value of trying, and not giving up. Lessons readers learn can be quickly applied to their own lives: speak up for yourself; sometimes it's okay for your friend to spend time alone; if you get your work done, you'll have time to play.

At times, a main character may explicitly state a theme at the end of the story. Other times, themes can be easily inferred from a solution to the problem.

Look for students to:

○ Articulate one of the book's lessons/themes based on most of the story's events.

Examples of Books at Level K

The Franklin series by Paulette Bourgeois

Jamaica's Find by Juanita Havill

Andy Shane and the Very Bossy Dolores Starbuckle by Jennifer Jacobson

The Sofia Martinez series by Jacqueline Jules

The Story of Ferdinand by Munro Leaf

The Ling & Ting series by Grace Lin

Days with Frog and Toad by Arnold Lobel

The Day Jimmy's Boa Ate the Wash by Trinka Hakes Noble

The Nate the Great series by Marjorie Weinman Sharmat

The Black Lagoon Adventures series by Mike Thaler

Plot and Setting

Series books abound at this level. Familiarity of a similar plot from book to book within a series offers support for readers. Books are about 60 pages in length and are divided into four to eight chapters. Each chapter has an event or two told in detail.

Stories at this level tend to have a problem/solution plotline. The first chapter usually serves to introduce the reader to characters and setting. Then, as early as the end of the first chapter or beginning of the second chapter, the problem is made clear to the reader.

As the book progresses, the problem is complicated or worsened until it is finally solved at the end. For example, in *Robert and the Triple Rotten Day* by Barbara Seuling, Robert is having a day that is going from bad to worse: his teacher picks someone else to take care of Sally, the class snake; he ruins a diorama; and he has to take a trip to the dentist. By the end, though, his mom treats him with some of his favorite desserts, and his friend Paul is a good listener and helps him feel better about his day.

Settings tend to be familiar to the reader (homes, schools, playgrounds). Settings may shift within a story several times, but these shifts are supported by an announcement of the new setting in the text as well as by illustrations. Even though a story may be told across a handful of settings, the settings change only occasionally within a chapter.

Look for students to:

- Retell multiple important events using text and/or pictures.
- Understand cause and effect.
- Identify multiple aspects of a scene's main problem.
- Name the setting.

Character

At this level, typically the reader will need to differentiate one or two main characters and several other secondary characters from one another, though they are unlikely to be well developed. Within the first pages of almost any books in the Horrible Harry series, for example, we meet Harry, Doug, Song Lee, and a few other classmates.

Even main characters in books at this level tend to have only one or two dominant traits that complement each other (rather than conflict). Some of the character's traits, thoughts, and feelings are explicitly named within the text and illustrated in the pictures. Cam (in the Cam Jansen series) has a photographic memory. In *Robert and the Triple Rotten Day*, "Susanne Lee [is] so bossy," "Kevin bites his nails," and "Lester had once been a bully, but [is] better now" (9). Other traits and feelings can be inferred, such as Cam's being brave and a good friend to Eric.

The main characters usually don't change in significant ways, though they may show another side of themselves by the end of the story or experience a change in feelings.

Look for students to:

- Identify one or more less obvious traits and/or feelings of a main character.
- Describe how a main character's feelings have changed and its significance.

Vocabulary and Figurative Language

Most vocabulary that readers encounter is likely to be familiar to them. Vocabulary that may be unfamiliar to the reader is often supported by context and/or by the illustrations on the same page.

Some words and phrases can be used figuratively in the text at this level. Readers will need to monitor for meaning and realize that sometimes when a word is used in a new way it has a different meaning from the one they already know.

There are occasional instances where phrases may be unfamiliar to the reader, but these are supported by text and/or pictures.

Look for students to:
- Use scene-level context to explain the meaning of a word or phrase.

Themes and Ideas

Stories at this level tend to be light and humorous. Common themes and ideas are those that are easily accessible to the young reader.

The lessons that readers will learn from reading texts like these can be quickly applied to their own lives. In *Robert and the Triple Rotten Day*, Robert learns that sometimes things have a way of working out in unexpected ways; in *Pinky and Rex and the Bully* by James Howe, Pinky learns how important it is to be yourself and stand up for yourself. The lessons are usually very clear from the events in the story and are at times even something a character explicitly says or thinks. In genres other than realistic fiction, such as in books from the Cam Jansen mystery series, a lesson or theme is less explicit.

Look for students to:
- Articulate one of the book's lessons/themes based on most of the story's events.

Examples of Books at Level L

The Cam Jansen series by David A. Adler

The King & Kayla series by Dori Hillestad Butler

The Pinky and Rex series by James Howe

The Horrible Harry series by Suzy Kline

The Milo and Jazz Mysteries series by Lewis B. Montgomery

The Amelia Bedelia series by Peggy Parish

The Ricky Ricotta's Mighty Robot series by Dav Pilkey

Robert and the Triple Rotten Day by Barbara Seuling

The Oliver and Amanda series by Jean Van Leeuwen

A Brand-New Day with Mouse and Mole by Wong Herbert Yee

Plot and Setting

Series books also prevail at this level, a boon to readers who can continue to build reading stamina and skills while supported by familiar characters, plotlines, and settings. Each chapter may include several well-developed events, requiring readers to carry forward significant details. There is a wider range in length of books, with many similar to Level L—around 60 pages—and some exceeding 100 pages.

Plotlines are still relatively simple, but unlike at the last level, where problem/solution structures abounded, at Level M some books are beginning to also be character-driven.

While simple fantasy books, such as *Stuart Goes to School*, begin to appear at this level, settings are generally familiar to the reader (home, school, and so on). Settings may shift within a story several times. Settings will also shift within a chapter. In certain series, such as the Magic Tree House, readers will need to visualize unfamiliar settings but are given a great deal of picture support any time they need to do so.

Books at Level M have stretches of narration where nothing is really "happening" in the plot; the author may be setting the scene or narrating a character's internal thinking. Look, for example, at the first two pages of *Stuart Goes to School*, where the author introduces the story with narration as opposed to character action or dialogue.

Look for students to:

- Retell multiple important events using text and/or pictures.
- Understand cause and effect.
- Identify multiple aspects of a scene's main problem.
- Name the setting.

Character

As was true at Level L, main characters often have several similar traits. The reader will often need to distinguish several other characters from one another.

The personality traits, thoughts, and feelings of the character are often explicitly named within the text and illustrated in the pictures. Bossy, naughty, shy, bullying, moody—whatever it is, the reader gets it loud and clear. The main character usually doesn't change in significant ways but may show another side of themselves by the end of the story or experience a change of feelings or opinion. Often, the main character learns a lesson by the end of the story. In *Marvin Redpost, Why Pick on Me?* by Louis Sachar, Marvin is teased by another student, Clarence, who claims he's a nose-picker. His friends turn against him. By the end, though, he learns to use humor and honesty to deflect the situation. He teaches the other characters and the reader that nobody is perfect and that family can be valuable in times of trouble.

In some of the harder books at this level, such as those in the Judy Moody series, the reader may begin to think about how secondary characters affect the main character's feelings.

Look for students to:

- Identify one or more less obvious traits and/or feelings of a main character.
- Describe how a main character's feelings have changed and its significance.

Vocabulary and Figurative Language

Most vocabulary is familiar or heavily supported by context; some is unexplained. The cat in *Stuart Goes to School* by Sara Pennypacker is described as a "maniac" without examples. In *Judy Moody Saves the World!* by Megan McDonald, some vocabulary relates to endangered species—even words in Latin—that the reader should be able to understand from context.

Metaphors, similes, and sarcasm begin to be more prevalent. When words or phrases are figurative, readers will need to monitor for meaning and notice words being used in new ways. For example, in *Ivy and Bean* by Annie Barrows, Bean's mom tries to convince Bean to befriend Ivy. When she hears that, she responds, "All aboard! Next train for Boring is leaving now!" (11).

Look for students to:
- Use scene-level context to explain the meaning of a word or phrase.

Themes and Ideas

Stories tend to be light and humorous with common themes that are easily accessible. Lessons can quickly be applied to readers' own lives (e.g., Stuart in *Stuart Goes to School* learns the importance of being true to himself).

Other lessons are more universal, more abstract, and less accessible to readers. For example, in *Judy Moody Saves the World!* by Megan McDonald, the theme of "everyone can do his or her part to make a difference in the world" may be a stretch for some.

Look for students to:
- Articulate one of the book's lessons/themes based on most of the story's events.

Examples of Books at Level M

The Ivy and Bean series by Annie Barrows
Freckle Juice by Judy Blume
The Paint Brush Kid by Clyde Robert Bulla
The Bink and Gollie series by Kate DiCamillo
The Riverside Kids series by Johanna Hurwitz

The Captain Awesome series by Stan Kirby
The Judy Moody series by Megan McDonald
The Magic Tree House series by Mary Pope Osborn
The Stuart series by Sara Pennypacker
The Marvin Redpost series by Louis Sachar

Plot and Setting

Chapter books in a series are still common at this level, but there are also a number of notable stand-alone titles, such as *How to Be Cool in the Third Grade* by Betsy Duffey and *Donavan's Word Jar* by Monalisa DeGross. Books are about the same length as those at Level M: around 100 pages.

Plotlines can be more complex at Level N. To understand these more complex texts, a reader will need to continue to be attuned to multiple problems or aspects of the main problem. For example, in *How to Be Cool in the Third Grade*, Robbie's initial problem is that he wants to figure out what is cool in third grade. Robbie soon has a second, complicating problem: the bully, Bo Haney. In addition, new plot challenges, such as stories-within-stories, may start to appear at this level.

Level N plots are driven largely by the main character's motivation and attempts at getting what they want. To follow these kinds of plotlines, a reader needs to follow events and realizations that unfold internally and externally for characters. That is, plot is not just a series of events but also a series of revelations and changes within the main character.

Settings still tend to be familiar to the reader (home, school, and so on). Settings may shift within a story several times and will often shift within a chapter.

Look for students to:

- Retell multiple important events using text and/or pictures.
- Understand cause and effect.
- Identify multiple aspects of a scene's main problem.
- Name the setting.

Character

Characters will be more complex than at prior levels, with multiple traits and feelings. While in previous levels main characters might have changed feelings, now main characters may show different sides to themselves over the course of the book. For example, Amber in *Amber Brown Is Not a Crayon* begins the story by being a good friend to Justin, but as the stress of his moving away starts to weigh on her, she shows a jealous side to herself. By the end of the story, as she learns that she can keep in touch with Justin in his new home, she resumes her good friend role.

Secondary characters begin to play a more prominent role at this level. At times secondary characters will display more than one trait, thought, and/or feeling and will also affect the main character in significant ways. An example of this is in Tomie dePaola's memoir *26 Fairmount Avenue*. DePaola develops the secondary characters—his family, teachers, and friends—with humor and humanity. Their influences and effects on him are clear and important to understanding Tomie as the main character.

Look for students to:

- Identify several less obvious traits and/or feelings that reveal different aspects of a main character (shift from Level M).
- Describe significant changes in a main character (shift from Level M).
- Identify many feelings and/or traits of secondary characters (shift from Level M).

Vocabulary and Figurative Language

New vocabulary that readers encounter at this level is likely to be unexplained. The reader will need to work to gather its meaning from the larger context of the story. Words also continue to be used figuratively and have connotative meanings. Dialogue continues to be unassigned or tagged with a variety of adverbs or adjectives.

Metaphors and similes continue to appear, but here they become more essential to overall understanding. For instance, in *How to Be Cool in the Third Grade*, readers will need to comprehend sentences like, "He wished a black hole would open up in the floor and swallow him" and "Coolness was like armor, protection from harm and teasing" (35) to think about characters and events in the story. Reading sentences like these in a literal way could lead to confusion.

Look for students to:
O Use scene-level context to explain the meaning of a word or phrase.

Themes and Ideas

Some themes at this level are similar to those at prior levels, but at this level some themes and ideas will begin to be deeper, requiring a reader to understand important human problems or issues: Amber's parents are divorced, and Justin's father had to take a job away from home and live away from his family (*Amber Brown Is Not a Crayon*); Milo is teased by his parents to the point of feeling that he is not good enough and goes to extremes to try to be perfect (*Be a Perfect Person in Just Three Days!*); and Robbie deals with a bully (*How to Be Cool in the Third Grade*).

Look for students to:
O Articulate one of the book's lessons/themes based on most of the story's events.

Examples of Books at Level N

My Name Is María Isabel by Alma Flor Ada

A Matter of Fact Magic series by Ruth Chew

The Magic Finger by Roald Dahl

Amber Brown Is Not a Crayon by Paula Danziger

Donavan's Word Jar by Monalisa DeGross

How to Be Cool in the Third Grade by Betsy Duffey

Make Way for Dyamonde Daniel by Nikki Grimes

Catwings by Ursula K. Le Guin

Be a Perfect Person in Just Three Days! by Stephen Manes

The A to Z Mysteries series by Ron Roy

Plot and Setting

Picture support drops off significantly at level O, requiring the reader to create mental images and track events from the text alone. Books are also longer on average, with plots that include many events told in detail across multiple chapters. Chapter books in a series, like Beverly Cleary's Ramona books, are about as common at this level as stand-alone fiction titles, such as Johanna Hurwitz's *Baseball Fever*.

Plotlines can be more complex than at level N; when a problem is introduced, there are likely to be multiple causes to the main problem. Character-driven plots continue to be common, where plot is advanced largely by the character's motivation and their attempts at getting what they want.

Settings can be either places and times that are familiar to the reader (i.e., home, school) or some that may be unfamiliar (as in the fantastical "New Mouse City, the capital of Mouse Island" in the Geronimo Stilton series). Settings will shift several times within a chapter and within a story.

Movement through time is swift in many parts of texts at this level, making it both more important and more challenging to understand the amount of time that has passed between events in the plot. Longer stretches of narration where nothing is really "happening" continue to occur.

Look for students to:

○ Retell multiple important events **(shift from Level N)**.

○ Draw connections between multiple causes and effects, and demonstrate deep understanding of the scene **(shift from Level N)**.

○ Identify multiple aspects of the story's main problem **(shift from Level N)**.

○ Describe in some original detail the time(s) and place(s) **(shift from Level N)**.

Character

Protagonists are likely to be complex and memorable. Beverly Cleary's Ramona Quimby is imaginative, happy-go-lucky, and brave, but she is also sensitive. When she is not allowed to visit her little sister, Roberta, in the hospital due to her age, Ramona begins to feel depressed and sick. Ramona is upset for most of grade three due to a misunderstood comment made by her teacher, Mrs. Whaley. Her problems are usually resolved when she talks to her parents, sister, or teacher. Ramona and her big sister, Beezus, have a love/hate relationship. Secondary characters play a prominent role at this level. At least one secondary character will be complex, showing multiple traits, thoughts, and/or feelings.

Secondary characters are also likely to affect the main character in significant ways. They may help teach the main character a lesson and may help cause the main character to change or show another side of themselves. For example, the Gloria series, a spinoff of *The Stories Julian Tells* by Ann Cameron, hosts an array of secondary characters. Each of the short stories features different characters who have effects and influences on Gloria, the main character.

Look for students to:

○ Identify several less obvious traits and/or feelings that reveal different aspects of a main character **(shift from Level M)**.

○ Describe significant changes in a main character by synthesizing many details.

○ Identify many feelings and/or traits of secondary characters

Vocabulary and Figurative Language

New vocabulary that readers encounter at this level is likely to be unexplained. The reader will need to work to glean the meanings of unfamiliar words from the larger context of the story. For example, in the opening pages of the first chapter of *Gloria's Way* by Ann Cameron, the words *palaces*, *embroidered*, and *scalloped* are all used without explanation.

Words will be used figuratively and/or will have connotative meanings and will be essential to understanding the story. Metaphors and similes are prevalent and therefore essential to understanding character, plot, and setting. For example, Clementine, the narrator and main character of *The Talented Clementine*, uses figurative language often, as in the opening chapter when she says, "And that's when the worried feeling—as if somebody were scribbling with a big black crayon—started up in my brain" (3). Readers will need to form a mental picture of what is being described and compared to continue to understand the narrator's perspective.

Look for students to:

○ Use scene-level context to explain the meaning of a word or phrase.

Themes and Ideas

Some themes at this level are those that are easily accessible to young readers. However, a higher incidence of themes tap into universal human problems and social issues. Themes may include issues that are more challenging for readers to understand, for example, racism in *Chocolate Fever* and bullying in *Jake Drake, Bully Buster*. Thus, a reader's background knowledge and inferential thinking come into play more at this level than at previous levels.

Look for students to:

○ Articulate one of the book's lessons/themes based on most of the story's events.

○ Identify a social issue in the book and explain the complexity of that issue (**shift from Level N**).

Examples of Books at Level O

The Stories Julian Tells by Ann Cameron

The Ramona series by Beverly Cleary

Jake Drake, Bully Buster by Andrew Clements

Baseball Fever by Johanna Hurwitz

The Little Pear series by Eleanor Frances Lattimore

Pippi Longstocking by Astrid Lindgren

The Baby-Sitters Club by Ann M. Martin

The Spray-Paint Mystery by Angela Shelf Medearis

The Clementine series by Sara Pennypacker

Chocolate Fever by Robert Kimmel Smith

Plot and Setting

Plots include a host of major and minor events, making it more challenging to hone in on what is significant. New plot challenges, such as time travel and subplots, may appear in some books at this level. Consider Cynthia Rylant's *Gooseberry Park*, in which the first three chapters are told from the points of view of different characters in different settings with seemingly disconnected story lines. The reader needs to keep reading on, synthesizing and recalling all the events, until they come together and are explained in a later chapter.

Settings tend to be a combination of places and times that are familiar to the reader (home, school, and so forth) and those that may be unfamiliar (such as medieval times in *The Time Warp Trio: Knights of the Kitchen Table* by Jon Scieszka or a double-Dutch competition in *Koya DeLaney and the Good Girl Blues* by Eloise Greenfield).

Movement through time is much swifter in many parts of texts at Level P, and a reader will need to understand the amount of time that passes between events in the plot, despite the changes in pacing. Longer stretches of narration where nothing is really "happening" continue to occur.

Look for students to:

○ Retell multiple important events

○ Draw connections between multiple causes and effects, and demonstrate deep understanding of the scene **(shift from Level N)**.

○ Identify multiple aspects of the story's main problem.

○ Describe in some original detail the time(s) and place(s).

Character

Characters are likely to be memorable and complex. They may have traits, thoughts, and/or feelings that contradict or show both positive and negative sides of their personalities. Main characters change and learn lessons, as they do in books at prior levels.

Secondary characters play an increasingly prominent role. At least one secondary character will be complex, showing multiple traits, thoughts, and/or feelings. Secondary characters continue to affect the main character in significant ways. The secondary characters may help teach the main character a lesson and may help cause the main character to change or show another side of themselves. *Stone Fox* by John Reynolds Gardiner is a good example of this, because Willy's grandfather is a driving force motivating his action and maturation in the story.

Look for students to:

○ Identify several less obvious traits and/or feelings that reveal different aspects of a main character.

○ Describe significant changes in a main character by synthesizing details.

○ Identify many feelings and/or traits of secondary characters

Vocabulary and Figurative Language

Similar to those at the previous level, books written at this level contain vocabulary not explained within the sentence or surrounding context. Readers will likely encounter figurative language and/or words that have connotative meanings and may be essential to understanding the text. Metaphors and similes continue to be prevalent and, therefore, are more essential to understanding character, plot, and setting.

Titles such as those in Jon Scieszka's Time Warp Trio series are filled with words that are unique to a particular period. The books also contain a plethora of sarcasm and wordplay, which adds humor. A reader unattuned to this vocabulary and language will miss out on the fun and joy of these clever books.

Look for students to:

- Use scene-level context to explain the meaning of a word or phrase.

Themes and Ideas

Some themes that can be derived from books at this level are easily accessible to young readers; however, other themes also go much deeper and speak to the universal human condition and social issues, including inequality, greed, and loss. Often novels have a blend of more and less accessible ideas. For example, readers of *Koya DeLaney and the Good Girl Blues* may easily connect the sister-loyalty theme to their own lives, whereas the pros and cons of fame might be more challenging for readers to appreciate.

Look for students to:

- Articulate one of the book's lessons/themes based on most of the story's events.
- Identify a social issue in the book and explain the complexity of that issue.

Examples of Books at Level P

Stone Fox by John Reynolds Gardiner

Koya DeLaney and the Good Girl Blues by Eloise Greenfield

Almost Zero by Nikki Grimes

Book Uncle and Me by Uma Krishnaswami

The Alvin Ho series by Lenore Look

Felita by Nicholasa Mohr

The Captain Underpants series by Dav Pilkey

Gooseberry Park by Cynthia Rylant

The Time Warp Trio: Knights of the Kitchen Table by Jon Scieszka

The David Mortimore Baxter series by Karen Tayleur

Plot and Setting

The books are longer on average than those at Level P, with more density of text on a page and fewer (or no) illustrations. Plotlines continue to be complex at this level. Each of the several problems is likely to have multiple causes. Character-driven plots continue to be common, where plot is driven largely by the character's motivation and their attempts at getting what they want.

Settings tend to be a combination of places and times that are familiar and unfamiliar. For example, *Fourth Grade Rats* by Jerry Spinelli is set largely in the main character's home, his best friend's home, and at school. *Abby Takes a Stand* by Patricia McKissack is a historical fiction book set in Tennessee during the civil rights era, which relies on that setting to drive the story; that is, the events couldn't have happened anywhere else.

Movement through time will continue to vary throughout the book, with some chapters or time elapsed between chapters paced quickly, and other parts having long stretches of narration.

Look for students to:

- Retell multiple important events

- Draw connections between multiple causes and effects, and demonstrate deep understanding of the scene.

- Identify more than two of the story's problems or aspects of the main problem, and mention internal and external aspects (**shift from Level P**).

- Describe in some original detail the time(s) and place(s).

Character

Characters are likely to be memorable and complex. They may have traits, thoughts, and/or feelings that conflict or show both positive and negative sides of their personalities. Main characters change and learn lessons, as they did at prior levels.

Secondary characters continue to play an important role. Secondary characters can be complex, with multiple traits, thoughts, and/or feelings, and they may affect the main character in more significant ways than in past levels. Oggie, in Sarah Weeks' *Oggie Cooder*, is a peculiar character—he has invented "charving" (chewing and carving slices of American cheese). Everyone considers him to be strange until he gets attention from a television show on the lookout for odd talents. Secondary character Donnica Perfecto wants to steal his talent and become famous. Then, when she's unsuccessful, she decides to become his manager. In that role, she tries to change him into an exaggerated version of himself. When he starts feeling uncomfortable with the way she's trying to change him, he actually changes—he becomes more aware and is unafraid to speak up for what he believes is right, staying true to who he is.

Look for students to:

- Identify several less obvious traits and/or feelings that reveal character's complexity (**shift from Level P**).

- Describe significant changes in main character, comparing past traits and/or feelings with present ones (**shift fromLevel P**).

- Identify and comment on many feelings and/or traits of a secondary character (**shift from Level P**).

Vocabulary and Figurative Language

Similar to the prior level, new vocabulary that readers encounter at this level is likely to be unexplained. Metaphors and similes continue to be prevalent at Level Q and are more essential to understanding character, plot, and setting.

The use of figurative language and colloquial language can add "voice" to the text that can enhance the reader's sense of character, appreciation of humor, and overall engagement. For example, in *Fourth Grade Rats*, Joey refers to himself as "Number One." Understanding this epithet reinforces the reader's impression of Joey's cockiness—his belief that it's important to be selfish and look out for himself, even at the expense of others.

Look for students to:
- Use scene-level context to explain the meaning of a word or phrase.

Themes and Ideas

Some themes that can be derived from books at this level are easily accessible to young readers. However, other themes also address important human problems and social issues, for example, gender issues in *Fourth Grade Rats*. Themes may include more challenging issues for readers to understand, such as the concept of "becoming a man" in *Fourth Grade Rats*.

Look for students to:
- Articulate one of the book's lessons/themes based on most of the story's events.
- Identify a social issue in the book and explain the complexity of that issue.

Examples of Books at Level Q

The Field Trip Mysteries series by Steve Brezenoff

James and the Giant Peach by Roald Dahl

Just Juice by Karen Hesse

Bunnicula, Rabbit Tale of Mystery by James Howe

The Year of the Dog by Grace Lin

Archer's Quest by Linda Sue Park

There's a Boy in the Girls' Bathroom by Louis Sachar

Fourth Grade Rats by Jerry Spinelli

Oggie Cooder by Sarah Weeks

Last Summer with Maizon by Jacqueline Woodson

R

Plot and Setting

On average, books at this level are longer than those at Level Q, so readers must have greater stamina. Plots are more complex and thus require students to synthesize lots of information. Students may need to navigate flashbacks and foreshadowing, and subplots or multiple plotlines. The character deals with multiple problems, many of which are resolved rather than solved. The resolution will give closure to the problem without fixing it as a solution would.

Increasingly, books may be set in places that are unfamiliar or foreign to most young readers (for example, post–World War II Japan in *Sadako and the Thousand Paper Cranes*). At Level Q, there are still lots of accessible "home and school" settings; a main character might visit a more exotic setting once. At Level R, however, the entire story may be set in an unfamiliar place. These settings, in addition to being unfamiliar, can be essential to understanding the story. For example, consider Gary Paulsen's *Hatchet* that tells the story of Brian, the sole survivor on a tiny bush plane that crashes in the Canadian wilderness. This story couldn't take place in the middle of a city; the setting here serves almost as a character in and of itself.

Look for students to:

○ Retell the most important events from more complex plots (**shift from Level Q**).

○ Draw connections between multiple causes and effects, and demonstrate deep understanding of the scene.

○ Identify more than two of the story's problems or aspects of the main problem. and mention internal and external aspects.

○ Describe in some original detail the time(s) and place(s).

Character

Main characters are complex, with positive and negative traits. To fully understand the character, the reader needs to notice how a character's traits lead them to behave in certain ways and empathize with them.

A reader must be open to having their perspective about the character change over the course of the story and must be able to consider different points of view offered by the main character within the story. For example, in *The Family Under the Bridge* by Natalie Savage Carlson, the narrator describes a "hobo" named Armand who lives in Paris. Unlike in many portrayals of homeless individuals, Armand is painted in a very positive light—he's happy with his life, in charge of his decisions, and sees the positive side of being homeless (like not having any dry-cleaning bills or rent to pay). Other characters in the book, however, look down their noses at him. The reader needs to grapple with their own preconceived notions about homeless people, the way the narrator perceives the character, and the way other characters in the book view the character.

As with prior levels, as the protagonists interact with secondary characters, readers often have to understand secondary-character complexity and reconcile multiple traits that sometimes conflict with one other.

Look for students to:

○ Identify several less obvious traits and/or feelings that reveal a character's complexity.

○ Describe significant changes in a main character. comparing past traits and/or feelings with present ones.

○ Identify and comment on many feelings and/or traits of a secondary character.

Vocabulary and Figurative Language

Stakes become higher in terms of understanding vocabulary and lnaguage: knowing the more-challenging words and inferring the meanings of words and phrases used figuratively are critical to comprehension (e.g., *atom bomb* in *Sadako and the Thousand Paper Cranes* by Eleanor Coerr or *tasting sorrow* in *Because of Winn-Dixie* by Kate DiCamillo). Readers will be able to understand these words and phrases only when they take larger context into account (i.e., the entire chapter, or the whole story so far). Readers may encounter narrators and characters who speak in unfamiliar ways (e.g., the dialect of the narrator in *Shiloh* by Phyllis Reynolds Naylor or the speech patterns of the autistic boy in *Rules* by Cynthia Lord).

At prior levels, the more-challenging vocabulary enhanced understanding but didn't always "make or break" comprehension (e.g., "sneered" in *Fourth Grade Rats*).

Look for students to:
○ Use cumulative knowledge of the story to explain the meaning of a word or phrase (**shift from Level Q**).

Themes and Ideas

Themes relate to students' lives (e.g., making new friends in *Because of Winn-Dixie* or loss in *Sadako and the Thousand Paper Cranes*). However, deeper meaning in these books is often couched in themes relating to more-complex social issues, which require more sophisticated inferring and reflection. For example, savvier readers of *Sadako and the Thousand Paper Cranes* will pick up on themes relating to war (e.g., innocence, forgiveness, and redemption).

Symbolism is common and often essential to understanding the plot. Strong contextual support helps readers understand the abstract meaning of the symbol. For instance, the paper cranes in *Sadako and the Thousand Paper Cranes* are an essential thread woven throughout the entire story.

Look for students to:
○ Articulate a universal lesson/theme that can be applied to other contexts outside the text, and consider events from multiple plotlines (**shift from Level Q**).

○ Identify a social issue in the book and explain the complexity of that issue.

○ Interpret a symbol by considering it in the context of the story and explaining its significance (**shift from Level Q**).

Examples of Books at Level R

How Tia Lola Came to Stay by Julia Alvarez
Circle of Gold by Candy Dawson Boyd
The Family Under the Bridge by Natalie Savage Carlson
Sadako and the Thousand Paper Cranes by Eleanor Coerr
Nothing's Fair in Fifth Grade by Barthe DeClements

Because of Winn-Dixie by Kate DiCamillo
The Whipping Boy by Sid Fleischman
Shiloh by Phyllis Reynolds Naylor
Hatchet by Gary Paulsen
Charlotte's Web by E. B. White

Plot and Setting

Readers need to continue to navigate plots that are increasingly complex and thus require students to handle a heavier load of inferring, synthesizing, and reflecting on the text. Students often must navigate flashbacks and foreshadowing and subplots or multiple plotlines. The internal journey of the character and the obstacles for the character continue to be important driving forces of the plot. For example, in *The Great Gilly Hopkins* by Katherine Paterson, young Gilly's deep-seated sense of abandonment by her mother, her anger, and her yearning for a mother figure are what drive her to act as she does throughout the book. If a reader isn't attuned to her internal journey, they miss out on the pathos of the novel.

Unfamiliar settings should be expected, and readers will need to work to understand them. The setting often has an impact on the plot and characters. The setting may also help to communicate a mood or tone of the scene. In *Taking Sides* by Gary Soto, for example, Linc's new neighborhood and the neighborhood he comes from are important to the plot. A driving force of the plot centers around his move to the "right side of the tracks," his journey of trying to fit in without losing who he was in his old neighborhood, and his struggle with whether to take a side.

Look for students to:

○ Retell the most important events from more complex plots.

○ Draw connections between multiple causes and effects, and demonstrate deep understanding of the scene.

○ Identify more than two of the story's problems or aspects of the main problem, and mention internal and external aspects.

○ Describe the time(s) and place(s), and understand the setting's significance or mood and its effects on character(s) (**shift from Level R**).

Character

Main characters are complex, possessing both positive and negative traits. To understand the character completely, the reader needs to synthesize traits and develop an interpretation of the character. As at prior levels, as the protagonists interact with secondary characters, readers often have to understand secondary-character complexity and reconcile many traits that sometimes conflict with one another. The secondary characters' effects on the main character are important to understanding the plot.

Readers need to change their perspectives on characters in the course of the book. In *The Great Gilly Hopkins*, Gilly begins as an unlikable character: she's a selfish troublemaker who resists love and lacks compassion. As the book progresses, however, a reader needs to step into Gilly's shoes to start to understand her dimensions. The reader begins to understand her aching for a mother. The reader is let in on her past, how she's let her guard down before, and how that's scarred her. By the end of the novel, a reader may practically weep at learning that she can't stay with Mrs. Trotter, a woman who loves her unconditionally as a mother should. Readers who stay fixed on the person Gilly was in the first few pages miss out on really understanding the story's complexity and depth.

Look for students to:

○ Identify and interpret several less obvious traits and/or feelings that reveal a character's complexity (**shift from Level R**).

○ Describe significant changes in a main character, comparing past traits and/or feelings with present ones.

○ Identify and comment on many feelings and/or traits of a secondary character.

Vocabulary and Figurative Language

Knowing challenging words is critical to comprehension. At this level, the prevalence of challenging vocabulary increases. The reader is likely to encounter complex words that deal with a time period, another language, or a challenging concept. *In the Year of the Boar and Jackie Robinson* includes *Confucian, conduct, patriarch, fortune, slights,* and *unsightly* on page 2 alone. Page 60 of *From the Mixed-Up Files of Mrs. Basil E. Frankweiler* includes *hodgepodge, mediocre, residence, auctions, amassed, conclusive, Michelangelo, Sistine Chapel, acquired,* and *masterpieces.*

Look for students to:

O Use cumulative knowledge of the story to explain the meaning of a word or phrase.

Themes and Ideas

The emotional maturity a reader brings to books at this level will enable them to have compassion for the characters and grasp the salient human and societal themes their lives represent. Readers come across issues such as racism; a young girl's emotional scars; and a young man's struggles with identity, culture, and class. Each of these protagonists shines a light on larger social challenges.

Gilly in *The Great Gilly Hopkins* provides an example of the leap readers must make: she's not a likable heroine in the beginning. Readers have to stick by her side, until she finally heals and grows enough to act thoughtfully. The reader gains access to the larger ideas of heartbreak, family, the restorative power of love, redemption, and more.

Look for students to:

O Articulate a universal lesson/ theme that can be applied to other contexts outside the text, and consider events from multiple plotlines (**shift from Level Q**).

O Identify a social issue in the book, explain its complexity, and recognize stereotypes (**shift from Level R**).

O Interpret a symbol by considering it in the context of the story and explaining its significance.

Examples of Books at Level S

In the Shade of the Níspero Tree
by Carmen T. Bernier-Grand

Quinceañera Means Sweet Fifteen
by Veronica Chambers

From the Mixed-Up Files of Mrs. Basil E. Frankweiler
by E. L. Konigsburg

In the Year of the Boar and Jackie Robinson
by Bette Bao Lord

Journey to Jo'burg by Beverley Naidoo

The Great Gilly Hopkins by Katherine Paterson

Taking Sides by Gary Soto

The Gold Cadillac by Mildred D. Taylor

Save Me a Seat by Sarah Weeks and Gita Varadarajan

The Midnight War of Mateo Martinez by Robin Yardi

Plot and Setting

Readers must continue to retain the details and meaning of increasingly complex plots that require students to synthesize information. Students often have to navigate flashbacks, foreshadowing, subplots, and/or multiple plotlines. The emotional/psychological or internal journey of the character as they respond to other characters and instigate events remains a driving force.

Readers will need to work to understand unfamiliar settings: Joey Pigza is sent to a special school "downtown" for kids with special needs (*Joey Pigza Swallowed a Key*); Rob lives in a motel with his father, and the concept of a motel as a home may be foreign to most readers (*The Tiger Rising*). Setting often affects plot and characters; it may help to communicate the scene's mood or tone. Sometimes, the setting may even be viewed as symbolic. In *The Tiger Rising*, Kate DiCamillo uses qualities of light—dark, overcast skies and rays of sun—to create a mood.

> **Look for students to:**
>
> O Retell the most important events from more complex plots.
>
> O Draw connections between multiple causes and effects, and demonstrate deep understanding of the scene.
>
> O Identify more than two of the story's problems or aspects of the main problem. and mention internal and external aspects.
>
> O Describe the time(s) and place(s), and understand the setting's significance or mood and its effects on character(s).

Character

By Level T, characters are more fully drawn with internal feelings and physical traits; their actions may be contradictory. To fully understand a character, the reader needs to synthesize traits and develop an interpretation of the character. The interpretation can answer fundamental character questions: is he or she kind? Trustworthy? Struggling? Readers will also need to consider what motivates characters.

As with past levels, readers often have to understand secondary characters' facets and be insightful about people having clashing traits. The secondary characters' effects on the main character are important to understanding the plot. A reader has to develop various perspectives on main and secondary characters to understand them; perspectives may change over the course of the book. Readers also need to determine whether the author intends characters to be held in high regard (Willie May in *The Tiger Rising*), to have a mix of strengths and shortcomings (Rob's father), or a low level of ethical behavior (the motel owner). Readers need to begin to interpret characters' morality and to be cognizant of how authors often try to create characters with contrasting value systems.

Authors may give characters symbolic roles, so readers need to look at the cast of characters in this light, too. Character names can be significant. Sistine (in *The Tiger Rising*) refers to Michelangelo's masterpiece and is important to the novel's themes.

> **Look for students to:**
>
> O Identify and interpret several less obvious traits and/or feelings that reveal a character's complexity.
>
> O Describe significant changes in a main character, comparing past traits and/or feelings with present ones.
>
> O Identify and comment on many feelings and/or traits of a secondary character, and name how a secondary character impacts a main character (**shift from Level S**).

Vocabulary and Figurative Language

More words are used figuratively. *The Tiger Rising* is almost poetic: "Sadness . . . You keeping all that sadness down low, in your legs. You not letting it get up to your heart, where it belongs. You got to let that sadness rise on up" (37), and "As he filled the grave, something danced and flickered on his arm. . . . It was the sun. Showing up in time for another funeral" (111). Although the first-person narrator of *Joey Pigza Swallowed the Key* has a simpler vocabulary, a great deal of metaphor and simile is still used: "'Help meeee. Help meee,' she'd squeak like the fly with the human face in that crazy bug movie" (11).

Look for students to:

- Use cumulative knowledge of the story to explain the meaning of a word or phrase.

Themes and Ideas

Readers will need emotional maturity to grasp themes relating to more complex social issues (e.g., loss, death, sadness, and freedom in *The Tiger Rising*). Those reading *Joey Pigza* will read from the perspective of a special-needs child, encounter an abusive caregiver, and witness accidental violence. Symbolism continues to be present. Numerous elements in *The Tiger Rising* have symbolic significance: the tiger, the overcast or sunny sky, the carved wooden bird, the rash on Rob's legs, the sage character Willie May, and the name Sistine. Understanding these symbols will deepen understanding of the story's bigger ideas and themes.

Look for students to:

- Articulate multiple universal lessons/themes that can be applied to other contexts outside the text, and consider events from multiple plotlines (**shift from Level S**)

- Identify a social issue in the book, explain its complexity, and recognize stereotypes.

- Interpret a symbol and its complexity, name the abstract idea the symbol represents, and relate its significance to the whole book and/or title (**shift from Level S**).

Examples of Books at Level T

Sounder by William H. Armstrong

The Barn by Avi

The Tiger Rising by Kate DiCamillo

Joey Pigza Swallowed the Key by Jack Gantos

Garvey's Choice by Nikki Grimes

Babe & Me by Dan Gutman

The Lion, the Witch, and the Wardrobe by C. S. Lewis

Where the Mountain Meets the Moon by Grace Lin

Drita, My Homegirl by Jenny Lombard

Bridge to Terabithia by Katherine Paterson

Plot and Setting

Readers need to continue to navigate complex plots that require picking up on significant events, synthesizing, and monitoring understanding when the text throws a curve ball. The curve ball might be a device such as a flashback, foreshadowing, a challenging subplot, or multiple plotlines. The character's obstacles and internal journey continue to be driving forces of the plot. Stamina is needed for long stretches of narration.

Readers will need to work to understand unfamiliar settings, which often have an impact on the plot and characters. For example, Jean Craighead George's *My Side of the Mountain* is about a child who runs away from his New York City apartment to live on a mountain. This setting is well developed and inseparable from the story: the challenges and triumphs of the main character simply couldn't happen anywhere else.

The setting may also help to communicate a scene's mood or tone and, in some instances, may even be viewed as symbolic. Kate DiCamillo uses symbolic settings, such as the castle dungeon in *The Tale of Despereaux*. Jerry Spinelli's *Wringer*, about a boy grappling with becoming "wringer boy" (one responsible for wringing pigeons' necks) has as its setting a "festive picnic atmosphere." This setting is crafted as a stark juxtaposition to the main action of the scenes.

Look for students to:
- Retell the most important events from more complex plots.
- Draw connections between multiple causes and effects, and demonstrate deep understanding of the scene.
- Identify more than two of the story's problems or aspects of the main problem, and mention internal and external aspects.
- Describe the time(s) and place(s), and understand the setting's significance or mood and its effects on character(s).

Character

To fully understand a complex, fully drawn character, the reader needs to synthesize traits and develop an interpretation of that character and understand the points of view of the main and secondary characters. As the protagonists interact with secondary characters, readers have to infer the feelings and motivations of each.

A reader also has to look for clues and cues in the dialogue and text details that signal character change and revise their "take" on the character accordingly. It's necessary to walk in the shoes of many characters to fully understand each of them. For example, Byron, a secondary character in *The Watsons Go to Birmingham—1963*, is at first a bully but then a protector of his younger brother by bullying his younger brother's bully. As readers, it's hard to know whose side to take. Later in the story, Byron softens and shows a more nurturing side as he helps his brother recover from the traumatic historical events that are a centerpiece to the novel.

Look for students to:
- Identify and interpret several less obvious traits and/or feelings that reveal a character's complexity.
- Describe significant changes in a main character, comparing past traits and/or feelings with present ones.
- Identify and comment on many feelings and/or traits of a secondary character, and name how a secondary character impacts a main character.

Vocabulary and Figurative Language

Knowing more challenging words is critical to understanding setting, characters, and theme; challenging vocabulary and figurative language is prevalent. Words are sometimes period specific and are sometimes used in a figurative or poetic way. In *The Watsons Go to Birmingham—1963* by Christopher Paul Curtis, the older brother relaxes his hair with a "butter." In *Loser* by Jerry Spinelli, a reader often encounters language such as, "He felt as if the picture he lived in had been tilted," or "scooping out the fruit of his life and plopping it into her lap" (143, 150)— poetic descriptions meant to signal a changing perspective and one character trusting in another.

Look for students to:

○ Use cumulative knowledge of the story to explain the meaning of a word or phrase.

Themes and Ideas

Readers must bring emotional maturity to their reading and use the more realistic characters and well-crafted narratives as a springboard to extend their understandings of themes and ideas. If readers grasp the story's richness of ideas, characters, symbols, and metaphors to consider larger ideas of justice, conformity, love, and lifestyles, they can apply lessons they learn to those in other books and in their lives.

Issues of racism and bullying present more violence and cruelty than at earlier levels. Symbolism of characters and setting continues to play a central role.

Look for students to:

○ Articulate multiple universal lessons/themes that can be applied to other contexts outside the text, and consider events from multiple plotlines.

○ Identify a social issue in the book, explain its complexity, and recognize stereotypes.

○ Interpret a symbol and its complexity, name the abstract idea the symbol represents, and relate its significance to the whole book and/or title.

Examples of Books at Level U

The Watsons Go to Birmingham–1963 by Christopher Paul Curtis

The Tale of Despereaux by Kate DiCamillo

My Side of the Mountain by Jean Craighead George

Planet Middle School by Nikki Grimes

The Grand Plan to Fix Everything by Uma Krishnaswami

Inside Out and Back Again by Thanhha Lai

Number the Stars by Lois Lowry

The Righteous Revenge of Artemis Bonner by Walter Dean Myers

Loser by Jerry Spinelli

Warp Speed by Lisa Yee

Plot and Setting

Readers need to continue to navigate plots that are complex and are centered around a variety of internal and external problems or conflicts. Readers often must navigate flashbacks and foreshadowing and subplots or multiple plotlines. The internal journey of the character and the obstacles for the character continue to be important driving forces, as in Jerry Spinelli's *Stargirl*. When Stargirl Caraway comes to town, everyone is in awe of her uniqueness and individuality, until they turn on her. The story is about her growing relationship with Leo and her attempts to stay true to who she is and resist being "normal."

The setting often has an impact on the plot and characters. The setting may also help to communicate a mood or tone of the scene. Whether you consider an 1832 voyage on the *Seahawk* for Charlotte in Avi's *The True Confessions of Charlotte Doyle*; Camp Green Lake for Stanley in Louis Sachar's *Holes*; or Hogwarts for Harry, Hermione, and Ron in the first few books in the Harry Potter series, the setting is essential to the story line and does more than provide a place for the main action to happen. Settings are almost like characters themselves.

Look for students to:

- ○ Retell the most important events from more complex plots.

- ○ Draw connections between multiple causes and effects, and demonstrate deep understanding of the scene.

- ○ Identify more than three of the story's problems or aspects of the main problem, and mention internal and external aspects (**shift from Level U**).

- ○ Describe the time(s) and place(s), and understand the setting's significance or mood and its effects on character(s).

Character

Main characters are complex. Their inner feelings don't always match their actions, and they are often striving to figure out a few things, not just one. To fully understand the character, the reader needs to synthesize a character's feelings and behavior as events unfold.

As with past levels, as the protagonists interact with secondary characters, readers often have to understand secondary characters' complexity and see each one's point of view. The secondary characters' effects on the main character(s) are important to understanding the plot. Readers have to stay attuned to how characters change and grow across the course of the story.

Look for students to:

- ○ Identify and interpret several less obvious traits and/or feelings of a main character that reveal their complexity, and analyze relationships between characters (**shift from Level U**).

- ○ Describe significant changes in a main character, comparing past traits and/or feelings with present ones.

- ○ Identify and comment on many feelings and/or traits of a secondary character, and name how a secondary character impacts a main character.

Vocabulary and Figurative Language

Becoming Naomi León is filled with metaphors, similes, and other descriptive, figurative language. In the Harry Potter series, readers will need to learn and remember invented vocabulary. In Scott O'Dell's *Island of the Blue Dolphins*, for example, the main character, Karana, has a way of speaking metaphorically that readers need to adjust to. When describing her brother she says, "He was small for one who had lived so many suns and moons, but quick as a cricket" (1).

Look for students to:

O Use cumulative knowledge of the story to explain the meaning of a word or phrase.

Themes and Ideas

Emotional maturity will help readers understand the multiple challenges pressing upon protagonists. In *Becoming Naomi León*, a young girl loves and protects a brother who was born with physical differences. She must also face up to her manipulative, alcoholic mother who, among other things, refers to her son as "damaged goods," endure teasing at school, search for her father, and try to assimilate the two cultures to which she belongs. The ideas and societal themes are adult: bullying, alcoholism, neglect, custody battles, prejudice, machismo, materialism, and the strains on the modern American family.

Characters, objects, and setting play a central role in understanding deeper themes and ideas. The holes that Stanley is meant to dig in *Holes* are more than just holes; the author is hinting at bigger ideas surrounding crime and punishment. Readers who don't grasp symbolism in Level V books miss out on a vital layer of meaning.

Look for students to:

O Articulate multiple universal lessons/themes that can be applied to other contexts outside the text, and consider events from multiple plotlines.

O Identify a social issue in the book, explain its complexity, and recognize stereotypes.

O Interpret a symbol and its complexity, name the abstract idea the symbol represents, and relate its significance to the whole book and/or title.

Examples of Books at Level V

The True Confessions of Charlotte Doyle by Avi

Pictures of Hollis Woods by Patricia Reilly Giff

The Thing About Luck by Cynthia Kadohata

Mrs. Frisby and the Rats of NIMH by Robert C. O'Brien

Harry Potter and the Sorcerer's Stone by J. K. Rowling

Holes by Louis Sachar

Crash by Jerry Spinelli

Locomotion by Jacqueline Woodson

Secret Coders by Gene Luen Yang and Mike Holmes

Beyond the Mango Tree by Amy Bronwen Zemser

Plot and Setting

Readers need to continue to navigate plots that are complex and thus require synthesis. Flashbacks, foreshadowing, subplots, and/or multiple plotlines continue to be prevalent. The internal journey of the character and the obstacles for the character continue to be important driving forces of the plot. The plots often depict higher doses of hardship than at prior levels. The protagonists often have to weather multiple challenges that test their strength.

The setting often has an impact on the plot and characters. The setting may also help communicate the mood or tone of a scene, and it may be symbolic.

Look for students to:

- Retell the most important events from more complex plots.

- Draw connections between multiple causes and effects to understand the importance of the scene deeply, and understand foreshadowing (**shift from Level V**).

- Identify more than three of the story's problems or aspects of the main problem, and mention internal and external aspects.

- Describe the time(s) and place(s), and understand the setting's complex significance, mood, or symbolism and its effects on character(s) (shift from Level V).

Character

Main characters are complex. Their quests often mirror the adolescent's struggle to define self, find courage, and fit in with peers. Many of the characters are on the threshold of leaving childhood and becoming adults, and stories at Level W will commonly have obstacles that add a weighty burden to the part of life that is already challenging: worrying whether your mom survived war and learning to live in a land where you're an outsider (Kek in *Home of the Brave* by Katherine Applegate), struggling with the legacy of a murderous father and a dying best friend (Max in Rodman Philbrick's *Freak the Mighty*), discovering you are the child of Poseidon and are forced on a treacherous quest (Percy in *The Lightning Thief* by Rick Riordan).

To fully understand a character, the reader needs to synthesize traits and develop an interpretation of the character. As with past levels, as the protagonists interact with secondary characters, readers often have to understand the secondary characters' complexities and reconcile many traits that sometimes conflict with one another. The secondary characters' effects on the main character are important to understanding the plot. A reader needs to be alert to character changes and be prepared to revise interpretations as the story unfolds in order to truly understand the character.

Look for students to:

- Identify and interpret several less obvious traits and/or feelings of a main character that reveal their complexity, and analyze relationships between characters.

- Describe significant changes in a main character, comparing past traits and/or feelings with present ones.

- Identify and comment on many feelings and/or traits of a secondary character, and name how a secondary character impacts a main character.

Vocabulary and Figurative Language

Home of the Brave is a novel in verse, filled with descriptive, figurative language. In *Freak the Mighty*, Kevin ("Freak") is an intelligent, articulate child who uses sophisticated language, alludes to classical fantasy, and creates his own dictionary, which is included as an appendix. In *The Phantom Tollbooth*, Norton Juster uses humorous invented words and challenging vocabulary: "'Ordinance 175389-J: It shall be unlawful, illegal, unethical to think, think of thinking, surmise, presume, reason, meditate, or speculate while in the Doldrums'" (24). Places are named "Dictionopolis," "Expectations," and "Digitopolis," and people "Lethargarians," "Dischord," and "The Dynne." Authors at this level expect readers to have a sophisticated sense of language.

Look for students to:

- Use cumulative knowledge of the story to explain the meaning of a word or phrase.

Themes and Ideas

Emotional maturity will enable readers to grasp themes relating to more-complex social issues. The symbolism of characters, objects, and setting is key to understanding deeper themes and ideas.

Whether encountering allusions to Greek mythology (*The Lightning Thief* by Rick Riordan), books steeped in history (*Roll of Thunder, Hear My Cry* by Mildred D. Taylor or *The Witch of Blackbird Pond* by Elizabeth George Speare), or handling the symbolism and deep themes of high-fantasy novels (*A Wrinkle in Time* by Madeleine L'Engle), readers must have deep prior knowledge or be willing to work to learn about new times, places, and genres.

Look for students to:

- Articulate multiple universal lessons/themes that can be applied to other contexts outside the text, and consider events from multiple plotlines.

- Identify a social issue in the book, explain its complexity, and recognize stereotypes.

- Interpret a symbol and its complexity, name the abstract idea the symbol represents, and relate its significance to the whole book and/or title.

Examples of Books at Level W

Home of the Brave by Katherine Applegate

Walk Two Moons by Sharon Creech

Igraine the Brave by Cornelia Funke

The Phantom Tollbooth by Norton Juster

A Wrinkle in Time by Madeleine L'Engle

Handbook for Boys by Walter Dean Myers

Freak the Mighty by Rodman Philbrick

The Witch of Blackbird Pond by Elizabeth George Speare

Roll of Thunder, Hear My Cry by Mildred D. Taylor

Dragonwings by Laurence Yep

Understanding Fiction Readers

A Goal-by-Goal Guide to Readers' Comprehension of Increasingly Complex Texts

How can a teacher know if a child is comprehending if there is no single "right" answer and the way a reader transacts with the text changes its meaning?

Developing an understanding of text characteristics offers you a crucial context for understanding what to expect of readers. To determine whether students "get it," we have to know what "it" is. For instance, if a text has flashbacks, we'd need to look at student retellings and note whether they show an understanding of the way the author moves the story through time. If the text has complex characters, we should be sure the reader is not simply offering one character trait but describing the character's multiple dimensions. If the book is rich and multilayered, with several plots and well-developed characters who change, grow, and learn lessons, then we should expect a reader to interpret multiple themes from the story, not just one. That is why the first half of Part II (pages 54–81) was dedicated to looking closely at texts.

This knowledge of text characteristics and understandings about what the author intended represents only a portion of what it means to comprehend, of course. As discussed in Part I, readers bring themselves to the reading of the text, and therefore there is no single meaning to "get" out of a text (Rosenblatt 1978). For example, the way that one reader views Gilly from Katherine Paterson's *The Great Gilly Hopkins* (1978) might be to think her selfish and rude because Gilly pushes others away and avoids relationships; another reader might infer that Gilly acts how she does because she is protecting herself and is afraid to be vulnerable, for fear of being hurt. Neither reader is wrong; their inferences are both grounded in the reality of the story. The differences between the two ways of seeing Gilly might in part be the result of the readers' prior experience with people in their own lives; the combination of personal experience and the details the author provides in the text produces different things for different readers.

How can a teacher know if a child is comprehending if there is no single "right" answer and the way a reader transacts with the text changes its meaning? I think the key is knowledge of text levels and a grasp of how readers of books at different levels demonstrate understanding based on *qualities* of a response. For example, with a student reading *The Great Gilly Hopkins,* what I'd be thinking about is: (a) that the text is considered Level S, and I know that in Level S texts, main characters are well developed with multiple positive and negative traits that change over time, and (b) that I should listen for more than one trait and note whether the student is far enough along to view the character in multiple situations over time, in which case I'd be listening for their ability to articulate the change.

In other words, as a teacher of reading, it is less the case that I am trying to get children to arrive at *a specific answer* about Gilly and more that I am trying to coach children into *ways of thinking* about texts (in this case, characters). The goal is teaching readers to know what to look for in texts, which will lead them to more complete comprehension.

Unlike the first half of this part, which is organized by levels, this second half is divided into goals. Recall the hierarchy of goals from *The Reading Strategies Book* discussed in Part I (page 11) and the four goals relating to comprehension of fiction: Plot and Setting, Character, Vocabulary and Figurative Language, and Themes and Ideas (Serravallo 2015). At the start of the section, you'll see a table that highlights the shifts in expectations for reader response that align to the shifts in characteristics of texts. You will then find a spread for each skill (e.g., for the goal of Plot and Setting, the four skills are retelling important events, synthesizing cause and effect, identifying problems, and visualizing setting) showing a progression of student responses from increasingly complex texts.

What's Ahead?

You can use the four Progression of Skills tables (on pages 86–87, 96–97, 104–105, and 108–109, thumbnails below), as quick references to see how changes in text characteristics result in changed expectations (also referred to as "look-fors" in the first half of this part) for readers. Each table is followed by examples that illustrate how students reading texts at different levels responded to their reading. Each response comes from a book you may or may not know—it doesn't matter either way. What these student work samples will help you to see is how the qualities of the responses change as students encounter more complex texts with more complex elements. I've offered descriptions of what to look for in the responses as captions for each student work sample. You can use these examples as illustrations of the "look-fors" and to use when studying your students' writing and/ or speaking about their reading.

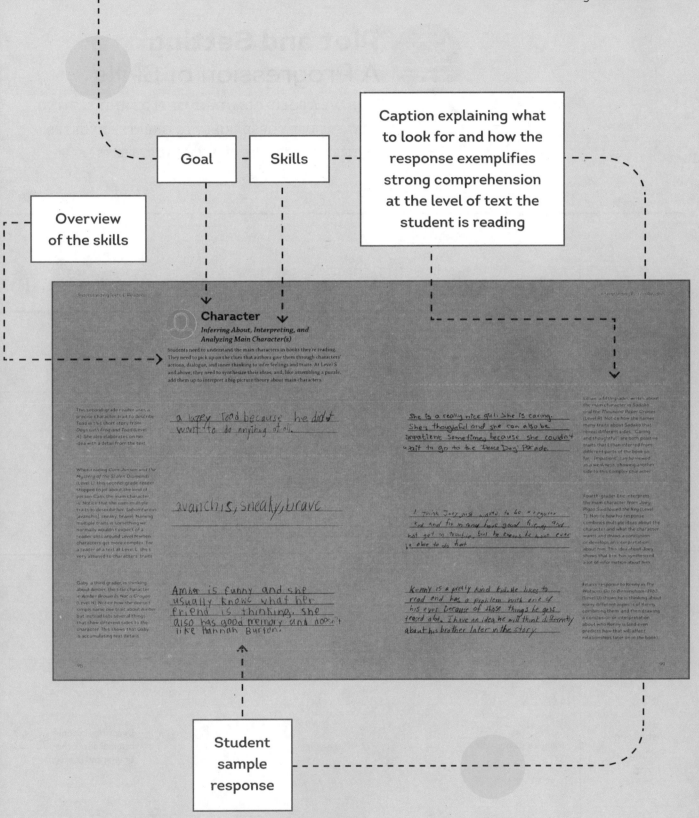

Goal

Skills

Caption explaining what to look for and how the response exemplifies strong comprehension at the level of text the student is reading

Overview of the skills

Student sample response

Character

Inferring About, Interpreting, and Analyzing Main Character(s)

Students need to understand the main characters in books they're reading. They need to pick up on the clues that authors give them through characters' actions, dialogue, and inner thinking to infer feelings and traits. At Level S and above, they need to synthesize their ideas, and, like assembling a puzzle, add them up to interpret a big-picture theory about main characters.

a lazey Toad because he didnt want to do anything at all.

avanchris, sneaky, brave

Amber is funny and she usually knows what her friend is thinking. she also has good memory and doesn't like Hannah Burton.

She is a really nice girl. She is caring. She's thoughful and she can also be impatient Sometime, because she couldn't "wait to go to the 'Peace Day' Parade.

I think Joey just wants to be a regular kid and fis in and have good friends and not get in trouble, but he knows he wont ever be able to do that

Kenny is a pretty kind kid. He likes to read and has a problem with one of his eyes. Because of those things he gets teased alot. I have an idea he will think differently about his brother later in the story

85

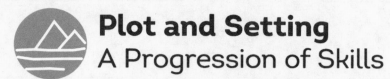

Plot and Setting
A Progression of Skills

TO HAVE A SOLID COMMAND OF PLOT AND SETTING, READERS USE THESE SKILLS TO GREATER DEGREES AS THEY READ MORE CHALLENGING TEXTS.

SKILLS	J	K	L	M	N	O	P
Retelling Important Events	Retells multiple important events, using text and/or pictures.					Retells multiple important events.	
Synthesizing Cause and Effect	Understands cause and effect using text and/or pictures.					Draws connections between multiple causes and effects, and demonstrates deep understanding of the scene.	
Identifying Problems	Identifies multiple aspects of a scene's main problem using text and/or pictures.					Identifies multiple aspects of the story's main problem.	
Visualizing Setting	Names setting.					Describes in some original detail the time(s) and place(s).	

Q R S T U V W

Retells the most important events from more complex plots.

Draws connections between multiple causes and effects to understand the importance of the scene deeply. Understands foreshadowing.

Identifies more than two of the story's problems or aspects of the main problem. Mentions internal and external aspects.

Identifies more than three of the story's problems, or aspects of the main problem. Mentions internal and external aspects.

Describes the time(s) and place(s). Understands the setting's significance or mood and its effects on character(s).

Describes the time(s) and place(s). Understands the setting's complex significance, mood, or symbolism and its effects on character(s).

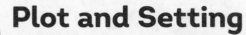

Plot and Setting
Retelling Important Events

It's important for a reader to be able to look across a section of text (a scene or chapter), or the whole text, and retell in sequence what's most important. At Level J, the reader needs to retell several events. At Level O, there is a decline in picture support and, therefore, an increase in the challenge of retelling events. At Level R and above, foreshadowing, multiple plotlines, and subplots are more common, making it more challenging for readers to tease out the most important main events.

Notice how this second grader, Nathan, is able to retell multiple important events in sequence from an early-in-the-book scene in *Cam Jansen and the Stolen Diamonds* (Level L). Even if you haven't read the book, the retelling will make sense to you.

> Cam was with her friend Eric at a busy shoping mall and Erics mother was shoping. Soon the alarm rang off at parkers jewlry store A man with a mystashe was running out of the store.

This third grader's retelling of an important scene in *Chocolate Fever* (Level O) shows that he is able to retell multiple important events from the story. The retelling is clear and sequential, and one event clearly leads to the next. Retelling is more challenging in Level O than in Level L because picture support drops considerably, so more of the events recalled come from text alone.

> Mac drives to the cabin and promises to protect Henry. Dogs show up and lick Henry. The police arrive and the thieves are taken away. Mac takes Henry to deliver the candy.

Courtney is Gilly's real mother. One day she got a postcard from Courtney saying she heard Gilly moved and she wished it was here. Gilly was talking back saying "I'm coming Courtney."

As plots get more complex, it becomes harder for a reader to understand why an event happens. In these cases, a reader may have to deal with flashbacks or foreshadowing or multiple events leading up to a moment. This fifth-grade reader of *The Great Gilly Hopkins* (Level S) shows she understands how events fit together.

Plot and Setting
Synthesizing Cause and Effect

Being able to determine cause and effect is vital to following a story's plot. For readers to be able to piece together causes and effects, they need to be able to carry information with them as the story unfolds and consider past moments in the plot to explain present ones. This requires readers to synthesize, remember, and attend to text details. At Levels J–N, one event clearly connects to another. Beginning at O, readers need to see how multiple causes relate to multiple effects. By W, readers should demonstrate an understanding of foreshadowing.

Emily, a second grader, read *Frog and Toad* (Level K) and was able to explain a cause-and-effect relationship between two events.

when frog pord water on the hot and let it dry it srunk and fit toadihead

---

This student, reading *Jake Drake, Bully Buster* (Level O), draws connections between multiple causes to explain a character's action in one part of the story. There wasn't only one reason why Jake says that Link made "it" (a project)–there is more than one, and the reader names both. This shows he's able to synthesize more of the text to truly understand the "why" of the present scene.

because he wanted Link to be his friend and Link did make it!

Suds is mad at Joey because Joey was not trying hard enough to get the girl Joey liked to like Suds. I think that Joey tryed and that the girl just doesn't like Suds. Maybe because he is not a rat.

Morgan is reading *Fourth Grade Rats* (Level Q) and stops to jot about a part when Suds is mad at Joey. She names multiple reasons -Joey was not trying hard enough, Joey isn't really a rat. She's demonstrating an understanding of how there can be more than one cause for each event in a story.

This moment is important because theft looking for this little girl and Zinkoff is trying to find her even though he's scared of the dark alley and because Zinkoff is doing lots of grown up things. He's not a loser.

This response to a moment in *Loser* (Level U) shows how Adriana, a fifth grader, is considering multiple causes and effects. She's applying what she knows about Zinkoff (that others have called him a loser, but here he's not one), how he's afraid of the dark (learned earlier in the story), and that others are searching for this lost girl in addition to Zinkoff.

Plot and Setting

Identifying Problems

Conflicts often drive stories. Characters are motivated to do something, get something, or figure something out. Obstacles stand in the way. Characters persevere and eventually overcome the obstacles. Assessing a reader's ability to understand the problems in a story, and then teaching them to pay attention to how problems are solved or resolved, greatly supports their ability to determine importance, retell, and synthesize important parts.

Emily, a second grader, is able to accurately identify a main problem in *Frog and Toad* (Level K). This is the main problem because most of the plot revolves around trying to solve or resolve this problem. The use of the word *and* means that she's not looking at the problem simplistically; she can see multiple ways the problem is impacting the characters. The problem she articulated also aligns to the title of the short story, "Alone."

> frog wanted to be alone and Toad wanted to help and be with him.

Ashley, a third grader, read *Stuart Goes to School* (Level M). Notice how she describes multiple aspects of the problem—not only did Stuart's actions cause him to disappear from the classroom, but he wound up on the roof of the school and couldn't get down. All three of these relate to one main problem.

> The first problem was that the teacher Disapperd. The second problem was she was on the roof of the school. The third problem was that she could not get off the roof

Fill is woryed hes preJudiced hes also woryed about danyal because he diden't have a Jacket and it was all his fault.

Spelling aside, this second grader is thinking about Phil's ("Fill") problems in the story *The Jacket* (Level R). Notice she names multiple problems (worried {woryed} that he's prejudiced as well as acknowledging that Daniel {Danyal} doesn't have a jacket because of him). The reader understood these problems from her reading of the text alone, because picture support at this level is minimal.

Trying to adjust to this new place, understanding what people are saying. It's hard for him to communicate. He isn't used to the season change. So he is very confused and a bit unhappy. He's trying to to trust others but its very difficult to him.

Notice how this reader of *Home of the Brave* (Level W) considers more than three problems the main character is experiencing. She's thinking about internal problems (confused, unhappy, problems with trusting others) as well as external problems (trouble with understanding the language and the season changes).

Plot and Setting
Visualizing Setting

Visualization is perhaps the most important reading skill, and some readers apply it more naturally than others. Children who visualize well usually not only talk about the details the author provides but also activate prior knowledge and elaborate beyond the text. Students need to know that authors expect them to picture many more details than they provide. Even if some students don't intuit this, they can be taught to do it.

Ben, a third grader, accurately names the time and place (setting) in his book, *Stuart Goes to School* (Level M).

afterNoon and in the classRoom

This fourth-grade reader accurately describes the time (medieval times) and place (a dark path) and adds in some original details showing that the reader is visualizing in *The Time Warp Trio: Knights of the Kitchen table* (Level P).

They are in medieval time's on a dark path the air is magy and spooky.

In Japan it is really hot and humid. But when the sun goes down it look really beautiful to see the sunset. Also there was lots of lanterns over the Ohta River. The candles shown very brightly.

At Level R, Angela does more than simply name the setting at the beginning of *Sadako and the Thousand Paper Cranes.* She includes a more detailed description of the time, place, and scene.

Max's bedroom is in the cellar because the author wanted the reader to think Max is a monster just like his dad. It's dark, lonely and isolated

Trevor, a fifth grader, writes about the setting in *Freak the Mighty* (Level W). Notice that this response includes details about mood ("dark, lonely, and isolated") and acknowledges the author's craft ("the author wanted the reader to think . . ."). The sense of a setting's mood and significance should begin around Level S.

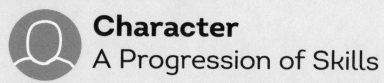

Character
A Progression of Skills

To have a solid command of character, readers use these skills to greater degrees as they read more challenging texts.

SKILLS	J	K	L	M	N	O	P
Inferring About, Interpreting, and Analyzing Main Character(s)	Identifies one or more less obvious traits and/or feelings of a main character.				Identifies several less obvious traits and/or feelings that reveal different aspects of a main character.		
Synthesizing Character Change	Describes how a main character's feelings have changed.	Describes how a main character's feelings have changed and its significance.			Describes significant changes in a main character by synthesizing many details.		
Inferring About, Interpreting, and Analyzing Secondary Character(s)					Identifies many feelings and/or traits of secondary characters.		

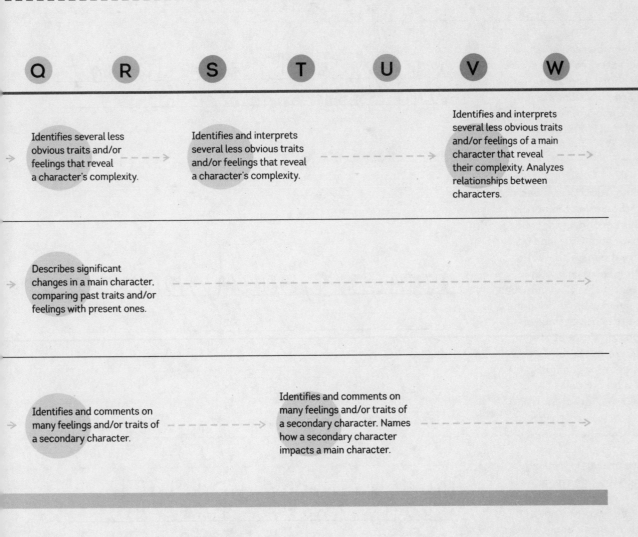

Q   **R**   **S**   **T**   **U**   **V**   **W**

Identifies several less obvious traits and/or feelings that reveal a character's complexity.

Identifies and interprets several less obvious traits and/or feelings that reveal a character's complexity.

Identifies and interprets several less obvious traits and/or feelings of a main character that reveal their complexity. Analyzes relationships between characters.

Describes significant changes in a main character, comparing past traits and/or feelings with present ones.

Identifies and comments on many feelings and/or traits of a secondary character.

Identifies and comments on many feelings and/or traits of a secondary character. Names how a secondary character impacts a main character.

Character

Inferring About, Interpreting, and Analyzing Main Character(s)

Students need to understand the main characters in books they're reading. They need to pick up on the clues that authors give them through characters' actions, dialogue, and inner thinking to infer feelings and traits. At Level S and above, they need to synthesize their ideas, and, like assembling a puzzle, add them up to interpret a big-picture theory about main characters.

This second-grade reader uses a precise character trait to describe Toad in this short story from *Days with Frog and Toad* (Level K). She also elaborates on her idea with a detail from the text.

> a lazey Toad because he did'nt want to do anything at all.

When reading *Cam Jansen and the Mystery of the Stolen Diamonds* (Level L), this second-grade reader stopped to jot about the kind of person Cam, the main character, is. Notice that she uses multiple traits to describe her: (adventurous {avanchis}, sneaky, brave). Naming multiple traits is something we normally wouldn't expect of a reader until around Level N when characters get more complex. For a reader of a text at Level L, she's very attuned to characters' traits.

> avanchis, sneaky, brave

Gaby, a third grader, is thinking about Amber, the title character in *Amber Brown Is Not a Crayon* (Level N). notice how she doesn't simply name one trait about Amber but instead lists several things that show different sides to the character. This shows that Gaby is accumulating text details.

> Amber is funny and she usually knows what her friend is thinking. she also has good memory and doesn't like Hannah Burton.

She is a really nice girl. She is caring. She's thoughtful and she can also be impatient sometimes because she couldn't wait to go to the "Peace Day" Parade.

Lillian, a fifth grader, writes about the main character in *Sadako and the Thousand Paper Cranes* (Level R). Notice how she names many traits about Sadako that reveal different sides. "Caring and thoughtful" are both positive traits that Lillian inferred from different parts of the book so far. "Impatient" can be viewed as a weakness, showing another side to this complex character.

I think Joey just wants to be a regular kid and fit in and have good friends and not get in trouble, but he knows he wont ever be able to do that

Fourth-grader Eric interprets the main character from *Joey Pigza Swallowed the Key* (Level T). Notice how his response combines multiple ideas about the character and what the character wants and draws a conclusion or develops an interpretation about him. This idea about Joey shows that Eric has synthesized a lot of information about him.

Kenny is a pretty kind kid. He likes to read and has a problem with one of his eyes. Because of those things he gets teased a lot. I have an idea he will think differently about his brother later in the story.

Eitan's response to Kenny in *The Watsons Go to Birmingham-1963* (Level u) shows he is thinking about many different aspects of Kenny, combining them, and then drawing a conclusion or interpretation about who Kenny is (and even predicts how that will affect relationships later on in the book).

Character

Synthesizing Character Change

Typically a character changes in some way over the course of the narrative. At lower levels, the change tends to be a change of feeling(s) or opinion(s). By Level N, characters often reveal new trait(s) or change based on some discovery or some event that causes the character to see the world differently. Regardless, synthesizing character change leads to a stronger understanding of the story because characters are so crucial to the development of the narrative.

This second-grade reader thinks about the main character, Judy (Juty), in this short jot about *Judy Moody Saves the World* (Level M). Notice that the student is considering a change in *feelings*. Books at this level usually have characters who don't change in major ways, except they do experience changes in feelings. Her writing shows she's tracking these changes in the main character.

> Jutys mood was envious
> bat now she's excited.

Third-grader keili recognizes the main changes that Koya's showing at a critical scene in *Koya Delaney and the Good Girl Blues* (Level P). Her writing shows that she's thinking about multiple aspects of Koya (she wants to be good, but here she can't, so she has to let out her anger) and even recounts an earlier dream scene that was important to understanding the character's feelings.

> Koya has some anger and she lets
> it out like the monster in her
> dreams because she wants to be good
> but she can't so she has to let out
> her anger by flilinging the air
> shouting get out of my way.

Suds just can't take it any more he is acting terrible and being mean and he was a calm and polite boy but now it is diffrent.

Chloe, a fifth grader, read *Fourth Grade Rats* (Level Q) and demonstrates she understands how the main character has changed. She shows an ability to compare past to present feelings and traits ("was a calm and polite boy" to "acting terrible and being mean").

Crash used to be a popular football-playing bully. Now that he might lose Scooter, he's starting to seem more sensitive, especially to Penn

Fifth-grader Deepak's response to the changes in Crash (Level V), the main character from Spinneli's novel by the same name, shows that he understands changes in significant traits ("bully" and "sensitive") and is able to compare past to present. He also adds details about what's caused the change to happen-that he might lose Scooter, Crash's grandfather whom he's very close to, who might die.

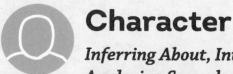

Character

Inferring About, Interpreting, and Analyzing Secondary Character(s)

Well-developed secondary characters start to appear at around Level N; before that there are usually one or two main characters and other peripheral characters. Inferring about, interpreting, and analyzing characters are tasks that require similar mental work, whether the reader is focusing on a character who is central to the story or one who is secondary. In fiction, readers must consider relationships among characters and the ways characters affect or impact one another.

This third grader is thinking about a secondary character from *Amber Brown Is Not a Crayon* (Level N). Notice how she names multiple feelings (worried) and traits (kind, understanding) of the character. She's also thinking not about the character in isolation but rather about how she relates to a main character (Amber/her daughter).

Amber's mom is kind and undestanding. She is also worried about her daughter's friendship with Jastin

---

Jessica, a fourth grader, writes about the secondary character Mac in *Chocolate Fever* (Level O). Mac is a Mack truck driver who takes the main character, Henry, under his wing after Henry runs away out of embarrassment because of the brown spots on his skin from eating too much chocolate. Notice how Jessica names traits of the secondary character ("funny" and "nice") and also the impact he has on Henry ("he was saying nice things to Henry").

I think Mac is a funny person who like to laugh and I think he is a nice person because he was saying nice things to Henry.

Joey's mom is a good person. She has been through a lot. She loves him so much and that's why she came back. He really feels loved and he wants to do better

John, a fifth grader, writes about a secondary character from *Joey Pigza Swallowed the Key* (Level T). Notice how he infers and comments on traits as he describes the character (she's a "good person," "She has been through a lot") and also describes her relationship to Joey and how Joey is impacted by her ("She loves him," "He really feels loved and he wants to do better").

Byron is mean, there's no doubt about it. He likes to bully people, but he has a soft side. He helpes kenny sometimes and helps Joey a lot. Weirdly, he likes to pretend to make movies.

From Eitan's writing about Byron, a secondary character in *The Watsons Go to Birmingham-1963* (Level U). you can tell he knows about him. He's seeing multiple sides – his tendency to bully but also his soft side. He shows that he is considering Byron's impact on other characters (Kenny, Joey).

Vocabulary and Figurative Language
A Progression of Skills

TO HAVE A SOLID COMMAND OF VOCABULARY AND FIGURATIVE LANGUAGE, READERS USE THESE SKILLS TO GREATER DEGREES AS THEY READ MORE CHALLENGING TEXTS.

SKILLS	J	K	L	M	N	O	P
Monitoring for Meaning and Using Context	Uses scene-level context to explain the meaning of a word or phrase.						

Q R S T U V W

Uses cumulative knowledge
of the story to explain the
meaning of a word or phrase.

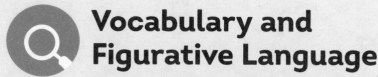

Vocabulary and Figurative Language

Monitoring for Meaning and Using Context

As fiction becomes more challenging, so do the words it contains—words used to describe story events, settings, and characters, and words used in narration and dialogue. Moreover, the frequency of challenging words increases. As texts become more challenging, readers will need to use larger context—first the page, then the scene, then whole chapters, and eventually the entire book—to infer the meaning of unfamiliar vocabulary. Therefore, understanding vocabulary and figurative language becomes increasingly integral to understanding the whole book, and understanding the story becomes increasingly important to understanding words and phrases.

Khoi, a first grader, read *Frog and Toad Are Friends* (Level K). When Toad says he feels "down in the dumps" as he looks around at his messy house that needs cleaning, Khoi explains his feeling of sadness with details from the text, which shows that he understands the meaning of the phrase within the context of the story.

> down in the dumps means that he is not going to have fun doing so much work tommorrw

---

Nathan, a second grader, explains the meaning of the phrase "caused a great commotion" from *Cam Jansen and the Mystery of the Stolen Diamonds* (Level L). Notice how he defines it ("made a big mess") and then elaborates with details from the context of the story. This shows he's able to derive meaning from the scene to figure out the meaning of this phrase.

> Made a big mess. By bumping in to people, making people drop there packages, causing problems.

He was so happy and excited because the doctor told him that he will be okay when they find him the right medication. It felt like Christmas.

John, a fifth grader, writes about figurative language in *Joey Pigza Swallowed the Key* (Level T). Notice how his explanation of the phrase, "I felt like Christmas was just a few days away," makes sense with what's happening in the scene, which involves conversations with Joey's doctor and family about a medication that will help him with ADHD that he's been struggling with for the entire story up to this point. He brings knowledge of the whole story to explain the meaning of the phrase.

It (according to Byron) is bad food they give you for free, from the top shelves. It would be embarrassing to Byron because, people would think that his parents are super poor.

Eitan, a fourth grader, writes about "welfare food"—mentioned by a character in *The Watsons Go to Birmingham-1963* (Level U). From his explanation of the term, you can tell that he goes beyond providing a definition and really explains what it means in this scene and why it's important to the characters. He is using knowledge of Byron from the whole story so far—his character has been well established as one who wants to keep up appearances among his friends.

When Crash says this he means that his home and himself were getting farther apart, and that the football Crash was fading away, and that the real Crash was starting to show.

Deepak, a fifth grader, reflects on the phrase, "Now there was a crack of daylight between them, like my shell was coming loose" from Spinelli's *Crash* (Level V) (127). His response shows not only that he understands the way this figurative language is meant to relate to the characters and events but also that the phrase helps him better understand the character. He is using his cumulative knowledge of the whole story here. by explaining that the rough bully football Crash character he's consistently been uo to this point is changing to the "real" Crash at this pivotal moment.

Themes and Ideas
A Progression of Skills

TO HAVE A SOLID COMMAND OF THEMES AND IDEAS, READERS USE THESE SKILLS TO GREATER DEGREES AS THEY READ MORE CHALLENGING TEXTS.

SKILLS	J	K	L	M	N	O	P
Interpreting a Story by Naming Life Lesson(s) or Theme(s)	Articulates one of the book's lessons/themes based on most of the story's events.						
Identifying and Interpreting Social Issues						Identifies a social issue in the book. Accumulates and synthesizes many details to explain the complexity of that issue.	
Identifying and Interpreting Symbols							

Q   R   S   T   U   V   W

Articulates a universal lesson/theme that can be applied to other contexts outside the text, such as to other texts or the reader's own life. Considers events from multiple plotlines.

Articulates multiple universal lessons/themes that can be applied to other contexts outside the text, such as to other texts or the reader's own life. Considers events from multiple plotlines.

Identifies a social issue in the book, explains its complexity, and recognizes stereotypes.

Interprets a symbol by considering it in the context of the story and explaining its significance.

Interprets a symbol and its complexity. Names the abstract idea the symbol represents. Relates the symbol's significance to the whole book and/or title.

Themes and Ideas

Interpreting a Story by Naming Life Lesson(s) or Theme(s)

To truly comprehend a piece of fiction, readers need to be able to look across the whole text, synthesize key information in the plot and the journey of the characters, and articulate life lesson(s) or theme(s)—a universal message of some sort. As texts become more complex, lessons go from simple, accessible lessons about friends and family, to lessons that take multiple perspectives into account and grapple with issues such as bullying, divorce, or war.

This first grader read *Days with Frog and Toad* (Level K) and was able to come up with a lesson that relates to the main events of the plot.

> toad learns that if somebody wants to be alone it doesent always have to be sad he/she can also Be happy.

This third-grade reader jots about lessons she learned after reading *Jake Drake, Bully Buster* (Level O). Notice that she's starting to see that stories can have more than one lesson or message, something typically expected at Level T and above. Both of her big ideas are stated in universal language.

> I leand never to bully because you might be friend and when the do something to make you emarresy laugh. And dont get mad the first time only give them chances

We can learn that your never supposed to give up. Your supposed to push yourself forward no matter how hard it may be. But its not always going to be accomplished

Lillian, a fifth grader, infers a lesson that relates to the whole of Sadako's story in *Sadako and the Thousand Paper Cranes* (Level R). Notice that the lesson she inferred isn't a cliche and that she identifies complexity in the lesson. She holds up two ideas simultaneously: that you should push yourself and not give up, *but* that even when you do, you may still not accomplish what you're trying for. This shows she's considering different aspects of the plot.

No matter where you go, no matter how different the place, you are still you deep inside. Also that you can be hurt by tragic events and come back to love people once again.

Notice the complexity in this sixth grader's thinking about the themes in *Home of the Brave* (Level W). This child is considering themes from multiple perspectives or parts of the story. and each of these big ideas connects to many events throughout the story.

Themes and Ideas
Identifying and Interpreting Social Issues

Uncovering the lessons or themes in a text often paves the way for readers to determine a deeper meaning. As readers encounter texts at Level O and above, they are confronted with issues in their texts that require awareness of the world around them. We can help children see how the issues that affect our lives—specifically, social issues such as bullying, war, poverty, or sibling rivalry—show up in books we read.

This third-grade reader is thinking about the social issue of bullying in *Jake Drake, Bully Buster* (Level O). She identifies the issue (bullying) and draws conclusions/a lesson about what the author might be teaching about the issue. Her interpretation aligns with the story.

> Link is stoping bullying because Jake is not scard I Learnd that you should never bully because it could lead up to bad things.

Morgan, a fourth grader, writes about the issues of gender in *Fourth Grade Rats* (Level Q). In this quick jot, she shows how she is able to identify the stereotypes that are presented in the book-boys have to be "all tough," and girls have to like boys and are "all mushy." The student doesn't call this out as a stereotype, but that's okay. An acknowledgment of stereotypes is something we typically see from readers' responses beginning with their responses to Level S books.

> I think it means to be a boy you have to be a rat and be all tough and to be a girl you have to like a boy and be all mushy to boys when they get hurt.

I have learned that war is very cruel and can destroy people's lives. Therefor the world should stay peaceful.

Angela, a third grader, read *Sadako and the Thousand Paper Cranes* (Level R). At the end, she inferred this lesson, which shows an understanding of larger social issues (war, cruelty, peace).

Maria's father said that "messed up kids shouldn't go to school with regular kids." He is ignorant. No one should think that way.

John, a fifth grader, read *Joey Pigza Swallowed the Key* (Level T), a novel that centers around a main character learning to cope with special needs and fitting in and being understood by his family. Notice how John reacts and responds to the social issue in the story by calling out the stereotype ("He is ignorant") and offers his own reaction and comment ("No one should think that way").

Themes and Ideas
Identifying and Interpreting Symbols

When children first encounter symbolism in their books, usually around Level R, they may have a gut sense that concrete objects, settings, or characters stand for something bigger. For what, though, they may not be sure. But as they move into more challenging texts, they can learn to become capable of explaining how a symbol's significance permeates the story to communicate something larger, such as an abstract idea or concept.

Third grader Keili enjoyed *Koya Delaney and the Good Girl Blues* (Level P), a story about a girl who is wrestling with her emotions—always trying to portray happiness and perfection while she actually feels a range of emotions. At one point in the story, Koya has a dream. keili recognizes that the monster in the dream represents the angry feelings that are trapped inside the character.

> The monster might represent her anger trieing to get out when she's tring to keep her good self in her. because she doesn't like anger.

This fifth grader understands the significance of the paper cranes in the book *Sadako and the Thousand Paper Cranes* (R). She is recognizing how a concrete symbol (cranes) can represent hope. She uses her interpretation of the symbol to better understand the character.

> The cranes symbolize hope. When she has the cranes she feels power over her sickness and she feels like she might get better.

Understanding Fiction Readers

In the book, Loser, Claudia might represt a person to show how caring Zinkoff can be. The old women might represnt a person for Zinkoff to share his life with and to show a strong relashonship. The wailing man represented a person that is really cares and has a lot of feelings for someone.

Responding to a Level U text, this fifth grader considers many of the author's choices to be symbolic. In his response, he jots about multiple characters and how each character can represent a big idea or help add further insight to the main character. Considering characters and/or settings to be symbolic is often more challenging than considering objects to be symbolic.

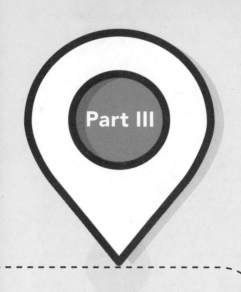

Nonfiction

TEXTS, READERS, AND COMPREHENSION

I n this book, *nonfiction* refers to informational text that is based in fact, and seeks to teach a reader about a topic relating to the natural and/or social world. An author of this type of nonfiction is someone who knows a lot about the topic, either because they have done research or they are experts in their field. It does not mean that the text is without bias or slant; nonfiction shouldn't be taken to mean "true" without question. It is the reader's job to read a text critically, understand what it says, and consider the validity of the points the author is making (Beers and Probst 2016).

Nonfiction can take many different forms.

Expository nonfiction texts are focused on a topic which is then divided into categories and subcategories. Some nonfiction is written in the form of a story, or narrative: biographies, autobiographies, and some historical accounts are examples. Other nonfiction texts teach readers how to do something and are more procedural (think: cookbooks, craft books, directions for how to play a game).

Some texts can't be classified as being exclusively one type of nonfiction. For instance, in Fay Robinson's *A Dinosaur Named Sue* (1999), a reader encounters narrative at various points in the book—several chapters convey the sequence of events that preceded and followed the discovery of an almost intact T. rex skeleton—mixed in with procedural text teaching about how a dinosaur is dug up, and expository sections about what a T. rex is.

Nonfiction texts often include technical vocabulary and terms that are important to learn to be able to understand the key information and ideas being presented. They may also have text features such as photography or realistic illustrations, indexes, tables of contents, graphs and charts, and diagrams to help convey information.

I share these definitions knowing that all experts do not agree. Some genre theorists and researchers consider informational texts to be a subcategory of nonfiction (Duke and Bennett-Armistead 2003), whereas others use the terms interchangeably as I do here (Beers and Probst 2016). Some introduce additional terms such as "literary non-fiction" and "traditional nonfiction" into the mix (Stewart 2018).

Throughout Part III of this book, you'll see lists of examples and read descriptions of nonfiction texts that are primarily exposi-tory, though texts described may occasionally include some narrative elements. When supporting students with expository nonfiction, the categories of Main Idea, Key Details, Vocabulary, and Text Features are helpful for studying texts, assessing readers, and setting goals. For students reading nonfiction that is primarily narrative (i.e., biogra-phies), the categories you read about in Part II focusing on fiction are more helpful (Plot and Setting, Character, Vocabulary and Figurative Language, and Themes and Ideas).

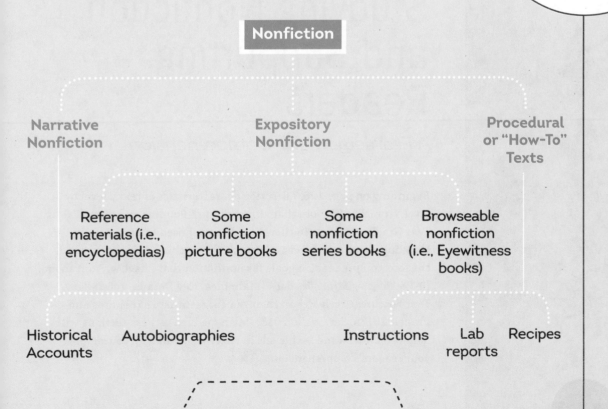

A Partial List of Nonfiction Text Types

Nonfiction

Narrative Nonfiction

Expository Nonfiction

Procedural or "How-To" Texts

Reference materials (i.e., encyclopedias)

Some nonfiction picture books

Some nonfiction series books

Browseable nonfiction (i.e., Eyewitness books)

Historical Accounts

Autobiographies

Instructions

Lab reports

Recipes

Listed below are the four goals for nonfiction comprehension that form the framework for the nonfiction section of this book.

Main Idea

Key Details

Vocabulary

Text Features

Studying Nonfiction and Supporting Readers

A Framework for Comprehension

Beginning on page 126, I describe characteristics of texts, level by level, from J to W. Note that although I use Fountas and Pinnell's Text Gradient™ levels in this book, I have chosen to organize my thinking about each level and associated teaching guidance around the four comprehension goals for nonfiction that I have written about in *The Reading Strategies Book* (Main Idea, Key Details, Vocabulary, Text Features), rather than their ten characteristics (Fountas and Pinnell 2017b; Serravallo 2015). My hope is that these sections will help you understand text levels in a way that will help you support your readers' comprehension.

Beginning on page 160, I provide a goal-by-goal overview of how expectations for comprehension shift and grow as students move through increasingly complex texts. Each spread is dedicated to a skill that is part of each goal. On these pages, you'll see sample written responses with captions to explain how they demonstrate increased sophistication based on complexity in the books they read.

Before getting to the level-by-level descriptions and the goal-by-goal student samples, an overview follows that describes each of the four main goals, the skills that are a part of them, and how these goals and skills are important to understanding nonfiction texts and readers of nonfiction.

A Crash Course on Main Idea

Richard Allington writes in *What Really Matters for Struggling Readers* (2000) that being able to summarize the main points of a text is key. He writes, "This is, perhaps, the most common and most necessary strategy. It requires that students provide a general recitation of the key content. Literate people summarize texts routinely in their conversations. They summarize weather reports, news articles, stock market information, and editorials. In each case, they select certain features and delete, or ignore, others" (122). A good summary is anchored by the main idea(s).

To determine main ideas, a reader needs to be able to synthesize multiple pieces of information from the text and/or text features. As texts become more complex, so do ideas. By fifth grade, a reader will need to be able to identify multiple main ideas that are often related. This requires the mental work of sifting and sorting through information to determine what's most important. In texts where the main idea(s) are more implicit, it also requires inferring.

This work is important and challenging. Stephanie Harvey and Anne Goudvis write, "Synthesizing is the most complex of comprehension strategies . . . . A true synthesis is an Aha! of sorts" (2000, 144). While simpler texts may offer support for determining main idea—e.g., clear headings or topic sentences—as texts become more complex, readers need to read closely, often inferring main ideas.

Studies have found that determining the main idea rarely happens by accident. Instead, students benefit from explicit strategy instruction. For example, Peter Afflerbach (1990) studied students' ability to construct the main idea from a text when they did and didn't have prior knowledge of the topic. When students reported having prior knowledge of the content domain, their ability to construct the main idea was more automatic. When students lacked prior knowledge, the study reported that they needed to use strategies. The author concludes, "Although sometimes automatic, expert readers' construction of a main idea is often a mediated, strategic task" (31).

Working with struggling readers, Jitendra, Hoppes, and Xin (2000) placed students in experimental and control groups. Those in the experimental group were taught through strategy instruction to identify and generate main idea statements. Students who were taught strategies showed increased reading comprehension, which was maintained over time. They also outperformed students in the control group on posttest and delayed posttest items. Six weeks later, students in the experimental group retained and were still able to use the strategies they learned.

This work of teaching explicit strategies for determining the main idea is a move away from having kids record every little factoid they come across in a book as they read. If students write while reading, we can steer them toward trying to group related facts, to determine which of an author's points are most important, and to distill these down to a clear main idea sentence. This will encourage deeper understanding of the author's main points and free the student up to question and critique content and even teach it to others.

A Crash Course on Key Details

Being able to distinguish the key details from the less significant details means holding the author's main idea in your mind as you read and proceeding through the text purposefully thinking, "Does this fact relate to the main idea?"

In their book *Strategies That Work*, Stephanie Harvey and Anne Goudvis write, "Determining importance means picking out the most important information when you read, to highlight essential ideas, to isolate supporting details, and to read for specific information. Teachers need to help readers sift and sort information, and make decisions about what information they need to remember and what information they can disregard" (2000, 117). They go on to say, "Readers of nonfiction have to decide and remember what is important in the texts they read if they are going to learn anything from them" (118).

One of the reasons that some students find nonfiction texts more challenging than fiction texts of the same level is that nonfiction texts are dense. Readers encounter fact upon fact upon fact in the main text and text features, and they need to control their pace, slow down, and figure out how all the information fits together. Readers also need to consider the relationship between the information and different facts—for example, does one fact add on more information about a previously stated fact? Or is the second one giving contrasting information to the first? Readers also must read nonfiction critically, "questioning their own beliefs and assumptions while struggling [to determine] what's true—or not—in the text" (Beers and Probst 2016, 19).

In expository texts, authors will often compare and contrast two related subtopics or ideas within a text. Readers will need to be able to understand which facts and information go with which subtopics or ideas as well as the relationships between the facts. Understanding what information is "key" to the section means understanding how the information fits together.

Skills That Enhance Understanding of Key Details

o Determining importance to support a main idea with key details from the text

o Comparing and contrasting key details

"Getting kids' attention is about creating interest; keeping their attention is all about relevance."

—KYLENE BEERS AND ROBERT PROBST (2016)

Skills That Enhance Understanding of Vocabulary

o Monitoring for meaning and using context

"*Vocabulary and comprehension go hand in hand. Our research shows that a higher vocabulary predicts or suggests that a student will comprehend at a higher level. This connection is not just an accident. Really, it is causal. We know that if you work to improve students' vocabulary, it actually improves their comprehension.*"

—NELL K. DUKE AND
V. S. BENNETT-ARMISTEAD (2003)

A Crash Course on Vocabulary

Vocabulary knowledge helps students access background knowledge, express ideas, communicate effectively, and learn about new concepts. "Vocabulary is the glue that holds stories, ideas, and content together . . . making comprehension accessible for children" (Rupley, Logan, and Nichols 1998/99).

Students' word knowledge is linked strongly to academic success because students with large vocabularies can understand new ideas and concepts more quickly than students with limited vocabularies. Word knowledge is strongly correlated to reading comprehension, indicating how crucial it is that students adequately and steadily grow their vocabulary knowledge. Students who lack adequate vocabulary have difficulty getting meaning from what they read, so they read less because they find reading difficult (Sedita 2005). The number of words that students need to learn is large; on average students should add 2,000 to 3,000 new words a year to their reading vocabularies (Beck, McKeown, and Kucan 2002).

Although it may be tempting to support children by teaching them a lot of words to make up for any perceived gaps, that alone will have less impact than the word learning students do when they are reading independently and listening to stories read to them (G. A. Miller 1999; Nagy, Anderson, and Herman 1987; Krashen 2004; Baumann, Kame'enui, and Ash 2003). Therefore, setting aside lots of time for independent reading and supporting students with strategies to help them understand new or unfamiliar words when they come upon them in texts will go a long way toward developing their vocabularies. Children benefit from encountering words repeatedly, in various contexts, both written and oral, to develop full and complete understanding of words' meanings (Nagy, Anderson, and Herman 1987; Vosniadou and Ortony 1983).

A Crash Course on Text Features

It's hard to read an informational text without encountering a variety of text features. Text features help break up long sections of dense expository writing and communicate important information in unique ways. The types of features readers may encounter are varied: graphs, charts, photos, illustrations, sidebars, and so on. Features such as tables of contents, indexes, glossaries, and more help the reader to navigate the book and understand the information in different ways.

Too often in elementary school, curriculum around informational reading stops at teaching students to *identify* these text features. However, text features exist to help readers derive meaning from, and to better comprehend, the information in the text. Therefore, it's essential that instruction around text features is not just about naming them—as in, "This is a map"—but more importantly about helping students *use* these features to get more information from a text.

In *Nonfiction Matters*, Stephanie Harvey writes about the importance of text features to the overall text. She says, "Features of nonfiction alert the reader to important information" (1997, 77). Depending on the level of the text, these features can also help add information to the main text or even summarize or synthesize key information within the text.

Skills That Enhance Understanding of Text Features

○ Deriving meaning from a text feature by synthesizing information from that feature, the text, and, if present, other text features

"In easier texts, text features tend to be explicitly aligned to the main idea; in harder texts, this connection is less explicit, and the features may actually seduce readers to give more significance to particular details than they deserve."

—LUCY CALKINS AND KATHLEEN TOLAN (2010)

Understanding Nonfiction Texts

A Level-by-Level Guide to Characteristics

By studying the information in this section, you'll learn about the text characteristics of nonfiction books at Levels J to W. This will help you to know children's informational texts so that when you are working with students in conferences or small groups, even if you don't know the specific book the child is reading, you'll have a sense of what to generally expect of books at that level. The knowledge will also help you plan when you *do* know the book the child is reading because focusing on the text characteristics, rather than the book itself, will help children to generalize your teaching from book to book.

Each spread focuses on one level. For each level, I offer a description of text characteristics, a "look-fors" checklist for studying student response to reading, and examples of books.

Understanding subtle shifts and increases in demands from level to level is helpful for a teacher to know what readers are encountering in texts.

A "look-fors" checklist that will allow you to apply the text-complexity knowledge to student written responses and conversation about books. This will help you apply what you know about text levels to *any* text at that level, even one you haven't read yourself. A more in-depth look at student development within and across levels begins on page 158. When the look-fors have changed from the previous level, the change is indicated with a "shift from" note.

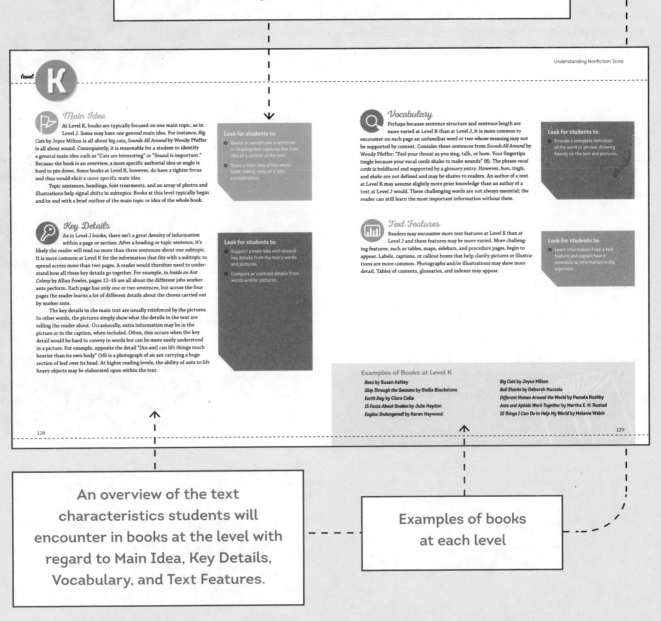

An overview of the text characteristics students will encounter in books at the level with regard to Main Idea, Key Details, Vocabulary, and Text Features.

Examples of books at each level

Main Idea

The main topic, and the main idea when there is one, are fairly obvious and explicit in books at Level J. The title usually clearly states the main topic of the whole book. Many books at this level tend to be "all about" a topic, without a narrowed focus or angle—for example, *Butterflies* as opposed to *Butterflies: The Great Migration*.

Within each section, the subtopic is also explicit. Boldface headings or clear topic sentences alert the reader to these subtopics. In some books, subtopics are presented in spreads. Often a table of contents will list the main subtopics, helping readers to preview and review the text.

Look for students to:

- Quote or paraphrase a sentence or heading that captures the amin idea of a section of the text.

- State a main idea of the whole book, taking most of it into consideration.

Key Details

At Level J, there isn't much density of information presented. After a heading or topic sentence, there may be just a few simple sentences, each containing one key detail. These key details explain the main idea and don't usually deviate from it with additional information. For example, in Penelope Arlon's *Farm*, a heading on one page says, "Farm Birds." Then each sentence gives one fact about one kind of bird: "A mother chicken, called a hen, can lay eggs for your breakfast" (4) and "Turkeys make funny gobbling sounds" (3).

Likewise, the key details in the main text are usually faithfully reiterated in the pictures. That is, the illustrations or photos generally don't convey additional information. Occasionally they do, but this is often in cases where the key detail would be too complex to explain in words and can be more easily understood when pictured. For example, in *Farm*, Arlon writes, "Mother pigs can have as many as sixteen piglets at one time" (12). Next to this is a photograph of a mother pig nursing six piglets. The photo teaches the reader that mother pigs feed their young.

Look for students to:

- Support a main idea with several key details from the text's words and pictures.

- Compare *or* contrast details from words and/or pictures.

126

Vocabulary

Vocabulary in books at Level J is often common knowledge. In *Play Ball!* by Vanessa York, one section readers will see includes words such as *weather*, *glove*, *teams*, and *at bat*.

Content-specific vocabulary is rare, and when it does appear, its meaning is heavily supported by context and/or pictures. In *Play Ball!* words such as *baseball diamond* and *inning* appear on pages with large photographs and additional sentences of explanation to support readers' understanding.

Look for students to:

○ Provide a complete definition of the word or phrase, drawing heavily on the text and pictures.

Text Features

Text features at Level J, usually pictures or illustrations, often support the main text on a page. Frequently they are colorful and realistic and convey exactly what the text states. In *Play Ball!* a photo of a batter at the plate is accompanied by a drawn box and label indicating the "strike zone" beneath her arms. The text on the page gives a supporting fact about the strike zone being where the pitch needs to land.

Tables of contents and inset boxes are common. Inset boxes often contain a photo or diagram. The Discover More series typically uses one main picture to support the main text and a series of smaller pictures, each accompanying its own fact.

Look for students to:

○ Learn information from a text feature and explain how it connects to information in the main text.

Examples of Books at Level J

Bears by Amy Levin

Insects by Carolyn MacLulich

Shadows by Carolyn B. Otto

Ants by Rebecca Rissman

Fantastic Frogs! by Fay Robinson

About Habitats: Oceans by Cathryn Sill

Fabulous Fishes by Susan Stockdale

All Kinds of People: What Makes Us Different by Jennifer Waters

Bats by Lily Wood

Play Ball! by Vanessa York

Main Idea

At Level K, books are typically focused on one main topic, as in Level J. Some may have one general main idea. For instance, *Big Cats* by Joyce Milton is all about big cats; *Sounds All Around* by Wendy Pfeffer is all about sound. Consequently, it is reasonable for a student to identify a general main idea such as "Cats are interesting" or "Sound is important." Because the book is an overview, a more specific authorial idea or angle is hard to pin down. Some books at Level K, however, do have a tighter focus and thus would elicit a more specific main idea.

Topic sentences, headings, font treatments, and an array of photos and illustrations help signal shifts in subtopics. Books at this level typically begin and/or end with a brief outline of the main topic or idea of the whole book.

Look for students to:
- Quote or paraphrase a sentence or heading that captures the main idea of a section of the text.
- State a main idea of the whole book, taking most of it into consideration.

Key Details

As in Level J books, there isn't a great density of information within a page or section. After a heading or topic sentence, it's likely the reader will read no more than three sentences about one subtopic. It is more common at Level K for the information that fits with a subtopic to spread across more than two pages. A reader would therefore need to understand how all these key details go together. For example, in *Inside an Ant Colony* by Allan Fowler, pages 12–16 are all about the different jobs worker ants perform. Each page has only one or two sentences, but across the four pages the reader learns a lot of different details about the chores carried out by worker ants.

The key details in the main text are usually reinforced by the pictures. In other words, the pictures simply show what the details in the text are telling the reader about. Occasionally, extra information may be in the picture or in the caption, when included. Often, this occurs when the key detail would be hard to convey in words but can be more easily understood in a picture. For example, opposite the detail "[An ant] can lift things much heavier than its own body" (16) is a photograph of an ant carrying a huge section of leaf over its head. At higher reading levels, the ability of ants to lift heavy objects may be elaborated upon within the text.

Look for students to:
- Support a main idea with several key details from the text's words and pictures.
- Compare or contrast details from words and/or pictures.

Vocabulary

Perhaps because sentence structure and sentence length are more varied at Level K than at Level J, it is more common to encounter on each page an unfamiliar word or two whose meaning may not be supported by context. Consider these sentences from *Sounds All Around* by Wendy Pfeffer: "Feel your throat as you sing, talk, or hum. Your fingertips tingle because your vocal cords shake to make sounds" (8). The phrase *vocal cords* is boldfaced and supported by a glossary entry. However, *hum*, *tingle*, and *shake* are not defined and may be elusive to readers. An author of a text at Level K may assume slightly more prior knowledge than an author of a text at Level J would. These challenging words are not always essential; the reader can still learn the most important information without them.

Look for students to:

- Provide a complete definition of the word or phrase, drawing heavily on the text and pictures.

Text Features

Readers may encounter more text features at Level K than at Level J and these features may be more varied. More challenging features, such as tables, maps, sidebars, and procedure pages, begin to appear. Labels, captions, or callout boxes that help clarify pictures or illustrations are more common. Photographs and/or illustrations may show more detail. Tables of contents, glossaries, and indexes may appear.

Look for students to:

- Learn information from a text feature and explain how it connects to information in the main text.

Examples of Books at Level K

Bees by Susan Ashley

Skip Through the Seasons by Stella Blackstone

Earth Day by Clara Cella

15 Facts About Snakes by Julie Haydon

Eagles: Endangered! by Karen Haywood

Big Cats by Joyce Milton

Bull Sharks by Deborah Nuzzolo

Different Homes Around the World by Pamela Rushby

Ants and Aphids Work Together by Martha E. H. Rustad

10 Things I Can Do to Help My World by Melanie Walsh

Main Idea

At Level L, the entire book may be focused on one main topic, or it may address several closely related topics. All information in the book may be angled toward one main idea.

Books at Level L may occasionally be divided into subsections that elucidate or support the main topic. When they are, they usually include headings. In Judith Bauer Stamper's *America's Symbols*, headings such as "Our Flag," "The American Eagle," and "The White House" clearly alert the reader to the subtopic of the page.

A concluding page or section may summarize a main idea of the whole book. These sections offer extra support for the reader because they reiterate the main idea of the book. *Antarctica* by Allan Fowler ends with this statement: "Even though Antarctica is a lonely continent, there are many amazing things to see and study there" (29).

Look for students to:

○ Quote or paraphrase a sentence or heading that captures the main idea of a section of the text.

○ State a main idea of the whole book, taking most of it into consideration.

Key Details

About five sentences or details occur per page on average. Details supporting one subtopic may carry across more than one page. In *How Kittens Grow* by Millicent E. Selsam, three to five simple sentences are on each page, supported by a full-color photograph. *Penguins* by Janet Reed has the same layout.

At Level L, readers may begin to encounter an occasional complex sentence that contains phrases not obviously related to each other. Words such as *unlike*, *also*, *instead*, and *then* may be used to link phrases. A reader will also have to work to understand pronoun antecedents. For example, in *Penguins*, one paragraph reads this way: "This is a king penguin. It is smaller than the emperor. It has two bright orange spots at each side of its head. They look like earmuffs" (8). The words *this*, *it*, *its*, and *they* require the reader to link the information from one sentence to the next.

Photographs and/or illustrations may be less supportive. Because they do not necessarily help explain a key concept, more responsibility falls on the reader to learn from the text. At this level, a typical layout features around five sentences and one photograph per page, so it's hard for the photo always to capture everything in the text.

Look for students to:

○ Support a main idea with several key details from the text's words and pictures.

○ Identify multiple similarities *and* differences, and categorize comparisons, using key details from the text (**shift from Level K**).

Vocabulary

The author assumes some prior knowledge but usually only of common words. In *How Kittens Grow*, *crawl*, *walk*, and *cries* are not defined, but content-specific words are.

Content-specific vocabulary words occur on each page. When important to learning key details and main ideas, they are mostly supported by context.

Look for students to:
- Provide a complete definition of a word or phrase, drawing heavily on the text and pictures.

Text Features

Prominent photographs or illustrations support important main-text information. On each page in *How Kittens Grow*, a half-page photograph or two smaller photographs accompany about four to five simple sentences. The picture usually shows most of the facts on that page.

More challenging features (tables, maps, sidebars, and procedure pages) begin to appear. Tables of contents, glossaries, and indexes appear. Allan Fowler's *Antarctica* has a map, a picture glossary, and a short index. *America's Symbols* has more features: a table of contents, glossary, index, headings, and captions. Other titles have few text features, relying mostly on large photographs or illustrations on each page, such as *What Do You Do with a Tail Like This?* by Steve Jenkins and Robin Page.

Look for students to:
- Learn information from a text feature and explain how it connects to information in the main text.

Examples of Books at Level L

Frogs! by Elizabeth Carney

The Power of the Wind by Mary Beth Crum

Horse Show by Kate Hayden

What Do You Do with a Tail Like This? by Steve Jenkins and Robin Page

Rescuing Stranded Whales by Marianne Lenihan

Amazing Animals: Elephants by Kate Riggs

Pumpkins by Ken Robbins

America's Symbols by Judith Bauer Stamper

Firefighters to the Rescue Around the World by Linda Staniford

Energy in Motion by Melissa Stewart

Main Idea

At Level M, as in Level L, the entire book is likely to be focused on a single main topic—e.g., manatees, ants, wolves—and organized into chapters, each dealing with a different related subtopic. All information in the book may be angled toward one main idea—for instance, that manatees are amazing animals. A reader may have to work hard to synthesize the increased amount of information within different chapters or sections to determine the main idea of the whole book.

For example, both Patricia A. Fink Martin's *Manatees* and Melvin and Gilda Berger's *Howl! A Book About Wolves* are organized by chapters. In *Manatees*, subtopics and subideas are found within each chapter. We learn, for example, where manatees live, why they are in danger, and how the cow takes care of her young calf. In *Howl!* we learn how wolves hunt, how they live in packs, and about different types of wolves.

Look for students to:

- Synthesize most details from pictures and words in a section of the text to state a main idea, using original language (**shift from Level L**).

- Take the whole book into account to state a main idea (**shift from Level L**).

Key Details

At Level M, each page and section has generally more density of information than there is at Level L. Most Level L books have around three to five sentences or details per page.

In addition, the reader should expect the complexity within each sentence to be greater than it is at Level L. Linking words and pronouns with unclear references require the reader to puzzle how the details within each section fit together. The reader has to consider, for example, whether the author is comparing two things (with signal words *like, but, unlike*), suggesting a causal relationship between two things (*then, later*), or presenting more information (*also, in addition*).

Look for students to:

- Support a main idea with several key details from the text's words and pictures.

- Identify multiple similarities *and* differences, and categorize comparisons, using key details from the text.

Vocabulary

As at Level L, readers reading Level M texts can expect to encounter multiple words per page that are content specific. Some of the simpler words will not be defined. More challenging words will likely be defined within the context of the page or in a glossary or illustrated in a visual image or other text feature.

For example, in *Manatees*, the terms *migrate* and *refuges* are defined in the text on the page where they appear, as well as in a glossary. On the same page, the terms *feeding grounds*, *scientists*, and *travel* are not defined.

Look for students to:

○ Explain or describe the meaning of a word or phrase using larger context, including text features (shift from Level L).

Text Features

The most common text feature in books at this level tends to be photographs. Enticing full-color pictures illustrate main topics and often take up entire pages. When examined closely, photographs provide more information to the reader. For example, on one spread of *Manatees*, the text describes how scientists track a manatee by attaching a tag to its tail. From the picture, the reader can learn that the tag is actually a wide band or belt that encircles the tail, with an antenna that probably sends the radio signal back to the scientist. These details aren't included in the text.

More challenging features—such as tables, maps, sidebars, and procedure pages—may appear a couple of times within a book at this level. Generally, text features appear once every few pages, if at all. Tables of contents, glossaries, and/or indexes are common, but books tend to feature one or two of these, not all three.

Look for students to:

○ Learn information from a text feature and explain how it connects to information in the main text.

Examples of Books at Level M

Howl! A Book About Wolves by Melvin and Gilda Berger

My First Book About the Internet by Sharon Cromwell

From Seed to Plant by Gail Gibbons

Who Eats What? Food Chains and Food Webs by Patricia Lauber

Manatees by Patricia A. Fink Martin

Diwali: Hindu Festival of Lights by June Preszler

Caring by Lucia Raatma

Martin Luther King, Jr. and the March on Washington by Frances E. Ruffin

Busy Bees by Margaretha Takmar

Hurricanes and Tornadoes by Kate Waters

Main Idea

Books at Level N tend to be longer than those at Level M, and they often cover multiple subtopics. However, all the information in a book tends to be angled toward one main idea. For example, *Endangered Animals* by Lynn M. Stone identifies animal species that are in danger, explains why, and describes what people can do to save them. Within each chapter, many different animals are introduced. Overall, a reader could synthesize the information to determine that one main idea in the book is: "We should do what we can to save endangered animals."

Books at Level N are usually divided into sections or chapters, which may have titles or headings. A main idea of each chapter or section is more implicit than it is at lower levels. *Endangered Animals,* for example, features chapters with titles that indicate a topic. The reader would still need to infer the main idea of a chapter, although each chapter often concludes with a sentence or paragraph that sums up its main idea.

Look for students to:

- Synthesize most details from pictures and words in a section of the text to state a main idea, using original language.

- Take the whole book into account to state a main idea.

Key Details

The density of information on each page is greater than it is in books at Level M. At Level N, it is common to find as many as seven or more details per page. More than one page is often dedicated to a main idea. This means that the reader needs to understand and synthesize a great deal of information across several pages.

In Kris Hirschmann's *Ants, Bees, and Other Social Insects*, for example, two or three subsections appear within a chapter, each with around eight facts. Connecting words demand that the reader understand links between information. For instance, in the sentence "So this cooling system is very important" (19), a reader needs to understand that the word *this* refers to the holes in the side of the ant mound that act like an air conditioner, a fact mentioned two sentences earlier.

Look for students to:

- Support a main idea with several key details from the text's words and pictures.

- Identify multiple similarities *and* differences, and categorize comparisons, using key details from the text.

Vocabulary

The author assumes some prior knowledge on the part of the reader. The reader can expect to encounter several content-specific vocabulary words on each page. Those that are important to learning key details and main ideas are often supported by context.

Across a couple of pages of *Ants, Bees, and Other Social Insects*, words like *communicate* and *chemical* are in bold and appear in a glossary. The words *activity* and *tunnel* are supported by visuals and context within the page. The author assumes some knowledge on the part of the reader, however. The words *pile*, *millions*, *termites*, *wasps*, and *weigh* are not defined.

Look for students to:

○ Explain or describe the meaning of a word or phrase using larger context, including text features.

Text Features

Photographs or illustrations support some, but not all, facts within the main text. See the spread in Seymour Simon's *Cool Cars* about Ford's Model T. On the pages, facts about the car's speed, its sales price, and the number of cars manufactured and sold are all included. The feature on the page is a historical photograph with some people in a car, so a reader will need to envision many of those details without visual support.

More challenging features such as tables, maps, sidebars, and procedure pages may appear once or twice. Tables of contents, glossaries, and indexes are common.

Look for students to:

○ Learn information from a text feature and explain how it connects to information in the main text.

Examples of Books at Level N

Gung Hay Fat Choy by June Behrens

One Tiny Turtle by Nicola Davies

The Cloud Book by Tomie dePaola

Save the Manatee by Alison Friesinger

Ants, Bees, and Other Social Insects by Kris Hirschmann

Tornadoes! by Lorraine Jean Hopping

Pompeii . . . Buried Alive! by Edith Kunhardt

The Real Poop on Pigeons by Kevin McClosky

Sod Houses on the Great Plains by Glen Rounds

Endangered Animals by Lynn M. Stone

Main Idea

The entire book at Level O is often focused on one complex, overarching main idea. It may be complex for a couple of different reasons. In one book, for example, to understand a compass, a reader has to grasp the more abstract concepts of magnetism and poles. A reader has to then glean the complex main idea by expertly reading multiple text features. Put simply, what is new for the reader is that they encounter *more—* more words per page, more facts, more complex concepts. They have to work harder to recall, retell, and comprehend.

The main idea of the whole book may be developed in several related subtopics. For instance, in Melvin Berger's *Germs Make Me Sick!* readers learn about viruses, bacteria, ways they enter the body, and how to keep oneself healthy.

When a book at this level is divided into sections or chapters, each section or chapter may have its own main idea. When this is true, the chapter titles may support the uncovering of main ideas of each chapter that relate to the main idea of the whole text.

Look for students to:

O Synthesize most details from pictures and words in a section of the text to state a main idea, using original language.

O Take the whole book into account to state a main idea and capture the complexity the author brings to the topic (shift from **Level N**).

Key Details

Around eight to ten sentences or details occur per page. A main idea is often carried across more than one page. For example, on a spread from Ellen Weiss' *The Sense of Taste*, it's noteworthy that words such as *undoubtedly*, *originally*, and *but* add to the complexity of the information presented. As at past levels, readers need to consider the relationships between details. At Level O, however, these types of words appear more often, and there are more details overall on each page.

Photographs and other images illustrate isolated details. In *Germs Make Me Sick!*, for example, a reader can get help visualizing the shapes that viruses and bacteria can take by using the illustration. However, the concept of being able to see them only "under the microscope" must be imagined.

Look for students to:

O Support a main idea with several key details from the text's words and pictures.

O Identify multiple similarities *and* differences, and categorize comparisons, using key details from the text.

Vocabulary

The author assumes some prior knowledge on the part of the reader. On one page in Miles Harvey's *Look What Came from Mexico*, the words *explorer*, *ruled*, and *independent* are not defined.

The reader can expect to encounter several content-specific vocabulary words on each page. Those that are important to learning key details and main ideas are often supported by context. In *Look What Came from Mexico*, terms such as *civilization* and *empire* are supported with glossary definitions.

Look for students to:

○ Explain or describe the meaning of a word or phrase using larger context, including text features.

Text Features

More challenging features such as tables, maps, sidebars, and procedure pages may appear at times. Some of these features offer information beyond that in the main text. The True Book and Investigators series are both filled with a variety of text features. Even at Level O, a reader will encounter maps, timelines, lists of statistics, and callout boxes. Tables of contents, glossaries, and indexes are common. The Let's-Read-and-Find-Out Science books (*Germs Make Me Sick!* by Melvin Berger is one example) typically do not include these features, but many other series at this level do.

Look for students to:

○ Learn information from a text feature and explain how it connects to information in the main text.

Examples of Books at Level O

Germs Make Me Sick! by Melvin Berger

Beacons of Light: Lighthouses by Gail Gibbons

Look What Came from Mexico by Miles Harvey

Owls by Kevin J. Holmes

Boy, Were We Wrong About Dinosaurs! by Kathleen V. Kudlinski

Wiggling Worms at Work by Wendy Pfeffer

Tropical Rain Forests by Darlene R. Stille

Where Do Polar Bears Live? by Sarah L. Thomson

At 1600 Pennsylvania Avenue by Crystal Wirth

You Can't Taste a Pickle with Your Ear: A Book About Your 5 Senses by Harriet Ziefert

Main Idea

As at Level O, the entire book at Level P is most often angled toward one complex main idea. For example, in Howard Gutner's *The Chicago Fire*, a reader learns the history of the late-1800s fire: its causes, the devastation it brought, and the rebuilding effort. In this book in particular, determining a main idea is extra challenging because the story is structured as a narrative. A main idea such as, "In a tragedy like the Chicago Fire, people can come together to rebuild, and even improve," would be an accurate statement. Notice the increased syntactical complexity compared to a main idea statement at, say, Level M.

A book at this level is usually divided into sections or chapters, which often have titles or section headings. Use of clever language in headings and titles begins to be more prevalent. Therefore, the main idea of each chapter or section is less explicit than at past levels. In these cases, a reader would need to consider the title, read the facts, and return to the heading to determine the main idea of the section.

A final page or section, or an introductory one, may summarize a main idea of the whole book. There may be concluding sentences within each chapter to sum up a main idea of that section. *The Chicago Fire* has concluding sentences after each section and at the end of the entire text: "If a great fire ever threatens Chicago again, the city will be ready" (16).

Look for students to:

- Synthesize most details from pictures and words in a section of the text to state a main idea, using original language.

- Take the whole book into account to state a main idea and capture the complexity the author brings to the topic.

Key Details

At Level P, it's likely a reader will encounter about ten sentences or details per page or spread. A main idea is often carried across more than one page. In *The Chicago Fire*, the first section is nine pages long.

Photographs and other pictures illustrate isolated facts on the page. Many important details are explained in the text alone. In *The Chicago Fire*, the illustrations are original prints from the late 1800s. A reader needs to study the images to understand them because there are no captions. It's also not always immediately clear how an illustration matches the text on that page.

Look for students to:

- Support a main idea with several key details from different pages or sections, using words, pictures, and text features (**shift from Level O**).

- Identify multiple similarities *and* differences, and categorize comparisons, using key details from the text.

Vocabulary

At Level P, the author assumes a good deal of prior knowledge on the part of the reader. The reader can expect to encounter many content-specific vocabulary words on each page. They will often need to work to learn these new words—by consulting a glossary in the back of the book, looking outside the book, or by pausing to study an illustration. For example, on one spread in Melissa Stewart's *Deadliest Animals*, a reader will encounter the words *pesky, diseases, malaria, West Nile virus, germs,* and *victims,* all of which must be figured out from context.

Look for students to:

○ Explain or describe the meaning of a word or phrase using larger context, including text features.

Text Features

Additional features within the main text such as tables, maps, sidebars, and procedure pages are common. Some of these features offer information beyond that in the main text. The types of text feature that a reader might encounter at Level P are varied, and the reader has to be ready to adapt to the diversity of styles and layouts in a book. The historical pictures in *The Chicago Fire*, the black and white illustrations in *Amelia and Eleanor Go for a Ride* by Pam Muñoz Ryan, and the sidebars, charts, and callout boxes in the Investigators series are some examples of this diversity. In addition, tables of contents, glossaries, and indexes are common.

Look for students to:

○ Learn information from a text feature and explain how it connects to information in the main text.

Examples of Books at Level P

Safari by Robert Bateman

The Let's Look at Countries series by Nikki Bruno Clapper

Arctic Babies by Kathy Darling

The Moon Book by Gail Gibbons

The Chicago Fire by Howard Gutner

Africa by Christine Juarez

The Our Physical World series by Ellen S. Niz

Inclined Planes by Andrea Rivera

Platypus by Joan Short, Jack Green, and Bettina Bird

31 Ways to Change the World by We Are What We Do

Main Idea

Books at Level Q tend to be broad in scope, cover a topic in depth, and tend to be longer than those at Level P. Determining a main idea is even more of a challenge than it is at previous levels, especially when ideas are more complex. A main idea may include a comparison, a cause-and-effect relationship, or multiple dimensions. A reader has to carefully consider all of the information and all subtopics and angles presented before determining one idea from the entire text. For example, in *All About Manatees* by Jim Arnosky, a reader could identify this main idea: "The manatee should be respected for the amazing creature that it is and protected from dangers that threaten its survival."

It is more work for a reader to determine the main idea of a section or chapters than it is at previous levels. Introductory sentences, headings, and titles may be less consistently supportive. In books such as *If You Lived When Women Won Their Rights* by Anne Kamma, the section headings framed as questions help the reader determine main ideas. However, in *Finding the Titanic* by Robert D. Ballard, titles such as "Chapter One: August 25, 1985" offer little support to determine an idea.

Look for students to:
- Synthesize most details from pictures and words in a section of the text to state a main idea, using original language.
- Take the whole book into account to state a main idea and capture the complexity the author brings to the topic.

Key Details

There are about ten sentences or details per page. These books are often arranged in chapters, with sections within those chapters. A chapter of related details may span five to seven pages. *Finding the Titanic* is a narrative nonfiction book with chapters that span five pages, on average.

At Level Q, as at past levels, photographs and other visuals illustrate only a small portion of the information in the main text. Readers have to work to absorb the information from the text alone. In addition, key details may be found in myriad text features—for example, in captions, labels, sidebars, and maps. For example, one page of *If You Lived When Women Won Their Rights* features a callout box that explains the U.S. Constitution, a political cartoon with a caption, and main text.

Look for students to:
- Support a main idea with several key details from different pages or sections, using words, pictures, and text features.
- Identify multiple similarities *and* differences, and categorize comparisons, using key details from the text.

Vocabulary

Readers of Level Q books should be ready to learn new vocabulary. Within a few pages, it's typical to encounter a half dozen or more content-specific words that involve challenging concepts. In *If You Lived When Women Won Their Rights*, the words and phrases *Constitution*, *African-American*, *antislavery*, *colored*, *master*, *voting inspector*, *trial*, and *Supreme Court* appear in the same section. Some terms are defined within the page; others are assumed to be familiar.

When vocabulary is unfamiliar, but not supported by text details, a reader needs to learn new words by consulting a glossary at the back of the book, looking outside the book, or pausing to study an illustration.

Look for students to:

○ Explain or describe the meaning of a word or phrase using larger context, including text features.

Text Features

Additional features within the main text (tables, maps, sidebars, and procedure pages) are common. Photos and other illustrations often have captions, which sometimes provide information beyond that in the main text. For example, in addition to the main text, a page from *All About Manatees* includes illustrations with labels offering plenty of information. A reader will need to work to figure out how the main text aligns with the content presented in these labels.

Text features are also more text-laden at this level. A reader needs to read, study, and think about the text features to determine meaning. At times, features offer additional facts, which need to be integrated with the main text.

Look for students to:

○ Learn information from a text feature and explain how it connects to information in the main text.

Examples of Books at Level Q

A Medieval Feast by Aliki

The Amazing Social Lives of African Elephants by Samantha S. Bell

Think Like a Scientist by Melissa Blackwell Burke

Hand to Paw: Protecting Animals by Jessica Cohn

Lost City: The Discovery of Machu Picchu by Ted Lewin

Extreme Weather by Torrey Maloof

Amazing Animal Journeys by Laura Marsh

America's Natural Landmarks by Jennifer Overend Prior

Meteors by Melissa Stewart

The Explore the Biomes series by various authors

The Reading Expeditions series by various authors

Main Idea

Books at Level R often cover vast amounts of information and include contrasting perspectives on topics and subtopics. Therefore, most books contain multiple complex main ideas. In a sense, a reader is required to see each chapter as a unique body of information and ideas. As well as summarizing these ideas, the reader has to track how they connect with ideas in other chapters and how these all contribute to a larger, overarching idea.

At this level, books are around fifty to sixty pages long, typically divided into chapters. Subsections within chapters are common. Chapters and sections may have titles or section headings, which can offer support to the reader.

Introductions and conclusions, when included, may or may not indicate a main idea of the whole book. For example, the author may write an introduction that first provides background information and context and then swerves into a different main idea. *You Wouldn't Want to Be an Egyptian Mummy* by David Stewart has this type of structure. In the introduction, the author writes about ancient Egypt and its history and explains why mummies were important to the ancient Egyptians. However, a reader goes on to discover that the main idea of the book is really a graphic depiction of the process of mummification, with an emphasis on its more disgusting aspects.

Look for students to:

- Synthesize most details from pictures and words in a section of the text to state a main idea, using original language.

- Take the whole book into account to state a main idea and two or three related subideas that capture the complexity the author brings to the topic (**shift from Level Q**).

Key Details

Text is dense, with around ten to fifteen sentences or details per page. Texts are often organized in chapters and in sections within the chapters. A chapter of related details may span as many as five to seven pages. This is true of titles in the True Book series, such as *The Digestive System* by Christine Taylor-Butler. Other books, such as *You Wouldn't Want to Be an Egyptian Mummy*, have busy pages that are packed with print, but each section is only a couple of pages long. On one spread in this book, for example, a few paragraphs of main text are surrounded by many smaller paragraphs. Each of these extra pieces could be considered subsections within the larger section, "What a Mummy Needs."

Look for students to:

- Support a main idea with several key details from different pages or sections, using words, pictures, and text features.

- Identify multiple similarities *and* differences, and categorize comparisons, using key details from the text.

Vocabulary

A reader of Level R nonfiction books needs to have some prior knowledge to navigate the wealth of challenging vocabulary and must be ready and resourceful to learn new words. Consider, for example, the words on one page in *The Digestive System*: *antibiotic*, *bacteria*, and *microbe* are defined in the glossary and appear boldfaced in the text. Others, such as *digestion*, need to be understood from context.

Look for students to:

- Explain or describe the meaning of a word or phrase using larger context, including text features, and demonstrate deep understanding of the word or phrase (**shift from Level Q**).

Text Features

The pages of books at Level R can feel quite busy. It's probably fair to assume that authors and publishers expect young readers at this level to tackle texts that resemble informational texts in the adult world. As well as the main text, the books features sidebars, tables, maps, and procedure pages. Photos and illustrations are often captioned, sometimes with information additional to that in a page's main text. A reader needs to be able to navigate different parts of the text, synthesize the information, and make sense of it all. Extra pages also offer text features beyond the main text (e.g., tables of contents, glossaries, and indexes).

Text features often add information (e.g., the "Shocker" facts in *Caught with a Catch* by Laura Layton Strom, or the "Handy Hint" boxes in *You Wouldn't Want to Be an Egyptian Mummy*). These types of features are often text-laden, requiring the reader to read and comprehend them almost as if they were their own section.

Look for students to:

- Learn information from a text feature and explain how it connects to information in the main text.

Examples of Books at Level R

The Great Kapok Tree by Lynne Cherry

Everything Dog by Marty Crisp

Forest Mammals by Bobbie Kalman

Glorious Days, Dreadful Days: The Battle of Bunker Hill by Philippa Kirby

Horses by Seymour Simon

You Wouldn't Want to Be an Egyptian Mummy! Disgusting Things You'd Rather Not Know by David Stewart

The Digestive System by Christine Taylor-Butler

The Detecting Disasters series by various authors

The One World, Many Countries series by various authors

Main Idea

As at Level R, at Level S readers routinely encounter complex ideas. Authors tend to cover a broad topic in great depth and detail, often from multiple angles or perspectives.

Some books, like *Ancient Greece* by Sandra Newman, are organized into chapters, with sections within those chapters. This structure supports a reader's ability to determine a main idea, yet the high page count of these books challenges readers to make sense of a lot of information presented over a number of pages. Seymour Simon's *Lightning* has no headings or chapters, so readers need to be on the lookout for topic sentences that alert them to shifting subtopics.

At Level S, introductions and conclusions become more important, in the sense that a reader can sometimes rely on them to telegraph or summarize a book's main ideas.

Look for students to:

- Synthesize most details from pictures and words in a section of the text to state a main idea, using original language.

- Take the whole book into account to state a main idea and two or three related subideas that capture the complexity the author brings to the topic

Key Details

From Level S onward, the content tends to be tough—laden with more abstract concepts, e.g., government, or technical subject matter such as biology or human anatomy. So it stands to reason that the density of key details will be greater. You can count on sentences being more complex and sections longer than they are at earlier levels.

Text features often give additional key details instead of merely supporting the information in the main text. The reader has to read and comprehend text-heavy features such as sidebars and boxes almost as separate sections and then synthesize the information with the main text on a page.

Look for students to:

- Support a main idea with several key details from many pages, sections, or chapters, and connect details and the main idea (**shift from Level R**).

- Identify multiple similarities *and* differences, and categorize comparisons, using key details from the text.

Vocabulary

Only the most challenging vocabulary is supported by context, a glossary, or a text feature. Without prior knowledge, a reader must get meaning from outside sources. Some words will appear in photo captions or highlighted text; almost all rely on context for explanation. Bold-faced words are often defined in a glossary; readers must seek out definitions to understand the text.

Look for students to:

o Explain or describe the meaning of a word or phrase using larger context, including text features, and demonstrate deep understanding of the word or phrase.

Text Features

Expect features to be text-heavy. For example, in *Ancient Greece*, a "Guide to Gods and Goddesses" includes pronunciation keys for the names of twelve gods and goddesses and facts about them. Even the photographs have captions that contain challenging vocabulary words.

At lower levels, the photographs and illustrations often reinforce key points. As mentioned in the Key Details section, at this level many text features offer information beyond what's in the main text. Historical photographs, timelines, and maps, for example, are all common.

Look for students to:

o Learn information from a text feature and explain how it connects to information in the main text.

Examples of Books at Level S

Building the Great Wall of China by Terry Collins

Extreme Animals: The Toughest Creatures on Earth by Nicola Davies

Coming of Age Around the World by Anita Ganeri

Mummies, Pyramids, and Pharaohs: A Book about Ancient Egypt by Gail Gibbons

Lewis & Clark: Explorers of the American West by Steven Kroll

Ancient Greece by Sandra Newman

Puffins by Susan E. Quinlan

Refugees and Migrants by Ceri Roberts

Lightning by Seymour Simon

Girls Think of Everything: Stories of Ingenious Inventions by Women by Catherine Thimmesh

Main Idea

At Level T, to fully grasp the author's intent and purpose, a reader needs to recognize the complexity of main ideas, duality of arguments, and opposing viewpoints these texts contain. Because books are likely to not only cover a topic but also give perspectives on it, readers need to be primed to grapple with several main ideas.

At Level T, with more varied content and ideas at play, reading and studying text features become increasingly important as readers work to understand how all the information fits together.

Look for students to:

- Synthesize all details from pictures and words in a section of the text to state a complex main idea, using original language (shift from Level S).

- Take the whole book into account to state a main idea and two or three related subideas that capture the complexity the author brings to the topic.

Key Details

Books at Level T have dense text, with up to fifteen details per page. Several details may be included within a sentence, as syntax becomes more complex. A chapter or section of related details may span several pages.

Within- and across-sentence complexity is greater at Level T than at previous levels. Sections may include subsections with different structures (narrative, expository, cause and effect, and so on). These alternating structures require a reader to constantly question the relationship among different pieces of information being presented. Readers may encounter stories, firsthand accounts, expository information in a Q&A format, and timelines.

Look for students to:

- Support a main idea with several key details from many pages, sections, or chapters, and connect details and the main idea.

- Identify multiple similarities *and* differences, and categorize comparisons, using key details from the text.

Vocabulary

Readers are expected to carry their understanding of vocabulary from one section or page to the next. For example, on one spread of *Wild Wetlands* by Janine Scott, the word *aquatic* is used early on in one context but then later in a different context and without support to figure out its meaning—the definition must be retained and applied to a new situation.

Earthquakes by Trudy Strain Trueit contains a glossary with definitions of key terms (i.e., *earthquake*, *tremor*, and *magnitude*), but many other terms and concepts that a reader needs to already know or figure out from context are not defined (i.e., *vibrations*, *energy is released*, *jolt hit*, *foundations*, *toppling like dominoes*).

Look for students to:

○ Explain or describe the meaning of a word or phrase using larger context, including text features, and demonstrate deep understanding of the word or phrase.

Text Features

Text features often serve as subsections of the main text. In *Earthquakes*, drawings of S waves and P waves offer an image of something mentioned in the text. However, the caption gives additional information that isn't in the text. A reader needs to synthesize that information with text on the next page: "They shake the ground both up and down and also back and forth. S waves may jostle trees, crack buildings, and keep cars from driving in straight lines" (21).

In addition, the labels on these drawings include new vocabulary: *compressions*, *dilations*, *undisturbed*, *medium*, *amplitude*, and *wavelength*. These terms are not explained in the text, a glossary, or elsewhere. Extra information without explanation makes an otherwise friendly graphic quite complex.

Look for students to:

○ Learn information from a text feature and explain how it connects to information in the main text.

Examples of Books at Level T

Capoeira: Game! Dance! Martial Art! by George Ancona

Life in the Oceans: Animals, People, Plants by Lucy Baker

Dancing Around the World by Nicolas Brasch

Animal Dazzlers: The Role of Brilliant Colors in Nature by Sneed B. Collard

Canada Celebrates Multiculturalism by Bobbie Kalman

Hurricanes: Earth's Mightiest Storms by Patricia Lauber

Animal Heroes: True Rescue Stories by Sandra Markle

To Space and Back by Sally Ride

Earthquakes by Trudy Strain Trueit

The Donner Party by Scott P. Werther

Main Idea

At Level U, as at Level T, a reader will need to assimilate several main ideas to fully grasp the author's intent and purpose. Readers have to learn to follow the author's train of thought to determine what they are ultimately trying to teach about the topic—but the journey is by no means direct. Authors writing books at this level assume their audience can handle the true complexity of science, social studies, and history topics and so routinely present diverging viewpoints on subtopics and often multiple main ideas to consider.

As at Level T, the reader needs to carefully read the *whole* page—sidebars, captions, and other text features give information that is essential to understanding a main idea. For example, one spread of Yvonne Morrison's *Earth Matters* includes sidebars, several paragraphs of expository text, a narrative to help to draw the reader into the content, photographs, callout boxes, and additional features that give facts and tips. A reader needs to take in all of this information to really understand the most important main ideas of these pages. At times, even the main ideas of the smaller sections are complex.

Look for students to:

O Synthesize all details from pictures and words in a section of the text to state a complex main idea, using original language.

O Take the whole book into account to state a main idea and two or three related subideas that capture the complexity the author brings to the topic.

Key Details

Books at Level U continue to be dense in text, with up to fifteen details per page in small font. Several details are included within a sentence, as syntax becomes more complex. A chapter or section of related details may span several pages. Consider, for example, a spread from *The Natural World: Under the Ocean* by Paul Bennett that includes sections, sidebars, and even captions that are extremely dense and filled with information.

At this level, readers often have to maintain comprehension while shifting not only from section to section but also from structure to structure (narrative, expository, cause and effect, and so on). One chapter of *The Challenger Disaster* includes a narrative about Christa McAuliffe and how she became a part of the *Challenger* crew, as well as an expository section about the mission, and subsection with technical information about causes and problems related to the delayed launch of the spacecraft.

Look for students to:

O Support a main idea with several key details from many pages, sections, or chapters, and connect details and the main idea.

O Identify multiple similarities *and* differences, and categorize comparisons, using key details from the text.

Vocabulary

Level U books are likely to use the same level of vocabulary found in technical books. The vocabulary will not always be defined. The reader must either know the terminology or be willing to search outside the text for meaning.

Particularly challenging vocabulary may be defined in a glossary, but a reader will still need to work to deeply understand the term in context and to describe or explain it. In *The Truth About Great White Sharks* by Mary M. Cerullo, *ichthyologists* and *cartilaginous fish* are defined in context, but readers will need to synthesize and infer to deduce the meaning of words such as *ancestors* and *ancient*.

Look for students to:
- Explain or describe the meaning of a word or phrase using larger context, including text features, and demonstrate deep understanding of the word or phrase.

Text Features

Level U text features are text-heavy and often serve as sub-sections of the main text. In *The Challenger Disaster*, photo captions are often a full paragraph of information, a text-dense timeline spans two pages, and inset boxes of sidebar information are prevalent. Multiple features work together and readers need to read, study, and re-read to understand the relationship among all of the information.

Look for students to:
- Explain how a text feature enhances understanding of the main text and/or how multiple text features work together (**shift from Level T**).

Examples of Books at Level U

The Natural World: Under the Ocean by Paul Bennett

The Navajo by Donna Janell Bowman

The Truth About Great White Sharks by Mary M. Cerullo

The Olympics by Matt Christopher

Remember the Ladies: The First Women's Rights Convention by Norma Johnston

Interrupted Journey: Saving Endangered Sea Turtles by Kathryn Lasky

Volcano: The Eruption and Healing of Mount St. Helens by Patricia Lauber

The Challenger Disaster by Tim McNeese

Earth Matters by Yvonne Morrison

Factory Through the Ages by Philip Steele

Main Idea

At Level V, as at Levels T and U, to fully grasp the author's intent and purpose, a reader needs to consider and deeply analyze several main ideas, some of which reflect opposing viewpoints on a topic.

Sidebars, captions, and other text features are essential to understanding a main idea, as at past levels. For example, *Immigrant Kids* is filled with historical photographs, which must be studied alongside the text. Information from the photographs must be synthesized with the main text to determine the text's main ideas.

Look for students to:

- Synthesize all details from pictures and words in a section of the text to state a complex main idea, using original language.

- Take the whole book into account to state a main idea and two or three related subideas that capture the complexity the author brings to the topic.

Key Details

Readers of Level V books can expect many sentences per page and many pages per chapter or section. Nonfiction authors writing at this level elaborate extensively to teach about a topic, concept, or event in depth. For example, in *The Titanic* by Deborah Kent, the author provides much detail about how the accident happened, not only in the main text but also in the pictures and engineering diagrams. These details include a plethora of technical terms that a reader needs to know to comprehend the information.

Readers have to be ready to shift from text structure to text structure (narrative, expository, cause and effect, and so on) and to reckon with information coming from different perspectives. See, for example, how the point of view shifts—from that of the creators of the *Titanic*, Smith and Andrews, to Harland and Wolff, who built the ship, to Lawrence Beesley, a passenger, whose story is told in a short piece of narrative text.

Look for students to:

- Support a main idea with several key details from many pages, sections, or chapters, and connect details and the main idea, possibly. quoting the text (**shift from Level U**).

- Identify multiple similarities *and* differences, and categorize comparisons, using key details from the text.

Vocabulary

Authors of books at Level V are likely to use the kind of rich vocabulary that one might find in technical books. For example, in *The Titanic*, the words *compartments*, *starboard flank*, *bulkheads*, and *bow* are not defined. The reader needs to either know the vocabulary or be willing to search outside of the text to fully understand the information being presented. Other sophisticated words that are not content-specific add to the challenge of navigating the text from a vocabulary perspective. Kent uses the words *inevitably*, *inconceivable*, *catastrophe*, *unsinkable*, *doomed*, and *ceased*, all on one page of *The Titanic*.

Look for students to:

o Explain or describe the meaning of a word or phrase using larger context, including text features, and demonstrate deep understanding of the word or phrase.

Text Features

As at earlier levels, at Level V the text features and structures are often text-heavy and often serve as subsections. In a spread from *The Civil Rights Movement in America* by Elaine Landau, a reader encounters a section about the Mississippi Freedom Summer, a photograph with a lengthy caption, an FBI poster of Freedom Riders Goodman, Chaney, and Schwerner filled with text, and another multisentence caption.

Look for students to:

o Explain how a text feature enhances understanding of the main text and/or how multiple text features work together.

Examples of Books at Level V

Founding Mothers: Women Who Shaped America by Melissa Carosella

Immigrant Kids by Russell Freedman

Lincoln: A Photobiography by Russell Freedman

America Votes: How Our President Is Elected by Linda Granfield

101 Things You Wish You'd Invented . . . and Some You Wish No One Had by Richard Horne and Tracey Turner

Extreme Scientists: Exploring Nature's Mysteries from Perilous Places by Donna M. Jackson

The Titanic by Deborah Kent

Abolitionists: What We Need Is Action by Torrey Maloof

Everglades Forever: Restoring America's Great Wetlands by Trish Marx

Moon Landing by Richard Platt

level **W**

Main Idea

Texts at Level W read more like middle-school textbooks or adult trade nonfiction, with a marked difference in density of information and handling of complicated scientific or historical concepts. There is also a plethora of text features. As at previous levels, to fully grasp the author's intent and purpose, a reader will often need to assimilate several complex main ideas, some of which reflect opposing viewpoints on the topic.

A reader of Level W books should expect a busy layout and sections spanning several pages. Reading the main text alone will yield only a partial understanding of a section. *Guilty by a Hair! Real-Life DNA Matches* by Anna Prokos is divided into chapters, each with its own true case. Within a ten-page chapter, a reader will encounter several subsections as well as a variety of text features such as firsthand accounts, maps, sidebars, and more. Putting all of this information together to infer main ideas is challenging work.

Look for students to:

○ Synthesize all details from pictures and words in a section of the text to state a complex main idea, using original language.

○ Take the whole book into account to state a main idea and two or three related subideas that capture the complexity the author brings to the topic.

Key Details

The density of information at Level W is remarkable. The author will elaborate extensively to teach about a topic, concept, or event in depth.

Readers have to be ready to shift from text structure to text structure (narrative, expository, cause and effect, and so on) and reckon with information coming from different perspectives. With differing structures, the reader will need to utilize different strategies to gather the key information and be flexible when reading. For example, in *Guilty by a Hair!*, the author, Anna Prokos, shifts from narrative—describing a case in mystery-genre style—to a procedural structure as she outlines the steps involved in using DNA evidence. Sidebars with facts and bulleted lists offer elaboration in an expository fashion.

Look for students to:

○ Support a main idea with several key details from many pages, sections, or chapters, and connect details and the main idea, possibly quoting the text.

○ Identify multiple similarities *and* differences, and categorize comparisons, using key details from the text.

Vocabulary

As at Levels U and V, the authors of books at Level W are likely to use the kind of specialized vocabulary that a reader might encounter in technical books on the topic. At times these words are defined; at other times the author expects a reader either to know them or to seek a source outside the book for a definition. In *Sea Otter Rescue: The Aftermath of an Oil Spill* by Roland Smith, words and phrases such as *adjustments*, *environment*, *shelter*, *slimmer margin of survival*, *unique*, and *frigid* appear in just two paragraphs of the text on one page, and none of them is defined.

Look for students to:

○ Explain or describe the meaning of a word or phrase using larger context, including text features, and demonstrate deep understanding of the word or phrase.

Text Features

As at earlier levels, at Level W, the text features are often text-heavy and serve as subsections. When a book is formatted without many text features, a reader can expect a denser, fuller page of main text. The busy layout of pages from books such as *The Industrial Revolution* means that a reader needs to approach the page with a plan and work to synthesize all the parts. The lack of features in books such as *The Human Body* by Seymour Simon means that a reader needs to subdivide the information on his or her own.

Look for students to:

○ Explain how a text feature enhances understanding of the main text and/or how multiple text features work together.

Examples of Books at Level W

Freedom of Speech and Expression by Bryon Cahill

Planes, Rockets, and Other Flying Machines by Ian Graham

Astronomy: Out of This World! by Dan Green

The Industrial Revolution by Melissa McDaniel

Heart and Soul: The Story of America and African Americans by Kadir Nelson

Cuban Immigrants: In Their Shoes by Tyler Omoth

Guilty by a Hair! Real-Life DNA Matches by Anna Prokos

Sea Otter Rescue: The Aftermath of an Oil Spill by Roland Smith

Taste of Salt: A Story of Modern Haiti by Frances Temple

Extreme Wildlife by Mark Thiessen

Understanding Nonfiction Readers

A Goal-by-Goal Guide to Readers' Comprehension of Increasingly Complex Texts

The role of background knowledge or schema that the reader brings to the text impacts comprehension.

Developing an understanding of text characteristics offers you a crucial context for understanding what to expect of readers. For instance, if we know texts at a given level reliably have multiple main ideas, we know when a student offers a simple, single main idea that they may be missing key information from across the book. If we know students are likely to encounter several content-specific vocabulary words that are crucial to understanding the key information, we'll know to ask them about what words they're learning or listen for them to include specific language when they are telling us about the text.

Students may phrase the main idea(s) in different ways or may define or explain vocabulary using unique terms. For example, one

154

reader might read Nicola Davies' awesomely gross book *What's Eating You? Parasites—the Inside Story* and state this main idea: "Although parasites seem gross, humans are not alone in having parasites, and most aren't harmful after all." Another reader might read the same text and conclude this: "The author wants us to learn about how parasites live and grow in human and animal habitats and ways to prevent parasites from inhabiting us." Both readers are correct—they simply latched onto different, important key information to conclude a possible main idea.

Assessing readers' comprehension and supporting their understanding is less about looking for *the one right answer*—because there is rarely just one!—and more about using knowledge of text levels and being familiar with the *characteristics* that a reader's response should have.

What's Ahead?

You can use the four Progression of Skills tables (on pages 158–159, 164–165, 170–171, and 174–175, thumbnails to the right) as quick references to see how changes in text characteristics result in changed expectations for readers.

Following each table, you'll find examples that illustrate how students reading texts at a range of levels responded to their reading. Next to each student work sample is an annotation that describes what to notice about the response and how and why the response is an example of strong comprehension at the level in question. Each response comes from a book you may or may not know—either way, it doesn't matter, because the purpose of these samples is to understand *qualities* of student response. You can use these examples as illustrations of the "look-fors" you read about on pages 126–153. They will be helpful when studying your students' writing and/or speaking about their reading.

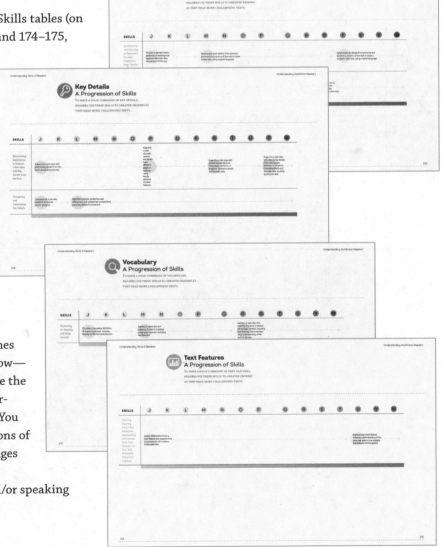

Goal

Skills

Caption explaining what to look for and how the response exemplifies strong comprehension at the level of text the student is reading

Overview of the skills

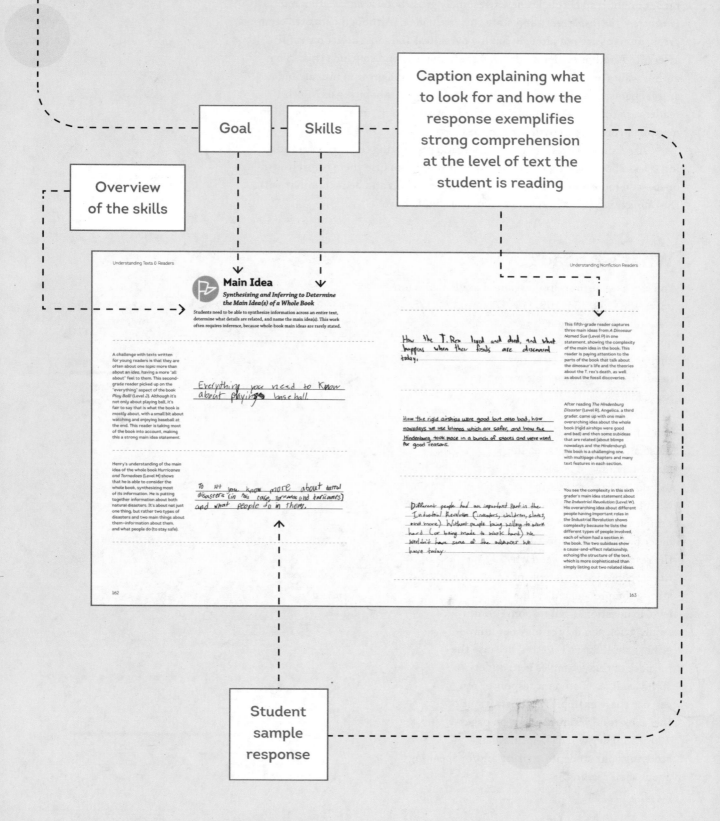

Main Idea

Synthesizing and Inferring to Determine the Main Idea(s) of a Whole Book

Students need to be able to synthesize information across an entire text, determine what details are related, and name the main idea(s). This work often requires inference, because whole-book main ideas are rarely stated.

A challenge with texts written for young readers is that they are often about one topic more than about an *idea*, having a more "all about" feel to them. This second-grade reader picked up on the "everything" aspect of the book *Play Ball!* (Level J). Although it's not only about playing ball, it's fair to say that is what the book is mostly about, with a small bit about watching and enjoying baseball at the end. This reader is taking most of the book into account, making this a strong main idea statement.

Henry's understanding of the main idea of the whole book *Hurricanes and Tornadoes* (Level M) shows that he is able to consider the whole book, synthesizing most of its information. He is putting together information about both natural disasters. It's about not just one thing, but rather two types of disasters and two main things about them—information about them, and what people do (to stay safe).

> Everything you need to know about playing baseball

> To let you know more about natural disasters (in this case, tornadoes and hurricanes) and what people do in them.

> How the T. Rex lived and died, and what happens when their fossils are discovered today.

> How the rigid airships were good but also bad, how nowadays we use blimps which are safer, and how the Hindenburg took place in a bunch of places and were used for good reasons.

> Different people had an important part in the Industrial Revolution (inventors, children, slaves, and more). Without people being willing to work hard (or being made to work hard) we wouldn't have some of the advances we have today.

This fifth-grade reader captures three main ideas from *A Dinosaur Named Sue* (Level P) in one statement, showing the complexity of the main idea in the book. This reader is paying attention to the parts of the book that talk about the dinosaur's life and the theories about the T. rex's death, as well as about the fossil discoveries.

After reading *The Hindenburg Disaster* (Level R), Angelica, a third grader, came up with one main overarching idea about the whole book (rigid airships were good and bad) and then some subideas that are related (about blimps nowadays and the *Hindenburg*). This book is a challenging one, with multipage chapters and many text features in each section.

You see the complexity in this sixth grader's main idea statement about *The Industrial Revolution* (Level W). His overarching idea about different people having important roles in the Industrial Revolution shows complexity because he lists the different types of people involved, each of whom had a section in the book. The two subideas show a cause-and-effect relationship, echoing the structure of the text, which is more sophisticated than simply listing out two related ideas.

Understanding Texts & Readers

Understanding Nonfiction Readers

162

163

Student sample response

A number of variables impact what students are able to comprehend from a text, and based on them, one individual child is likely to be able to read a range of levels and text types with independence.

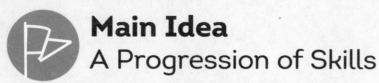

Main Idea
A Progression of Skills

To HAVE A SOLID COMMAND OF MAIN IDEA, READERS USE THESE SKILLS TO GREATER DEGREES AS THEY READ MORE CHALLENGING TEXTS.

SKILLS	J	K	L	M	N	O	P
Synthesizing and Inferring to Determine the Main Idea(s) of a Page, Section, or Chapter	Quotes or paraphrases a sentence or heading that captures the main idea of a section of the text.			Synthesizes most details from pictures and words in a section of the text to state a main idea, using original language.			
Synthesizing and Inferring to Determine the Main Idea(s) of a Whole Book	States a main idea of the whole book, taking most of it into consideration.			Takes the whole book into account to state a main idea.		Takes the whole book into account to state a main idea and capture the complexity the author brings to the topic.	

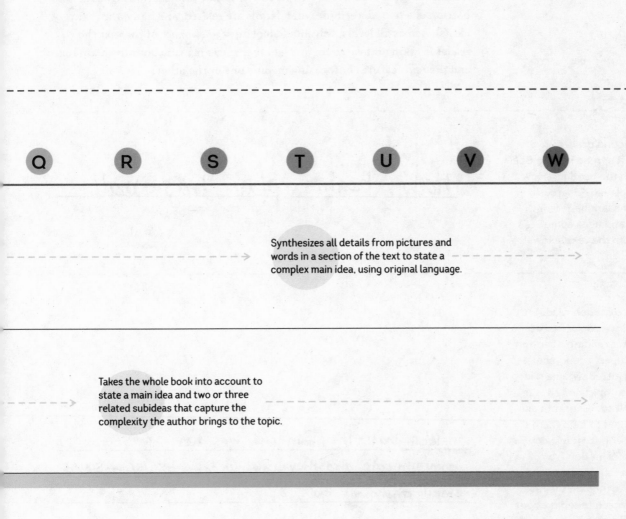

Q   R   S   T   U   V   W

Synthesizes all details from pictures and words in a section of the text to state a complex main idea, using original language.

Takes the whole book into account to state a main idea and two or three related subideas that capture the complexity the author brings to the topic.

Main Idea

Synthesizing and Inferring to Determine the Main Idea(s) of a Page, Section, or Chapter

It's important for readers to be able to synthesize information across a portion of a text, determine what details are related, and name the main idea(s). Across all levels, you should look to see *how much* of the text the reader is taking into account and whether they are using both the main text and the text features or focusing on only one or the other.

Marcus, a second grader, summarizes a spread in *Play Ball!!* (Level J) with the heading "How is the game played?" Marcus borrows some language from the heading and uses some language from the text below it.

How teams play baseball.

Meteja, a third grader, read *Ants, Bees, and Other Social Insects* (Level N). After reading a section titled "How Insects Talk," she stopped and jotted this main idea. In the book, a topic sentence in bold saya, "All social insects use smell and sound to help them communicate," but Meteja doesn't simply use information from this sentence-she adds in "and many more" to include the next subsection, which teaches about ways that bees communicate through a variety of motions. Including "and motions" rather than "and many more" would have made this response even stronger. As it stands, though, I do think she's understanding the main idea of the section.

Well that the main idea was how they communicate and they communicate by using sound smell and many more

---

One main idea is that Sparta and Athens had been fighting for awhile and Greece was not as powerfull after that then it once was.

As texts get more complex, the length of the chapter increases. In *Ancient Greece* (Level S), fifth-grader Kevin encounters chapters that are around seven pages long, with running text, and multiple text features. In Chapter 6, titled, "From Greece to Rome," he read about warrior training, the Peloponnesian War, Alexander the Great, and the Hellenistic empires after Alexander. This main idea statement uses completely original language and reveals the complexity of the idea being presented in the chapter. He includes both the fighting and the impact it had on power and rule.

What I can conclude about the tools for DNA testing is that they are very important because they can preserve, pick up, and find important clues to a case.

Reading *Guilty by a Hair!* (Level W), fifth-grader Sonja synthesizes the information in a section, including pictures and words, to show the multiple ways that DNA testing is important to cases (1. Preserving, 2. Picking up on clues, and 3. Finding clues). In texts at this level, look for readers' using words like *and* and *but* in their main idea statements as a way to show they are grappling with the complexity of the ideas and see the many aspects of it.

Main Idea

Synthesizing and Inferring to Determine the Main Idea(s) of a Whole Book

Students need to be able to synthesize information across an entire text, determine what details are related, and name the main idea(s). This work often requires inference, because whole-book main ideas are rarely stated.

A challenge with texts written for young readers is that they are often about one *topic* more than about an *idea*, having a more "all about" feel to them. This second-grade reader picked up on the "everything" aspect of the book *Play Ball!!*(Level J). Although it's not *only* about playing ball, it's fair to say that is what the book is *mostly* about, with a small bit about watching and enjoying baseball at the end. This reader is taking most of the book into account, making this a strong main idea statement.

> Everything you need to Know about playing baseball.

Henry's understanding of the main idea of the whole book *Hurricanes and Tornadoes* (Level M) shows that he is able to consider the whole book, synthesizing most of its information. He is putting together information about both natural disasters. It's about not just one thing, but rather two types of disasters and two main things about them-information about them, and what people do (to stay safe).

> To let you know more about hatrul disasters (in this case, tornados and hurricanes) and what people do in them.

How the T. Rex lived and died, and what happens when their fossils are discovered today.

This fifth-grade reader captures three main ideas from *A Dinosaur Named Sue* (Level P) in one statement, showing the complexity of the main idea in the book. This reader is paying attention to the parts of the book that talk about the dinosaur's life and the theories about the T. rex's death, as well as about the fossil discoveries.

How the rigid airships were good but also bad, how nowadays we use blimps which are safer, and how the Hindenburg took place in a bunch of places and were used for good reasons.

After reading *The Hindenburg Disaster* (Level R), Angelica, a third grader, came up with one main overarching idea about the whole book (rigid airships were good and bad) and then some subideas that are related (about blimps nowadays and the *Hindenburg).* This book is a challenging one, with multipage chapters and many text features in each section.

Different people had an important part in the Industrial Revolution (inventors, children, slaves, and more). Without people being willing to work hard (or being made to work hard) we wouldn't have some of the advances we have today.

You see the complexity in this sixth grader's main idea statement about *The Industrial Revolution* (Level W). His overarching idea about different people having important roles in the Industrial Revolution shows complexity because he lists the different types of people involved, each of whom had a section in the book. The two subideas show a cause-and-effect relationship, echoing the structure of the text, which is more sophisticated than simply listing out two related ideas.

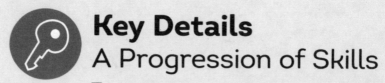

Key Details
A Progression of Skills

To HAVE A SOLID COMMAND OF KEY DETAILS,
READERS USE THESE SKILLS TO GREATER DEGREES AS
THEY READ MORE CHALLENGING TEXTS.

SKILLS	J	K	L	M	N	O	P

| Determining Importance to Support a Main Idea with Key Details from the Text | Supports a main idea with several key details from the text's words and pictures. | | | | | | Supports a main idea with several key details from different pages or sections, using words, pictures, and text features. |
| Comparing and Contrasting key Details | Compares *or* contrasts details from words and/or pictures. | | Identifies multiple similarities *and* differences, and categorizes comparisons, using key details from the text. | | | | |

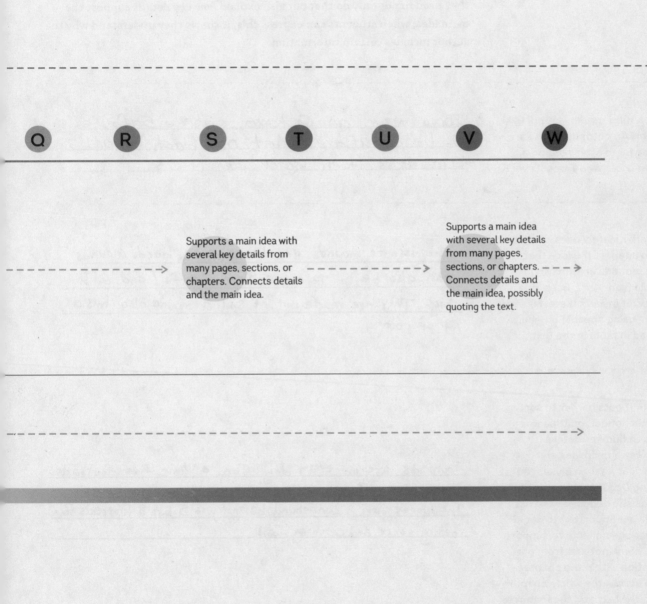

Q R S T U V W

Supports a main idea with several key details from many pages, sections, or chapters. Connects details and the main idea.

Supports a main idea with several key details from many pages, sections, or chapters. Connects details and the main idea, possibly quoting the text.

Key Details

Determining Importance to Support a Main Idea with Key Details from the Text

Readers must be able to distinguish details that are essential ("key") because they support a main idea from those that are more tangential. Over time, they need to not only do that but also explain *how* key details support the main idea; when students can express this, it shows they understand why the author includes certain information.

Andrew, a third grader, supports his main idea—"An octopus stays safe"—with three facts after reading a section in *Tricks and Traps* (Level K).

> Some ways an Octapus can be Safe is 1, be camaflage, 2. Jets out black ink, and 3. Can make itself bigger then it is.

Third-grader Mateja uses multiple details to support the idea that "termite mounds are amazing." her details from *Ants, Bees, and Other Social Insects* (Level N) show precision, using specific numbers mentioned in facts in the text.

> The termite mounds are large, rock hard. Mounds can also be up to more than 20 ft! and 6.1m high. They are made out of soil a mound also has a lot of room

---

At Level R, it gets harder to sort through the longer, multipage chapters to find key details that support a main idea and aren't ancillary. When Elyse read *Everything Dog* (Level R), one of the main ideas she deduced was that "footpads are important to dogs." The details she collects to support that idea come not just from one small section within the chapter but from across the whole chapter, including the text and the features.

> Footpads are on every dog. They all have five footpads. Dogs always walk on their toes not on the soles. The Norwegian Lundshund has not just 5 but 8 footpads for scaling rocks and catching food.

Many things came from the amazing culture of ancient Greece. We have Greece to thank for Arts, Sciences, and Athletics (Olympics). Even a kind of government we use came from Greece.

In this sixth grader's retelling of key facts from the book *Ancient Greece* (Level S), you can see that Cadence does more than just list the facts. Instead, she makes it clear *how* the facts connect to the overarching idea that the culture of Greece is amazing. Her phrases, "We have Greece to thank" and "Even . . . came from Greece" show that her facts are almost angled toward the idea, in support of it.

• During Birmingham marches, King was imprisoned. Still, he wrote a famous letter that got attention and which helped the movement.
• Huge turnout in 1963 for the March on Washington shows the cause is spreading
• July 2, 1964 – L.B. Johnson signed the Civil Rights Acts – a result of protestor actions.

This sixth grader lists several specific facts from across many parts of a section in the book *The Civil Rights Movement in America* (Level V). The main idea Yuki is supporting is "Although African Americans faced hardships and challenges, they still made invaluable contributions." The idea itself is complex, and the supporting information clearly connects back to it: "Still . . ." and " a result of protestor actions" show that he's linking the facts back to both the hardships and the contributions aspects of the main idea.

Key Details

Comparing and Contrasting Key Details

Understanding connections between key details is another important skill students need. To fully comprehend the text, they must be able to compare similarities among details and contrast differences.

When reading Level J texts, readers should be able to compare or contrast, not necessarily both. Of course, if they can do both, great! But doing one or the other is still a sign of strong comprehension because often the texts they are reading do not compare and contrast information on the same page. This second grader read *Play Ball!* and was able to find a key difference between what the "team at bat" does and the "team in the field" does.

> The team batting tries to make a point by running all four bases. The other team tris to stop them.

Franco, a third grader, was able to find multiple similarities and differences between two types of storms in *Hurricanes and Tornadoes* (Level M). In comparing and contrasting, he toggles back and forth between a fact for one and a fact for both. When they have something in common, he states it in the same sentence: "They both have lightning." At this level, students should start to learn how to categorize their comparisons—for example, talking about differences in how they are formed, similarities about the destruction they cause, or differences in where they can be found.

> They both have lightning. Hurricane is bigger. Tornado has stronger winds. Hurricane happens over ocean\sea. Tornado happens in farm areas. Both winds go in circles.

Bell and Edison both worked hard. Bell worked all night, every night. Edison - day and night. They both invented multiple things. Bell. telephone, iron lung; Edison incandescant lamp, movie camera

This sixth grader, Gemma, organizes her comparing and contrasting within categories as she reads *So You Want to Be an Inventor* (Level R). First, two inventors' work (both: hard; Bell: all night; Edison: day and night), then their inventions. She is likely organizing and comparing information as she reads.

Marches, sit-ins, and boycotts were all nonviolent and organized. All showed how African Americans could come together to protest. Sit ins -- lunch counters. Marches -- streets. Boycotts - refusing to buy goods or use a service.

It's not surprising a reader of texts at this very challenging level (V) would encounter more than two things to compare. *In The Civil Rights Movement in America,* this sixth grader found two similarities between three protest methods ("Marches, sit-ins, and boycotts were all nonviolent") and then explained a single key difference between each. This shows his understanding of the information and how information within a section relates to other information within that same section.

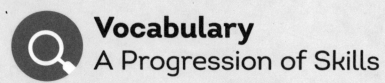

Vocabulary
A Progression of Skills

To HAVE A SOLID COMMAND OF VOCABULARY READERS USE THESE SKILLS TO GREATER DEGREES AS THEY READ MORE CHALLENGING TEXTS.

SKILLS	J	K	L	M	N	O	P

| Monitoring for Meaning and Using Context | Provides a complete definition of a word or phrase, drawing heavily on the text and pictures. | | | Explains or describes the meaning of a word or phrase using larger context, including text features. | | | |

Q R S T U V W

Explains or describes the meaning of a word or phrase using larger context, including text features. Demonstrates deep understanding of the word or phrase.

Vocabulary
Monitoring for Meaning and Using Context

As nonfiction becomes more challenging, so do the words it contains. Moreover, the frequency of challenging words and phrases increases. Initially, a reader uses immediate context to give an accurate definition of a word. As texts increase in complexity, readers will need to take information from multiple pages or even sections into account, using the text and text features. At lower levels, readers will be able to offer a complete definition, but as context expands and words are used in multiple places within a text, readers should be able to explain or describe the terms they are learning.

The word *run* is used in *Play Ball!* (Level J) in a way that is specific to baseball. This reader provided a complete definition with detail and used both the text and a picture on the page to help.

It's when you get to him plate before the other guy catches the ball. You score.

In *Hurricanes and Tornados* (Level M), fourth-grader Melissa does more than just pull words from the sentence in which the term *meteorologist* appears. Instead she's combining clues in the text ("weather scientists" and" look at photographs of the earth" and "measure wind speed" and "they warn people in the hurricane's path" as well as a photograph of a meteorologist in front of computer screens with weather data) and offers a brief explanation in her own words.

Meteorologist find information of Hurricanes and tornadoes and they warn the people who are close to it

---

To have anyone actually live there (make a home)
For example, it would be too cold for anyone to stay.

The word *habitable* in *Antarctica* by Mel Friedman (Level Q) is not a bolded term that has an easily referenced glossary definition. It appears midway through the book, after the reader learns about the extremely dry and cold conditions of the continent. The immediate context is, "If there really were a southern continent, it would be too far south to be habitable" in a section about British explorer Cook. Laura, a fourth grader, gives a clear definition and then provides an example from the text to further explain its meaning.

An airship is a gasfilled ship. It looks more like a balloon, though. In a compartment at the bottom of the ship people rode for their jeorney

In *The Hindenburg Disaster* (Level R), the term *rigid airship* is an important term to understand. Support for understanding it appears across many pages in both the text and the features. Olivia, a fourth grader, provides a detailed explanation and description, offering many details to show she understands ("looks more like a balloon" and "compartment at the bottom of the ship people rode" and "a gasfilled {gas-filled} ship").

Abolitionists are people (man or woman, black or white) Who disagreed with slavery and wanted slaves to be free. They helped them escape. 60,000 slaves escaped with help so it's important to know about them.

Sixth-grader Monique offers a very complete explanation of the term *abolitionist* during her reading of *If You Lived When There Was Slavery in America* (Level U). She provides multiple details from the text when she explains the term, and goes on to point out why it's important to understand this term in a book about slavery.

Text Features
A Progression of Skills

TO HAVE A SOLID COMMAND OF TEXT FEATURES, READERS USE THESE SKILLS TO GREATER DEGREES AS THEY READ MORE CHALLENGING TEXTS.

SKILLS	J	K	L	M	N	O	P
Deriving Meaning from a Text Feature by Synthesizing Information from That Feature, the Text, and, If Present, Other Text Features	Learns information from a text feature and explains how it connects to information in the main text.						

Q   R   S   T   U   V   W

Explains how a text feature enhances understanding of the main text and/or how multiple text features work together.

Text Features

Derives Meaning from a Text Feature by Synthesizing Information from That Feature, the Text, and, If Present, Other Text Features

Readers must be able to unpack information from text features and connect that information to information in the main text. It's not enough to name what the text feature is ("That's a map!"). Instead, readers should comprehend and derive meaning from the feature.

This second-grade reader looks closely at the feature (in this case, a photograph) in *Tricks and Traps* (Level K) to learn something that isn't explicitly said in the text: "An octopus stretches to look so big." The reader then combines that with another fact that is in the text: "An octopus can look like a rock."

> An octopus stretches to look so big and it can scare away the predators. An octopus can look like a rock.

When reading *Germs Make Me Sick* (Level O), fourth-grader Jewel demonstrates that she's learning information from the text feature and combines what she learns with the main text. In the illustrations, you see seven differently shaped bacteria and viruses. She is combining information such as "you cannot see" and "different types of germs" with the descriptions of how the germs look ("spider legs," "balls," "tadpoles").

> There are different types of germs, that you cannot see some look like metal straws, spider legs, bread, balls, tadpoles and spikey balls

---

If you wanted to know more you could go on
websites like www.the-kennel-club.org.uk or
read books like The Atlas of Dog Breeds of the World.
I could learn the differences in breeds and what
kind of dog I may want to have for a pet.

At the end of the book *Everything Dog* (Level R), fifth-grader Elyse stops to jot and think about a page that offers extra resources- books and websites- for learning more about the topic. She's considering what extra information she'd get from each of the suggested resources and how that information connects to what she's learned in the book.

Boys and girls were separated
in class but sometimes
came together for assemblies.
They learned reading and
writing but also life skills
like cooking (girls). Their
hands are stained in the
picture so maybe they had
other jobs, like working in
a factory.

Immigrant Kids (Level V) offers readers a collection of historical photographs, most taken by Jacob A. Riis, a New York City newspaper reporter, alongside descriptive paragraphs explaining the immigrant experience. Studying these photographs, and thinking about the images alongside the descriptive paragraphs, is central to understanding the book. Sixth-grader Aarush clearly studies details in the photograph (such as the stained hands) and combines it with other information he learne in the text (that many young) children had factory jobs). He also lists other information about boys and girls being separated, and the types of things children learned in school. The number of details he offers shows deep understanding of the text feature.

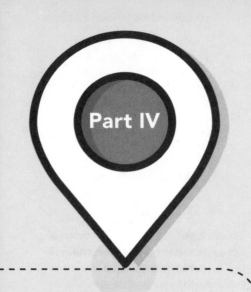

Part IV

Assessment and Instruction

BRINGING YOUR UNDERSTANDING OF TEXTS AND READERS TO THE CLASSROOM

A s so many literacy experts have declared, *levels are a teacher's tool* (Fountas and Pinnell 2017a; Peterson 2001; Mooney 2004; Calkins 2000; DeFord, Lyons, and Pinnell 1991; Fisher, Frey, and Lapp 2012; Szymusiak, Sibberson, and Koch 2008). In Part I, we explored the foundations of text leveling and comprehension. In Parts II and III, you learned about what to expect of books, level by level, and what to expect of readers, goal by goal. Now, in Part IV, you'll explore how to bring your knowledge of readers, texts, levels, and comprehension to make informed choices in the classroom by

- Learning about students' interests, language, culture, background knowledge, and more
- Assessing and evaluating comprehension
- Matching readers with just-right books

- Conducting goal-setting conferences to establish a goal for each student

- Using a variety of teaching structures and comprehension strategies to support students with their goals over time

In the reality of the classroom, these five items don't necessarily happen in order, and they don't usually happen in isolation, either. For example, you likely don't hold off on letting students borrow books until you've done formal assessments of all of them. When you are teaching, presumably, you have ears and eyes open and are assessing students as well, considering how they are responding to your instruction and what your next move will be. You'll be getting to know students as readers, reconsidering how you've organized your library, talking to kids about their reading goals, and teaching new strategies based on what you learn.

However, the linear nature of a book means I've got to put something first, so I've chosen getting to know students followed by assessing and evaluating comprehension because they are so foundational to everything we do in the classroom. That said, I could have just as easily started with classroom libraries and matching kids to books (that's how I had it organized yesterday), because I remember the August ritual of unpacking boxes and arranging books for the children I'd be meeting just a few weeks later, knowing that after I met and got to know them, we'd likely do some rearranging together. In truth, my students always visited my classroom library on Day 1 of school, before I knew very much about them. So, feel free to approach Part IV's five sections either in the order they appear or in an order that matches what you most want to learn first. Then, after reading all five, consider how they work together under the umbrella of assessment, instruction, and supporting meaningfully engaged reading experiences for your students.

> *"Understanding what you've read is the goal of reading."*
>
> —RICHARD ALLINGTON AND RACHAEL GABRIEL (2012)

Knowing Students

Interests, Language, Culture, Background Knowledge, and More

In Part I, I wrote about the importance of considering reader variables to understand comprehension. Here, I go a step further. There is no substitute for getting to know our students well. When we do that, students trust us, feel comfortable and cared for, and want to work hard.

It also helps us to be better reading teachers.

Factors such as motivation, background knowledge, culture, and English language proficiency should all be on our radar when considering how to help students find books they'll love, and how to evaluate students' comprehension and support them with appropriate goals and strategies. That means, in addition to more traditional types of reading assessments such as listening to students read aloud or asking them to respond to comprehension prompts, it's important to take time to learn about students in a more well-rounded way. What follows are some of my favorite ways for doing that.

There is no substitute for getting to know our students well. When we do that, students trust us, feel comfortable and cared for, and want to work hard.

Conferences

There is no substitute for the one-on-one conference! Conferences allow students to feel seen and heard and allow you to get to know them as individuals and support them with what they need most. Use conferences to listen to kids read aloud, discuss their book choices, ask them what's going well for them and what they need help with, celebrate their growth, find out what they want to work on next, and perhaps, most importantly, develop relationships.

Reading Histories

Ask students if there was a time when reading was the pits, and if there were times when reading was great. You might start by asking, "What comes to mind when you hear the word *reading*?" "What was your reading life like last year? This summer?" (Calkins and Tolan 2015).

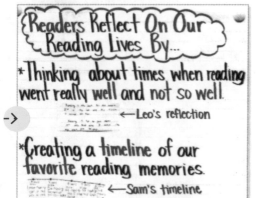

Reading Interviews

Reading interviews ask students to describe their beliefs about their own reading proficiencies, how the way they currently read is influenced by how they've been taught in the past, and what they've experienced in the past (Goodman, Watson, and Burke 2005). Teachers using the Burke Reading Interview (BRI) ask students a series of ten questions, including, "Who is a good reader you know? What makes that person a good reader?" "When you come to something you don't know, what do you try?" and "How would you help someone who is having trouble reading?"

Identity Webs

Talk to students about the various factors that make up a person's identity: race, culture, language, religion, ethnicity, gender, religion, and so on. Ask them to create an identity web to introduce themselves to you and to their peers in the classroom. (For more information, see Daniels and Ahmed's *Upstanders: How to Engage Middle School Hearts and Minds with Inquiry* [2014].)

Sara Ahmed's identity web from *Upstanders*

Heart Maps

Many of us know the value of student-created heart maps, as written about by Georgia Heard (2016). Students create a heart on a sheet of paper and then write words and phrases about the things that hold importance in their lives: family, pets, places they've visited, times of significance in their lives. Not only are these heart maps helpful for students to return to as a source for writing inspiration, but they also can help us as teachers to get to know our students and what matters most to them.

Home Visits

When my daughter Lola was two years old and about to enter Montessori preschool, we had our first home visit from a teacher. While Puja was with us, we told her about Lola: her likes, dislikes, and interests. Lola showed her new teacher around our apartment, and Puja learned about what life was like for her outside of school. Everyone felt that much closer on the first day of school, as if we were all already friends. (Read Ernst-Slavit and Mason's helpful advice about successful home visits: https://bit.ly/2Lg4d32.)

Letters from Parents

Ask parents to write you a letter introducing their child, in whatever language they feel most comfortable. If it's in a language with which you're not familiar, use a school-based translator or online translation software. You can be open-ended or suggest questions that might help, such as, What should I know about your child? How does your child feel about school? Does your child ever choose to read at home? Does anyone read to or with them?

Discussions About the Learning Environment

It's becoming more commonplace to offer flexible seating options for students in the classroom, honoring the reality that the conditions in which people work and learn best may vary. In college, I always chose to study in my dorm room, whereas others chose the library, and still others chose a noisy coffee shop. Consider your own preferences: When you read at home, is it always in a hard-backed chair, like those students sit in at their desks? Ask students about how they will be most successful and get their best learning done. They might think about seating options, noise level, music, and lighting.

Collaborative Team Teachers Ms. Wang and Ms. Lukjanczuk offer their students many seating options, from kneeling desks to high stools to camp chairs. At the start of the year, students rotate through all the options to decide which works best for them and then make a selection. If the teacher notices a student isn't getting their best work done, she suggests trying a new seating option. Removable nametags, cups with Velcro on the bottoms, and Tupperware bins to house notebooks and books allow kids to move to select new seats with minimal disruption.

Assessments of Language Proficiency

Knowing what students understand about English will help you teach them as readers. In addition to any language assessments your school may use that offer a language proficiency score, be sure to also do your own assessment to figure out what language goals students can be working on. My go-to resource for understanding stages of language acquisition is Cappellini's *Balancing Reading & Language Learning* (2004).

Kidwatching

Watch children during reading time and take notes on behaviors that may indicate they are engaged (smiling, focused, leaning in) or disengaged (book closed, visiting the bathroom, watching what's outside the window). Watch them at other times, too. Notice when they are most engaged. (Doing this can help you as a reading teacher, even if their most engaged times are during recess, art class, or science exploration. You could ask yourself, "What is it about activity X that engages the student? How can I re-create those conditions or qualities during reading time?" (Goodman and Owocki 2002).

Supporting Students' Needs

It's important to be aware of whether students' basic needs are being met, and consider ways to support them if they need it. Did your student eat breakfast? Do they wear glasses? (And, if so, did the glasses make it into the backpack today?) Do they need to sit closer in order to hear? Are their parents going through a divorce? Is a new baby in the house making it hard to get a good night's sleep? Does the student feel accepted by peers? Sometimes challenges with reading, comprehension, or concentration and engagement have their roots in something else.

Academic Language Tracker

Listen in, transcribe, and/or audio-record during times a student is with peers. Notice their language usage. Think about what the student knows and understands about structures of English, and consider how you'll support them in reading and writing so that academic language isn't a barrier (Goodman and Owocki 2002; Gibbons 2014).

Families in the Classroom

Invite family members to the classroom to share about their backgrounds, cultures, traditions, and celebrations. If they aren't able to come in, you can ask for photographs to be sent in, and students can share things about their own unique backgrounds (Souto-Manning and Martell 2016).

"I Wish My Teacher Knew . . ."

Ask students to respond to the prompt "I wish my teacher knew . . ." to express something about themselves that past teachers may not have known about them, but they want you to know so you can teach them better. - - - - -→

Anna

I wish my teacher knew that I am proud to be weird. And that I am obsessed with anime shows and video games. And that I am a blue belt in taekwondo. I wish my teacher knew that I DO pay attention when I'm doodling. And that I only like tuna sushi. I wish my teacher knew that at home, I like to jump on the furniture. And that cats are the main thing I think about all day.

Expressions of Care

When we're time crunched, teaching begins the moment the morning bell sounds, and we transition quickly from activity to activity every moment after that. Taking time to greet each student during morning lineup and asking them about their lives ("How'd the soccer game go yesterday?" "Did the baby keep you up last night, or did you sleep okay?" "I know you were nervous about visiting your grandparents in the nursing home. How was it?") will let students know they matter to you and will also help you learn more about their lives outside of school. Some students will open up, some won't, but knowing they are seen and that you care goes a long way.

Interest Surveys

Talk to students and/or ask them to complete interest surveys at the beginning of the year and then again at points across the year. Students change so much in the ten months they are in our classrooms—they develop new friendships, pick up new hobbies, and read new and more challenging texts as the year goes by. I have found, therefore, that every three or four months, if I asked, I was able to learn new information about what authors they loved, what series they were drawn to, and what activities they were now doing outside of school. (For a downloadable interest survey, see http://hein.pub/UTR [click on Companion Resources].)

Reading Interest Survey

Name: Lola

Do you like to read? yes

How much time do you spend reading? 30 min /day

What are some of the books you have read lately? nonfiction about animals, picture books

Do you have a library card? How often do you use it? yes. I don't usually borrow books

Do you ever get books from the school library? yes. 2 every friday

About how many books do you own? too many to count!

What are some books you would like to own? joke books, anything with a good story

Put a check mark next to the kinds of reading you like best and topics you might like to read about:

___ history ___ travel ___ plays ___ sports
✓ adventure ___ romance ___ poetry ✓ science fiction
___ biography ___ war stories ___ car stories ___ supernatural stories
___ humor ___ mysteries ✓ folktales ✓ how-to-do-it books
___ art ___ westerns ✓ novels ✓ astrology
___ detective stories

Reading Interest Survey

Do you like to read the newspaper? no.

If yes, place a check mark next to the part of the newspaper listed you like to read:
___ headlines ___ editorials ___ sports
___ advertisements ___ columnists ___ entertainment
___ comic strips ___ political stories ___ current events
___ others (please list)

What are your favorite television programs? cartoons and some stuff on Disney

How much time do you spend watching television? only a few shows a week

What is your favorite magazine? Ranger Rick!

Do you have a hobby? If so, what is it? I like ballet. I also like arts+ crafts and science.

What are the two best movies you have ever seen? Toy Story, Frozen.

Who are your favorite entertainers and/or movie stars? When you were little, did you enjoy having someone read aloud to you? yes. I love being read to. I like anybody from Disney movies

List topics, subjects, et cetera that you might like to read about: animals, space, folktales

What does the word "reading" mean to you? fun!

Say anything else that you would like to say about reading: I like to read.

Involvement Outside the Classroom

This may not be possible for all of us, but if you can coach the basketball team, lead the mock-trial club, or volunteer in the afterschool program, you'll find that knowing students outside of the classroom helps you get a more well-rounded sense of them and also helps you learn about their interests.

Assessing and Evaluating Comprehension

After you have read and studied the information in Parts II and III about text levels and the readers' responses that reflect strong comprehension, you'll understand a theoretical model of comprehension and reading development that you can apply to your teaching. Assessing and evaluating students' comprehension will help you to

- Match students with just-right books (page 201)
- Match students with appropriate goals (page 219)
- Match students with appropriate strategies (page 225)
- Use teaching structures based on those goals (page 233)

The information you glean from these assessments will help launch you into purposeful instruction and your students into purposeful work around their goals for reading.

Creating a Whole-Book Assessment

Remember Vanessa from the first pages of this book and the story of how learning about her whole-book comprehension made a huge difference in our ability to match her with texts and with appropriate goals? When children's everyday reading lives consist of reading texts that are longer than what they'd read in a five- to ten-minute sitting, or around the time they are reading texts at Level J and above, it's helpful to transition from relying solely on short-passage assessments (i.e., running records and/or short texts with multiple choice) to including an assessment that asks students to engage with a whole book and demonstrate their understanding. You may decide to create your own whole-book assessments with books that you know and love and that you believe your children will respond well to.

When creating a whole-book assessment, the first thing to consider is which books you'll select. Because we've already established that prior knowledge and motivation are important variables to consider when getting an accurate "read" on a student's ability to comprehend, I believe it's important that students have a choice in the text they read for an assessment, whenever possible. When I selected books for the whole-book assessments I created, I read widely from a selection of texts at each level and looked for books that are good examples of the characteristics of that level, as well as books that would appeal to different types of readers. Sometimes that means one book is more action/adventure-oriented whereas another is slower and more character-driven. Other times I try to offer a choice between a realistic-fiction text and a fantasy-fiction text. For nonfiction, I try to find books about diverse topics: perhaps one geared more toward life science and another more toward history. As you read through your library, consider the different interests of the students in your class, and select two or more texts to represent each level that may appeal to different readers.

Next, you'll want to consider the possible comprehension goals you'll be assessing and the sorts of questions that you can ask to assess for comprehension skills connected to each goal. The tables on pages 190–193 contain some samples of questions and prompts that I find work well in a variety of situations. You may want to adapt the questions slightly to fit the book you're using (for example, instead of "What are some problems in the story?" you may want to ask "What are some problems that Amber is dealing with now?"). Strive to phrase questions in an open-ended way, inviting a response rather than a one-word answer. With open-ended questions, you'll also avoid overly scaffolding the student by inadvertently delivering key content information via your questions.

Finally, I read each book carefully and placed questions and prompts inside the book so that when students read the texts independently, they could briefly pause to respond in writing before resuming reading. I find that eight to twelve prompts or questions in each book gives me enough information to draw conclusions about readers, without bogging them down with too many interruptions or tasks while they read independently.

I try to create more than one opportunity for students to demonstrate their ability to answer questions from each goal. For example, I may ask a retell question after the first chapter, a problem-solution question after the third chapter, and a visualizing setting question in the fourth chapter. All three questions prompt students to demonstrate skills that are part of the Plot and Setting goal.

I embed the questions throughout the book so that a reader doesn't have to stop too frequently or for too long in any one chapter. To elicit a strong response, I try to place prompts in places where I know the reader will need to think about the whole text. I find places that lend themselves to the type of question I want to ask; for example, I might place a question about a character after there's been a lot of narrative description and/or the character has acted in a surprising way and I want to see if the student picks up on it. I might place a vocabulary question after a word has been used multiple times and there is sufficient context. Theme questions tend to go near or at the end, but a symbolism question might be within a scene where the symbol is particularly important. Where I place the prompts matters, but there is definitely more than one place I can embed a prompt to yield the specific information the prompt is meant to yield.

As you find places to prompt readers to demonstrate their thinking, trust your gut (and your professional expertise!), and search for the places where you, as a reader of the book, are doing the thinking that you'll ask the children to do.

Keep in mind that the prompts you use for your more formal assessments can also be used every day when you're assessing students informally, during conferences, or in small-group instruction. You could also use these prompts to invite conversation during whole-class read-aloud. In short, you'll want to keep these prompts handy and use them repeatedly in a variety of instructional and assessment contexts.

Tips for Creating a Whole-Book Assessment

- Choose books that exemplify characteristics of each level and will appeal to different readers. Try to offer two choices per level.

- Create eight to twelve prompts per book.

- Distribute prompts throughout the book.

- Come up with several prompts to assess skills connected to each goal.

- Keep prompts open-ended.

Sample Prompts to Assess Comprehension of Fiction

GOAL: PLOT AND SETTING

Skills	Prompts
Retelling Important Events	• Retell what happens in this chapter. • Retell the three or four most important events from the *whole* story so far. • Tell all the ways [character] has [action] so far in the story.
Synthesizing Cause and Effect	• Why does [event] happen? • What are the events that lead up to [event]? • Explain why [event] happens.
Identifying Problems	• What are some problems that [character] is having? • What's the problem in this story? • What problem(s) does [event or character] cause?
Visualizing Setting	• Describe the setting of this scene. Give details. • Describe the setting (time and place). • What do you picture based on the description on pages ____ – ____?

GOAL: CHARACTER

Skills	Prompts
Inferring About, Interpreting, and Analyzing Main Character(s)	• What kind of person is [character]? • What do [character] and [character] have in common? • What are some differences?
Synthesizing Character Change	• How is [character] acting differently than before? • How has [character] changed? • Explain the change that occurs in [character].
Inferring About, Interpreting, and Analyzing Secondary Character(s)	• What kind of person is [character]? • Describe the relationship between [character] and [character]. • How is [secondary character] important to [main character]?

GOAL: VOCABULARY AND FIGURATIVE LANGUAGE

Skills	Prompts
Monitoring for Meaning and Using Context	• What does [word/phrase] mean in this part/scene? • What does [character] mean when she says [word/phrase]? • Define the [word/phrase] using information from this chapter. • Explain what [word/phrase] means here.

GOAL: THEMES AND IDEAS

Skills	Prompts
Interpreting a Story by Naming Life Lesson(s) or Theme(s)	• What lesson does [character] learn by the end of the story? • What message or lesson did you get from reading this book? • What is something that [character] has learned so far in this story? • What lessons can we learn from [character]'s story?
Identifying and Interpreting Social Issues in a Story	• What have you learned about [issue] from reading this book? • What are you learning about the issue of [issue] here? • What have you learned from this story about what it means to [issue]?
Identifying and Interpreting Symbols in a Story	• What does [symbol] represent? • What do the [symbols] teach [character(s)] about life?

Sample Prompts to Assess Comprehension of Nonfiction

GOAL: MAIN IDEA

Skills	Prompts
Synthesizing and Inferring to Determine the Main Idea(s) of a Page, Section, or Chapter	• Look back across this chapter/section/page. What is it mostly about? • What is the most important idea the author wants you to learn from this section? • What is one main idea from this section?
Synthesizing and Inferring to Determine the Main Idea(s) of a Whole Book	• What is the most important idea you learned from reading this whole book? • What are two or three main ideas the author wants you to learn from reading this whole book?

GOAL: KEY DETAILS

Skills	Prompts
Determining Importance to Support a Main Idea with Key Details from the Text	• Which details support the idea that [main idea]? • The author claims [main idea]. Which details from this section support that idea?
Comparing and Contrasting Key Details	• What is similar about [topic] and [topic]? • What is different about [topic] and [topic]? • Compare and contrast [topic] and [topic].

GOAL: VOCABULARY

Skills	Prompts
Monitoring for Meaning and Using Context	• Using text and pictures, what does [word] mean? • Explain what [word] is and how it adds to what you're learning about [topic]. • Define [word]. • Describe [word] using information from pages ____–____.

GOAL: TEXT FEATURES

Skills	Prompts
Deriving Meaning from a Text Feature by Synthesizing Information from That Feature, the Text, and, If Present, Other Text Features	• How would you use [feature] and [feature] to help you learn more about [topic]? • What does the [feature] titled "____" help you to learn? • Study the [feature]. What information can you learn from it? • Why is the [feature] important when thinking about the section titled "____"? • How does the information from [feature] add to what you're learning about ____?

Procedures for Administering a Whole-Book Assessment

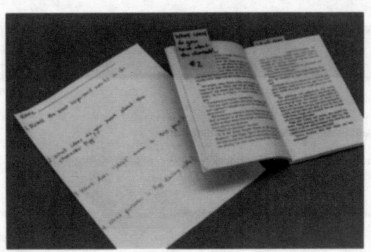

After placing prompts inside selected books, I offer students a choice from texts that I think they will be able to read with accuracy, fluency, and comprehension. I've found that, in general, students demonstrate comprehension of whole texts at slightly lower levels than the level at which they demonstrate proficient comprehension on shorter text assessments. Therefore, if you currently use a short-passage assessment (running records, computer-based multiple-choice assessments, etc.), you may offer text choices one or two levels below that level for this assessment.

After a student chooses a book, I ask them to read it independently. When they arrive at a question, I ask them to stop, think about the book so far, and answer the question on a separate sheet of paper. You can also create response forms that have the questions on them, if you think students would benefit from that extra support. (See page 196 for some possible modifications you can consider for kids who need them.)

Create your own response form, and note pages in the book where students should stop and respond. You may put the prompts on sticky notes or labels inside the book or simply write a prompt number and have the prompt on the form. Allow students time to read and respond to prompts independently. Evaluate responses after they've completed the reading.

Determining Rate and Stamina

Asking students to log their reading each time they sit to work on their assessment—start and end page and number of minutes read—can provide information about reading rate, a helpful piece of the comprehension puzzle. Students who read very slowly may have difficulty comprehending. They could be slowing down to monitor, rereading often, or getting distracted and having a difficult time engaging with the text. This isn't always the case, of course—readers read at different rates naturally—but it is one thing to be aware of. A slow reading rate combined with shaky responses to the prompts could indicate a text that is overly challenging.

Visit http://hein.pub/UTR to download a copy of this reading log.

Reading Log

Name:

Book:

Date	Start Page	End Page	Start Time	End Time

Students who average much below three-quarters of a page per minute are the ones to flag for further study and observation. A reading log shouldn't be used every day (it may start to feel like drudgery for the student and for you), but for a short period of time it can serve as a helpful assessment, self-reflection, and goal-setting tool.

Assessing Self-Monitoring

In addition to responding to prompts and logging reading, I find it helpful to ask students to reflect on their experience reading the text when they are done with the book. You could ask them to respond to a few questions in writing or verbally, which would help you assess their ability to monitor their own comprehension and engagement with the text (see sample page at right).

That's it. Unlike other assessments that require students to read aloud to the teacher, or where the teacher sits side by side with the student, prompting for more information, this assessment is designed to give you a sense for what the student can do independently. The prompts in the books are already a sort of scaffold, so I try to refrain from any other involvement if I can help it, because I'm trying to learn what a student can do *independently* to best match them to texts and goals. Asking students to complete the assessment independently also frees you up to work with other students who are not currently reading an assessment book. The reading of the assessment book will take as long as it takes—remember, it's a whole book so it could take anywhere from a single reading period to a week—so it's important that you are free to continue teaching the other students.

Name: _____

What did you think of the book?
_____
_____
_____

Do you think the book was just right, easy, or hard?
_____
_____
_____

Would you choose others like it?
_____
_____
_____

Do you think you understood it? How do you know?
_____
_____
_____
_____

Visit http://hein.pub/UTR to download a copy of this reflection form.

Administering a Whole-Book Assessment

1. Offer each student a choice of books to read from the selection with preplanted prompts.

2. Give the student the book and corresponding response form.

3. Allow the child to read the text and respond to prompts independently.*

*See sidebar on page 196 for possible modifications for students who may need them.

Assessment Modifications

The whole-book assessment, as it's described, requires little involvement from the teacher while the student takes it, thus safeguarding instructional time for you to work with other students.

For some students, you may know that the way they respond in writing to their reading does not give you the same information as when they respond orally. For students who need it, you may choose to modify how they are recording their thinking during the assessment to account for that. If a student has a paraprofessional who works alongside them each day, the assistant could scribe the student's responses as they speak them, as long as the paraprofessional doesn't help with content. You may also consider having the student dictate responses using speech-to-text software.

With any modifications you make to support the student, keep in mind that the aim is to see what kids do independently and to capture their thinking as they read. For example, because the prompts are placed within the book, it'll be important for the student to respond to them *as they read,* not all at the end.

Evaluating Student Responses

After the student finishes reading the book, answering questions, and responding to prompts independently, it's time for you to review and evaluate their responses to determine if the text is a good fit (and, therefore, the student may be comfortable with other books with similar complexity) and what goal(s) to focus on to support deeper, more complete comprehension.

Using your knowledge of text complexity and what to expect of responses to indicate comprehension at each level (see Parts II and III), you'll evaluate each of the eight to twelve individual responses, one at a time. Each time you read a student response, you can ask yourself, "Does it seem like the student's response in this book matches up to the look-fors of this type of prompt at this level?"

The sample student responses and the student look-fors show what "exceptional" or deep comprehension looks and sounds like. Students whose responses match the look-fors and samples can be marked as "E," or "Exceptional." Those that are close—accurate but not quite as complete—might be marked as "proficient," or "P." Those that are shaky but not incorrect might be marked "approaching," or "A." And if the answer is just wrong, you could mark it as "I," or "Incorrect."

For example, a fifth grader read Roald Dahl's *Charlie and the Chocolate Factory* (Level R) and wrote about a secondary character, Willy Wonka:

He's old and a bit mean.

To evaluate this response, I'd look at the character look-fors at that level. They say, "Identifies and comments on many feelings and/or traits of a secondary character." Looking at that response, I think that the reader does name multiple traits—"Old" and "mean"—but not an effect he has on the main character. I could also look at samples of student work if I'm not sure. There, I find a sample student response from Jessica, reading a Level O text, and see that her response is more elaborate and precise and includes an impact of the secondary character on the main character. If readers are expected to do that at Level O, they certainly should be doing that work here at Level R, too. So I'd mark this response as "Proficient" (accurate but not quite complete) but not "Exceptional."

Here's another example, this time using nonfiction. A fifth grader read a Level S book about ancient Greece. When asked to explain the meaning of a key term, *worshipping*, the student responded:

Worshiping means to sacrifice to the gods to make them happy.

Is this response an indication of an "Exceptional," "Proficient," or "Approaching" level of understanding of vocabulary? According to the vocabulary look-fors at Level S, a student should be able to "use cumulative knowledge of the story to explain the meaning of a word or phrase." Does this student do that? I would classify this student's response as "Approaching" because the student gives a simple definition. I don't see that the student connected much of the information from across the book or showed that they deeply understood. This simple definition looks at just one aspect of the way the term is used in the book.

As you evaluate each response, you may want to keep a running list on a separate sheet of paper (see sample below), or mark E, P, A, or I next to each response.

It's helpful to know not only *how many* responses are considered "Exceptional" and how many "Incorrect," but more specifically to *which type of question* each of those evaluations corresponds. So, if you keep track on the response form, you may "code" each question with a type (i.e., Plot and Setting, Character, Vocabulary and Figurative Language, or Themes and Ideas), and if you keep track on a separate sheet of paper, you may list your evaluation of each question underneath headings.

Looking for Patterns to Determine a Goal

After you've taken time to evaluate each individual student response, the next step is to look for patterns. I like to look holistically at one type of question—say, all of the Character questions. In general, did the student's overall responses show understanding, or do I think the student is in need of support? If one or more of the responses is marked as "Approaching" or "Incorrect," I would support the student with a goal in that area. If a student answers no more than one-third of the total questions incorrectly, they can have up to two goals maximum. I would advise focusing on one (e.g., Plot and Setting) for a month or so and then moving to the second goal after the student seems to have developed more skills and is able to demonstrate comprehension in their first goal. You'll know that they are ready for a new goal based on your ongoing conversations with them as they read other self-selected books or books you've chosen for instruction.

Compile information about how a student's responses rated in each of the four possible goal categories.

Assessing Comprehension in Shorter Texts

Whole-book assessments are crucial to use if your students read whole books as a routine part of your reading instruction and practice. Whether students read books independently, in book clubs, or during guided reading, learning about what they can do independently during a whole-book assessment can help to inform all areas of instruction.

Some teachers may choose to use these same assessment procedures in shorter texts, and/or during the read-aloud. This could help give you a balanced view of how students respond to texts of different lengths, and how their listening comprehension compares to their independent reading comprehension. In addition, middle school teachers or upper elementary grade teachers who teach eighty or more students in rotating sections may also find that it takes too long to assess and evaluate student comprehension in whole books within a reasonable period of time for every student in their class. They may want to get a quicker sense of how students are comprehending texts, even if only on a short story or article.

You can follow the same procedures outlined in the previous sections to design your own comprehension assessments with shorter text that students can read independently and/or that you might read aloud to them. To prepare the assessment

- First, select a text or texts. Picture books, short stories, a first chapter of a longer book, articles, or nonfiction picture books can make for great assessment texts. Offer individual students a choice of text if they are reading it independently. If you're reading the text aloud to the students, you can poll your class to learn which book they'd most like to hear.

- Second, read the text and insert four to six questions and prompts assessing for all goal categories. You may choose to insert the questions along the way, or to ask all of the questions at the end of the text. Because the text is short, asking the questions at the end is more manageable than it would be in a chapter book or longer nonfiction book.

Evaluating Student Responses and Planning Goal-Directed Instruction

1. Check student responses against expectations for the level and sample student responses (from Parts II and III of this book).

2. Identify a goal or two.*

3. Teach one goal at a time, offering strategies. Plan to spend about four weeks on each goal.

*More than two possible goals? Repeat the assessment at a lower level. No goals? Repeat the assessment at a higher level.

After assessing comprehension, you'll want to evaluate their responses in a timely fashion and meet with students to reflect on their reading experience and to help them set goals, just as you would with whole-book assessments. Reread pages 196–197 for more information on evaluating student responses using the information from Parts II and III in this book.

Plot and Setting

WEEK 1	WEEK 2	WEEK 3	WEEK 4

Skill: Retelling Important Events

Skill: Visualizing Setting

Key Details

WEEK 1	WEEK 2	WEEK 3	WEEK 4	WEEK 5	WEEK 6

Skill: Determining Importance to Support a Main Idea with Key Details from the Text

Skill: Comparing and Contrasting Key Details

The length of time a student spends on a goal will vary, but it is likely to last several weeks. While working on the goal, they may learn strategies for one skill or several. See the two sample schedules—one covers four weeks, the other six.

Using What You've Learned About Readers

You've now learned about using your students' responses as a way to evaluate their comprehension—perhaps when they are reading long texts or short, perhaps when they are reading independently or when you're reading to them—and you've also learned about their interests and lives both inside and outside of reading. The information you gleaned from all of these assessments will help launch you into purposeful instruction and your students into purposeful work around their goals for reading.

In the next section, you'll read about the important work of matching students to just-right texts, including some advice about creating a classroom library that sets students up to find books they will be able to read and will want to read.

After you've evaluated the student responses and have a sense of what goal would be of most benefit to each student, it's time to confer with them to establish the goal and to begin offering strategies that will support the student in practicing the goal. These first conferences are known as *goal-setting conferences*. After students are set up with goals, these goals can help you to plan ongoing strategy instruction, which can be taught using a variety of teaching methods.

Matching Readers with Books for Independent Reading

I was recently asked to support a suburban New Jersey school district whose leadership was inspired to move away from its basal reading series in favor of a more balanced literacy approach that included supporting students as they read real children's literature of their choice. Any time I'm asked to support schools with that goal, my first step is to get purposeful independent reading up and going. When kids are reading books they want to read and can read, I can help teachers learn about the reading process and how to better understand their readers.

When I shared this first step with the principal, he told me they already had independent reading going, so, like any teacher would, I decided to do an assessment before teaching: before embarking on the professional learning, I spent a day with the school principal and district superintendent on a learning walk, visiting the classrooms during independent reading to observe, notice trends, and set realistic goals for our first year working together.

When helping students make book selections it is crucial that we consider interest and what the student brings to the text first and use text levels only as a guide.

201

In many of the classrooms we visited, students were reading books they had chosen from their classroom library. Each time we entered a classroom to observe, we would hang back and kidwatch. We noticed some students in each room reading, but we also often saw a good percentage of them completely disengaged. We observed students staring out the window; switching between chapter books mid-book; and getting up to ask to use the bathroom, drink water, or find a new book from the library. We saw students fake reading: looking intently at their book but not flipping the page once in the more than fifteen minutes we were in the classroom.

We decided to investigate further. Next, the three of us spent a bit of time talking to kids about their books. When we asked them to tell us about what they were reading, we found that students mostly offered superficial gists, speaking with less information and specificity about the book than what was written on its back cover, even when the student was halfway through the book. We asked them to read aloud and found that almost all of the students who read to us made several miscues that interfered with meaning within the first paragraph. As they read on, the rate of miscues didn't improve. Many also exhibited disfluent reading without much expression.

The leadership and I had a conversation about how students would need support in making book choices that really engaged them and that they could really understand. We also noted that teachers would need support to notice the difference between real reading and fake reading as well as engagement and disengagement and to learn how to support students with purposeful feedback as they read.

The kind of independent reading they currently had in place wasn't benefiting their readers as much as it could have.

In 2012, during the yearlong pilot study I mentioned earlier—when I sent hundreds of books to readers across the country and asked them to read a book, respond to comprehension prompts, and reflect on their comprehension—I found overwhelmingly that students thought that the book they read was just right for them, even when their responses to all or most of the questions showed very limited understanding of the book.

Others have found this problem to be true, too. Lucy Calkins has written about how in the early days of piloting reading workshops, she disagreed with the practice of leveling classroom library books, for fear that classroom libraries would turn into the SRA kits of our childhoods, where we'd race through a ladder of levels or compete with classmates to get to a higher one. However, her experiences visiting classrooms of colleagues in her leadership groups where student after student was in a book that was too hard, and all of their conferences with these students tended to be about selecting more accessible books, led her to come to the conclusion that levels can have some utility in helping guide children to choose books they can read (Calkins 2000; Calkins and Ehrenworth 2017).

Powerful instruction can and should happen as students read independently (Miller and Moss 2013). However, children need to be able to access the text.

For many years, teachers have taught students the "Goldilocks rule" or "five finger rule": Read a page, and put down one finger for each unknown word. If you have five fingers down the text is too hard. The problem with this? It leads students to consider word-level accuracy when selecting texts and focuses on only a short piece of the text. Fluency and comprehension also must count as we work to determine which texts are just right and why (Allington 2011a). The task of reading a 250-page book is not the same as reading one page out of the middle, so sampling just that one page is of limited help when students are trying to figure out if they will be able to handle the whole book.

The mismatch between what students choose and an appropriate text they can understand is perhaps most concerning with striving readers. Studies have shown that readers who read below grade level are likely to choose books that are well beyond their abilities, while more capable readers tend to choose books that are more in line with their abilities (Reutzel and Fawson 2002).

Because of my experiences as a teacher and as a literacy consultant in hundreds of classrooms, and because I am so influenced by Calkins and Allington, I do believe that levels can be a helpful tool when guiding children to book choices during independent reading. I give this advice knowing full well that many leading educators and authors that I respect greatly, including Fountas and Pinnell themselves, are opposed to the use of levels for independent reading. Some oppose it because of the way that levels are misused and misunderstood. Others oppose it because of the belief that levels should only be used for instructional-level instruction when the teacher selects the text, and that independent reading should be free/open choice. Still other opponents work primarily with middle school readers where, I agree, leveling texts begins to be less helpful. In this section I offer what I hope is a helpful and sensible addition to this debate for those who use independent reading time as

instructional time (i.e., those who use a Reading Workshop or Daily 5™/CAFE framework) and who confer or do small-group instruction using students' self-selected independent reading texts. I offer advice on how to use, not abuse, levels and the sorts of language to use with children so that choice always comes first and levels never become a reader's label.

For teachers, levels provide a helpful shortcut to acquiring information on the hundreds of books in each classroom library. If you are a teacher who has read (almost) every book in your classroom library, who has a sense of the challenges in each of the books, and who is willing to help support student book selection, then leveling texts may not be necessary at all. For many librarians who have deep knowledge of children's literature, levels aren't as necessary. But for the majority of teachers who are still learning about children's literature in general and the books in their ever-growing library specifically, I have found that levels have a practical utility.

For students, levels may have some usefulness too. I believe strongly that choice and interest come first when children select texts—and I address a bit later how important it is to not limit student selection based on levels. However, I do think that for children who are developing readers, throughout elementary and into the beginning of middle school, levels could serve as a quick way to give children some sense of the relative difficulty of each of the classroom library's books when they are making book selections for independent reading. If you do choose to make students aware of book levels, please pay close attention to my advice and cautions beginning on page 212. I could also understand, though, if you want to keep the levels for yourself. This would mean you plan to support students' book choices by making recommendations based on your deep knowledge of readers' interests as well as the complexity of the texts you're offering.

So, in sum, my advice stems from the following research and beliefs:

- Students need to be reading texts they can read with accuracy, fluency, and comprehension to make sure that independent reading time is the most effective (Allington 2011a).

- Independent reading *is valuable instructional time,* different from the DEAR time of our childhood when teachers read their own books quietly as we read ours, modeling their own reading habits (or used DEAR to get other teacher work done since the children were quietly engaged in a task). Today, we focus on independent reading time as an opportunity to support children with targeted instruction around their goals (Miller and Moss 2013; Calkins 2000; Moss and Young 2010).

In the rest of this section I offer you advice about how to audit your book collection to ensure that it reflects your readers and the world, how to organize the books in your library to entice your readers and help them quickly find books that they will love and that they can read, and how to use levels as a tool when helping students make their selections. When students notice their own engagement and comprehension in books they've found in the classroom with guided choice, they will be better set up to make choices from books in the school or local public library where levels won't (and shouldn't) be used.

Creating a Classroom Library

A well-organized, inviting classroom library is essential to setting students up to read with independence and to develop a reading life (Guthrie 2008; Worthy and Roser 2010; Mulligan and Landrigan 2018). The richer the array of offerings, the greater the opportunities for students to connect to the books they've chosen and really "own" what you teach them as they work toward their goals. By organizing your library, you can ensure that students are able to find immediately books that are appropriate for them in terms of interest and readability; this way, students spend more time actually *reading* the books than they do *choosing* them.

1: Survey and Audit Your Library Collection

Children deserve to see themselves and the world in your classroom library. When you're choosing texts to add to your collection, it's important to carefully consider whether the texts are both "mirrors" (reflecting the students in your classroom so that they can see themselves in the texts you're reading) and "windows" (to help your students see the rest of the world) (Bishop 1990; Botelho and Rudman 2009). In 1990, Rudine Bishop wrote, "When children cannot find themselves reflected in the books they read, or when the images they do see are distorted, negative, or laughable, they learn a powerful lesson about how they are devalued in the society of which they are a part." And it's not only children of color, or from families with LGBTQ members, families in poverty, or families who speak a language other than English at home who benefit from an inclusive collection of culturally responsive texts. Bishop makes the important point that when children who are part of privileged groups see only themselves represented in books, they may grow up with an "exaggerated sense of their own importance." In some insulated communities, books are one of few ways that children can experience the lives of people who are different from themselves.

This issue of publishers supporting and publishing diverse voices and advocating for these books to have a prominent place in our class, school, and public libraries is thankfully gaining more attention. With the advent of the We Need Diverse Books campaign and website, and a new peer-reviewed journal titled *Research on Diversity in Youth Literature* (https://bit.ly/2NDXYD8), as well as national organizations and conferences including the National Council of Teachers of English and the International Literacy Association making diversity in children's books a priority in their conference offerings and publications, this issue is timely.

To audit your own classroom library offerings, you may want to enlist the help of your students. Fifth-grade teacher and blogger Jessica Lifshitz described how she did this with her students (https://bit.ly/1sFxpCO). Teaching her students about a "diversity gap" in children's publishing, she had her students explore their own classroom library to consider representation. First, she had students look at the classroom library through the lens of gender diversity. Next, they considered how well the books represented racial diversity. In both cases, students randomly grabbed twenty-five books from the classroom library and took notes on a simple form that asked them to consider:

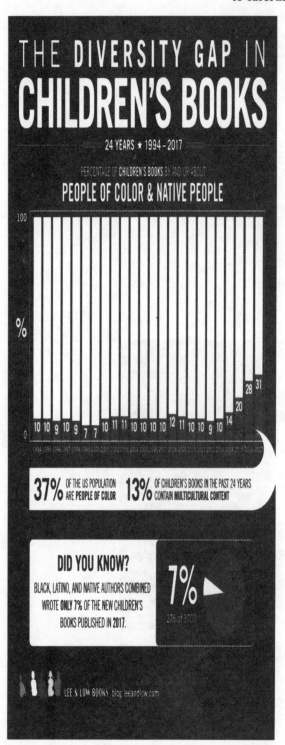

- Are there people on the cover of the book?

- If there are characters on the cover, are they white?

- If there are multiple characters, how many are white?

- If there are characters on the cover, are they male or female?

- If there are multiple characters, how many are male/female?

After looking at gender and race, she repeated the process with family structures and gender roles. Jess acknowledges that the process is not scientific and her students' findings do not represent her entire library, but rather a cross sampling. Still, their inquiry opened a dialogue about representation in books and made them more aware of biases in book publishing, in their own book selections, and in the books that their teacher had gathered for their library. Jess then bravely took suggestions from her students about what she could do to improve the offerings in the class library so that the books helped the children to see not only themselves but also the world. She reported that these conversations improved not only her classroom library but also her students' awareness about representation in books, on TV, in movies, in advertising, and online. Let's all be like Jess!

Another excellent resource for examining your collection, with your students or on your own, is SocialJusticeBooks.org. See, for example, this post by Louise Derman-Sparks: https://bit.ly/2fk0RtK.

In addition to the important inquiry into diversity, inclusion, and representation, you may also ask your students to identify their own interests, passions, and hobbies. Looking through the classroom library, students could see if their identities as readers are well represented, or if there are gaps. You could hand out book catalogs, invite students to go online to book retailers to highlight favorites, or visit your local independent bookstore and ask them to make lists of the books that most interest and excite them. Afterward, compare their interests to your collection (and use their lists for future purchasing). Revisiting the interest survey (page 185) and conversations you've had with students to learn about them (page 181) will also help you figure out which types of books they will be most drawn to. Reach out to your knowledgeable school librarian to help you find books to supplement your own classroom collection, and for recommendations of new titles to look out for as the school budget allows for new purchases. Read more about ways to acquire more books and make the most of the ones you have in the new professional book *It's All About the Books* (Mulligan and Landrigan 2018).

> *"While any book can be assigned a text level indicating its approximate placement along a text gradient, that alone is not sufficient information for making choices about which books to purchase or recommend for readers let alone for developing a meaningful literacy program for children."*
>
> —BARBARA PETERSON (2001)

2: Level Books—If You Choose

As I mentioned earlier, if you've read the books in your classroom library, can guide student book selection using that knowledge, and feel comfortable knowing what to teach during conferences, you may not need to level books.

If you choose to mark levels on books, place any levels or codes on the inside cover of the book. That way, kids see the cover illustration, title, and blurb and think about their own identity as readers first when choosing. Having levels tucked out of sight also protects students' privacy.

But if you would benefit from a way to surmise the relative difficulty of the books in your library at a quick glance, you may find marking them discreetly with a level will help. Whether you make children aware of the level or not is another choice.

If you're setting up a classroom library for the first time and have many books to level, I recommend asking colleagues, parent volunteers, or capable students for a helping hand. You can download one of the many apps available to scan ISBN codes on the back of books and/or use leveling websites to manually search by entering the title and/or author. I use www .fountasandpinnellleveledbooks.com, the only official source of books leveled by Fountas and Pinnell, as my first go-to.

Practice and experience, your own teacher judgment, and your developed knowledge of your books and leveling formulas are what I hope you learn to rely on most. Revisit pages 25–37 for a reminder of my advice about how to engage in work with colleagues to develop knowledge and confidence.

Also, a caution: as discussed in Part I, chances are that if you look up a book in two different sources, you may occasionally find that the levels listed in each are different or that it doesn't appear at all. In these instances you'll need to look at the book yourself, and use your own judgment. If you can, match them to leveled books in your library, and adopt the same levels.

Consider where you'll place the level on the book. I strongly encourage you to mark the book in an inconspicuous place, such as the inside front cover. For the purpose of student privacy, and also because we don't want children to see the level of the book they read as any sort of mark or badge on them as a reader, the level should be used by you (and possibly also by the student) to find books that will work; it's best if the level of the book is not visible to all.

3: Organize Books

I advise against using levels on the baskets. Instead, organizing them into categories can be more helpful to the development of your students' reading identities. This way, when students approach the classroom library their first thoughts are, "Who am I as a reader?" and "What are my interests?" rather than "What level book can I read?"

An interest survey (page 185), which you used to consider the types of books in your collection, can also be helpful with sorting books. Organizing your books in categories based on student interest reflects their identities in the classroom library.

For example, if Jeff Kinney's Diary of a Wimpy Kid series is hot in your class, consider a basket with a label that reads, "If You Loved Wimpy Kid, You'll Love . . ." If you have a class with many athletes, make sure to have a bin titled "Athletes Who Will Inspire You" and maybe a fiction basket called

"Sports Stories." You don't have to do all the sorting yourself—you could ask students for suggestions for the bins, and you can also start a bin by putting a label on an empty basket. Then, when kids finish a book that they think fits the category, they can add it to the new bin. You can also elicit student input about what content baskets they'd like to see and invite them to launch new baskets. Inviting students to label the baskets themselves helps build reading ownership.

Some clever basket and bin titles from teachers' libraries that are organized by topic, genre, and/or author categories rather than by level follow:

- Strong Girl Characters

- Before Justin Bieber These Guys Were Cool

- As Magical as Harry Potter

- Class 3-404's Favorites

- Eww, Gross! (Boogers, Body Odor, and Other Stuff About Your Body)

- Out of This World! (Science Fiction)

Be sure your library is open and accessible. For example, you may have it encircle the classroom meeting area, so students can visit it without traffic jams. Also, try to keep shelves low and baskets and bins lean, so that children can easily lift bins off the shelves to browse through them. For more on organizing classroom libraries, see the library tour on pages 210–211 and Mulligan and Landrigan's *It's All About the Books* (2018).

Library Tour

Ashleigh Rose works with her sixth-grade students in Washington, DC, to group books and label bins in a way that makes sense to them (students take ownership over organizing and labeling the bins). During their daily book talks her students decide for that day's book either (1) which bin they think it came from, or (2) which bin it should now live in. She reports that the organization and book talk practice have helped kids more easily find books on their own as opposed to when she organized her library in genre or author bins.

Bin labels in this classroom include: The Struggle Is Real; Finish the Mission; Young Kids Overcoming; You Might Cry, You Might Not; Fantastic Books and Where to Find Them; Stand Up (Against Bullies) Before You Fall; The Disaster Is Real; Undercover; In for a Scare; Got the Giggles; A Messed-Up Future; #squadgoals; Back Then in the Past; Parents Just Don't Understand.

Andrea, a teacher in Missouri, has about sixty different categories (some genre, some author, and some theme: war stories, animal stories [fiction], Holocaust, African American stories, Newbery Award, humor, school stories, mythology, friendship, poetry, sports, and so on) in her library of about 1,600+ books. In her first year teaching sixth grade, Andrea had a student who loved to read so much that she would collect and keep stacks of books on her desk that she couldn't let go of. She created one of the categories in honor of this student—a basket labeled "Juvina's Favorites."

Joann, a fifth-grade teacher in North Carolina, involves her students in organizing her bins and labeling them in ways that match their interests. - - - - - ->

Kathryn teaches in Illinois. She finds that organizing her books spine-out works better for her classroom than having them in bins. She likes to give her kids lots of choices, and by putting the books on the shelves, she has space to keep all of her books out. Each shelf has a basket at the end declaring the shelf's category; the rest of the books are spine-out. Students shop at the library by turning their head to one side and scanning the shelves.

Brittany teaches second grade in North Carolina. Series books abound for young readers, so many of her bins are series- or author-focused. The nonfiction area of the library is topic-focused. She involves her students in creating labels for the bins, which helps students develop ownership over their library.

4: Use, Don't Abuse, Levels When Matching Texts and Readers

Offering students choice in what they read is highly correlated to reading motivation and engagement and increased comprehension (Guthrie and Humenick 2004). By supporting students with their choices in the classroom, kids can learn to make choices outside of school as well, thereby increasing the likelihood that they will choose to read (Ivey and Broaddus 2001; Reis et al. 2007). Our first aim should be to support student choice and interest when helping them find books (D. Miller 2009).

High-success reading (reading texts with accuracy, fluency, and comprehension) is also highly correlated to student motivation and comprehension (Allington and Gabriel 2012). Students need choice, but if they are choosing books that are too hard, they need support in finding texts with which they will be more successful (Allington and Gabriel 2012).

I believe we can use levels to help guide student choice, but levels should never be used to shackle a reader. As I've already established, there are many reader and text variables to consider, and expert reading teachers need to know their readers and texts well enough to be flexible about what text might be a best fit in a particular circumstance. Saying to a student, "You are a Level ___ so you can only read Level ___ books," is deeply problematic. Instead, while I use my knowledge of what they demonstrated they were able to read with comprehension on a whole-book assessment, I keep it in mind alongside what I know about the reader. If the student wants to select a book that I think would be a stretch—fine. As their teacher, I'd need to know about that so that I could either plan to meet with the student in conferences or a small group, offering some strategies for tackling a more challenging text such as rereading or adjusting their pace, and/or set them up in a book club to offer more support. Or, if the student knows a lot about the topic already, then maybe they wouldn't need the extra support from peers or me. If the student is constantly picking books that are five or six levels higher than what I know they can comprehend, or if a student is regularly selecting books that they abandon after one chapter, it's important that I'm more involved in their book selection. In short, the levels help serve as a *guide*.

The student's reflection after reading a book shows that she is overly focused on reading levels as the sole determinant of what a just-right book is for her. In conferences ask, "Was this book just right? How do you know?" and listen for students talking about comprehension, interest in the topic, relating to the characters, and other non-level-based markers. An overfocus on levels does not create lifelong readers.

Reflection

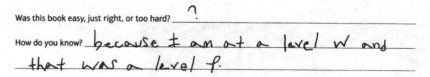

Was this book easy, just right, or too hard? _____

How do you know? _because I am at a level W and that was a level F._

When students choose books, their first thoughts as they enter the classroom library should be along the lines of, "Who am I as a reader? What kinds of books do I enjoy? What am I in the mood to read this week? What recommendations have I heard from friends that I want to check out? What series am I working on reading? What authors do I love?" and so on. You *don't* want children to ask themselves, "What's my level?" Ideally, they'll look for books that appeal to them, and then you can decide how you'd like to support them with choosing texts that are accessible. Either you can be there in the library helping them find books that will be a good fit, or you can let kids know that they can peek at the level where you've inconspicuously placed it on an inside cover. It's important to not say things like "This book is too hard—choose your level" as you're redirecting a student's choices and that you remember what I've written throughout this book—there is no such thing as one level fitting one student all the time. Knowing the level of the book, however, might help them to consider how hard it may be, relative to other books they've read that were the same level.

Model thinking aloud about using levels to help guide choices such as, "Oh, this one is a bit harder than the Anastasia Krupnik book that I just read, but given that it's set at sleep-away camp and I've been to sleep-away camp I think I'm up for the challenge," or, "This book is as hard as the ones I usually read, but it's historical fiction and set in Japan. I know nothing about Japan so I'm going to have to read more slowly and carefully to get through it."

Reconsidering Our Language Choices When Matching Readers to Books

TRY NOT TO SAY . . .	INSTEAD, SAY . . .
That book is too hard for you. Choose from your level.	That book is going to be harder than what you typically read. Let's think about how I/your friends can support you as you read, if you find you need it.
Make sure you're choosing only books that are at your level.	Your first step is to find books that look interesting that you think you'll love reading. You can peek at the inside front cover to see the book's level as one more thing to consider.
You can't read that book. It's too easy for you.	I usually have some books in my stack that feel extra comfortable, just like this one you've chosen here. As you pick your next book or two for the week, make sure it's going to set you up to work on your reading goal.
You're a Level ___ reader.	In many cases, the books that will be just right in terms of challenge will be marked with a Level ___ or ___ on the inside front cover. Of course, make sure you're thinking about what interests you as a reader first and foremost.
Yay! You moved up to Level ___.	I can tell you've been practicing your goal and you've been doing a lot of reading in school and at home. Do you think you'd like to try some more challenging books because the ones you've been reading are starting to feel easy? You may want to look for books that have a Level ___ or ___ on the inside cover. I'll check in with you next week to see how these new books feel.

If the book is at a higher level than what a student typically reads, they might think, "I'm up for it. I think this book is a bit harder than usual, but I'll just ask my teacher for help/read it with a friend/go slower/plan to reread a bit at home . . ." If the book is a bit easier than what they usually read, they might think, "This one looks fun. It might be a quick read. I'll pick an extra book or two this week because I don't plan to spend as long on this one."

Be sure to emphasize with kids that there is no such thing as a reader being leveled, and that the level on books are just one of the many things to consider when choosing them. Never refer to children by a reading level. Correct and redirect children if you ever hear them referring to themselves as a level.

Some children will need more support than others when it comes to choosing books that will be a good fit. Students benefit from thinking about what books they've read in the past that they loved, what books didn't hold their interest, and what the characteristics of those books were. They might complete reading reflections to consider who they are as a reader, and based on the reflections, you might suggest certain books. In classrooms where children and their teacher routinely discuss books, give book talks, and meet in partnerships and groups to talk about what they're reading, children will almost certainly have their eyes on titles that they're bound to love. For incredible guidance on book talking and recommending books to your students, I suggest Donalyn Miller's *The Book Whisperer* (2009).

If your classroom is one where reading reflections and book talks are the norm, then students will likely feel comfortable visiting the library to select books on their own. If not, students may want you to accompany them to the library and confer with them about their choices. With time, practice, and support, visiting the library will come to feel comfortable and familiar, and your students will grow into being able to make their own independent book selections.

Each week, have students visit the classroom library and choose a book or books for the week. If you can get the library and procedures running smoothly, you'll gain instructional time, and students will use independent reading for its intended purpose: to enjoy their reading and to practice strategies that you've taught to help them reach their goals.

If you're short on books, it might make sense to have all students choose their books on the same day, at the same time. That way, all students will return their books at the same time, and students can choose from those books, as well as from other books in the library. This method can be a bit chaotic, admittedly, because your entire class will descend on the shelves at once, but see what works best for you and your kids.

Barb Golub

If you're lucky enough to have plenty of books, stagger book-choosing times. (See the sample schedule to the right.) You might, for example, have one group per day visit the library during morning work time, or right after lunch when students are making bathroom and water fountain visits.

Ideally, book choosing happens outside of independent reading time. I've found that some students use visits to the library to avoid reading. Independent reading should be about just that: reading.

If students visit the library only once a week, they'll need enough books to get them through the week. You can easily calculate the number of books they'll need by taking their total number of minutes of independent reading in school and at home each day and the number of minutes students read on the weekend. Then figure a student will read about three-quarters of a page per minute (this estimate is based on word-per-minute research by Harris and Sipay [1990] and average word per page counts of books at various levels).

Assuming a student reads thirty minutes each day in school, and thirty minutes each night during the week, plus about thirty to sixty minutes on Saturday and Sunday, that's 420 total minutes of reading each week, which translates to 315 pages, assuming a reading rate of three-fourths of a page per minute. Here's a rough estimate of the number of books a student might read:

Assigning days for book shopping, and encouraging students to choose a week's worth of books, helps teachers manage traffic in their libraries. Other teachers have an "open" time each day, such as during morning work or immediately following recess.

LEVEL	AVERAGE # OF PAGES IN A FICTION BOOK	AVERAGE # OF PAGES IN A NONFICTION BOOK	# OF BOOKS NEEDED FOR THE WEEK
J, K, L	40–60	20–30	10–15
M, N, O, P	60–110	30–50	6–10
Q, R, S, T	75–120	40–60	2–8
U, V, W	150–250	50–70	1–5

Use the lower end of the range as a guide when students choose mostly fiction, the higher end of the range when they choose mostly nonfiction, and the middle of the range when they are choosing a balance of fiction and nonfiction. Nonfiction books have fewer pages than fiction books of the same level. Monitor students' reading habits and adjust as needed.

Matching Books and Readers:
Cautionary Tales from the Classroom

Carol, Literacy Coach, New Jersey

We teachers need to make sure we're not matching levels to readers rather than books to readers. Although we have focused on getting to know our readers by their skill sets, we are not as focused on getting to know books to match our students' interests. This was underscored in June when I offered to come into classrooms to rearrange classroom libraries by topic instead of levels. One teacher expressed concerns about mixing levels and rearranging books in bins by topic since she knew how important it was to match students to books they could read. "How will I get the right level books in their hands?" she asked.

As we led the children in naming possible topics, the excitement was palpable. The kids were talking about books with no strings attached as we listed possible categories for the book bins. Disasters, Bullies, Special Families, Baseball, World War II, Dogs, and my favorite—Books Teachers Don't Like—were among the labels that they placed on bins to begin the sorting. As the kids sorted the books, the teacher and I went through a couple of the piles and saw that, in fact, a variety of levels emerged in nearly all of the bins. We could sense the students' excitement around the new organization.

A different teacher I coach said that some readers picked books from their leveled bins but showed little interest in the books when it came time to reading and often wanted to return the books. Our conversation led to a discussion about how passion about books needs to come first. Additionally, I suggested that "selling" books to the kids was important. I came into the room to model selling books the following week after reviewing the levels of the students and considering what I knew about them personally. I had preselected a pile of books from the classroom library, including some new hi/lo books. I told the kids that I had several books that were favorites of mine and past students that I wanted to share with them. As I held up each book I gave a very brief book talk, adding comments: "This one's a little creepy, but I know some of you like creepy. . . ." "This one flies off the shelves at the town library . . . " "If you like blah blah blah, you'll love this," and so on, and

then I asked if anyone wanted the book. Unbeknownst to them, I gave the books out aware of the levels of book that are typically right for each child. They were literally jumping out of their seats to get the books. It was easy to bring the kids around to a conversation in which they decided that when they finished one of the books, they would let their classmates know so they could pass it along.

Ryanne, Second-Grade Teacher, Wisconsin

One of the biggest struggles I have had to face as an educator began a few years ago. I was told that my entire library had to be reorganized. Each book that I had carefully selected and grouped by themes, genres, series, and authors had to be dismantled and reorganized by levels. It took me over 20 hours to do this, and the entire time my heart was crying because I felt it was not in the best interests of my students. My classroom library was no longer an inviting place to browse for books out of interest and desire but a storage place for bin upon bin of leveled books. I tried to make the most of it by keeping my lamps, rugs, and comfy chairs, but it was not the same space. I was told to remove books that were not in the grade level span of my current students and that students were allowed to have in their book baskets only books that were at their independent level.

Curiously, I had a mix of students that year. Some I had looped through from the previous year—students who knew my expectations for reading and picking books by interest, not level. There were also students who had joined our learning community, having had a different teacher the year before. One day, one of the students I had looped, came to me with a look of serious concern on her face. She was distraught that a friend pointed out a book that he wanted to read but felt he wasn't allowed to read because it wasn't his "level." She told me she had offered the advice to the other child that if he wanted to read the book, he should just read it. Such wise words from an eight-year-old. I was so grateful for the conversation she had with her friend, and for the fact that she had shared it with me. The next opportunity I got, I sat down with that little boy and asked him about the book he wanted to read. It was a Level N; his teacher from the previous year had told him he could only read Level H books. The book was a nonfiction text called *Steam Engines*. He read it to me fluently and accurately with minimal support. He had so much knowledge about engines, cars, and the history thereof, that he *could* and *did* read this book. Repeatedly . . . because he enjoyed it. After this encounter, I found my voice and told *all* my students to think first about what they were interested in reading, not the level on the book.

Jennifer, Third-Grade Teacher, Wisconsin

To start the school year, I have an order of new books set to arrive during the first few days of the year. I like to make a big deal about books and share how exciting it is to get new books with my students right from the start. I play it up almost like I'm opening a birthday present and make sure I "ooh and ahh" over each and every book in that box. I was almost to the bottom of the box when I grabbed out a shiny new chapter book and I could see one of my stronger readers eyeing it up. I read the back cover and barely finished the last sentence when her hand shot up in the air. I was already nodding my head yes in anticipation of the question I expected to hear, "Can I have that one?!" She had a huge smile on her face from the time that book came out of the box, but I saw that smile slowly start to disappear as she instead timidly asked, "What level is it? Do you think it's mine?"

Later that same year, I had a student who was in intervention and was very aware of his reading level due to the emphasis placed on it while in intervention. He had been quite a reluctant reader all year. He would read but it was because he had to, not because he wanted to. We had started mystery book clubs, and he wasn't feeling the first book he chose. After conferring with him, I asked him to take some time and look for a new mystery book to try. We went over how he would be able to tell if it was a mystery, and I pointed him in the direction of my collection of series, where there are many mysteries to choose from but they are not arranged by level. (At the time, he was being directed to read Level L books in intervention, but I tried to give him the freedom of choice in my classroom and did what I could to move students away from the emphasis that had been put on levels in the past.)

He stumbled across a section of Geronimo Stilton books, and I could tell he was really getting interested. He was looking through each book and picked up a few of them. I checked back in with him and asked him to read a little to me. He struggled through some of the beginning and with just a little encouragement he was able to get through some tricky words. He stopped, a little confused at one part, and we talked about it—it was a joke, and he suddenly got it. He loved it and was suddenly in love with that series. He struggled through the first book but persisted because he was so smitten with that mouse! He then devoured almost every single title in that collection. He was using decoding strategies to figure out any tricky words; he would back up and reread when he was confused; he was making predictions and piecing together the clues. He was reading, and he was loving it! He even took a stack of three books with him when he ended up with in-school suspension because of a fight on the playground. He couldn't wait to tell me about the books and how many he was able to read that day. I think he truly enjoyed having a whole day to himself with his little stack of books. My point—Geronimo Stilton is a Level O. Had he known the level, he would have likely passed those books right up. In some classrooms, he wouldn't have even been allowed to pick it up. If he had brought that first book with him to intervention, he would have been told that book was too hard for him because of the level. Had he used the five-finger rule, he would have failed on the first page because of all the new names and words he had to figure out. If he didn't have the interest, he wouldn't have been engaged in his reading and surely wouldn't have been putting effort into using strategies to get through the tough stuff.

Conclusions About Matching Texts and Readers

The benefits for students are many when they read a wide range of texts, for a variety of purposes, and in a variety of contexts. When helping students make book selections for their independent reading, book clubs, and partnership reading—or when you select texts for instructional-level reading (guided reading, close reading lessons, and so forth), it is crucial that we consider interest and what the student brings to the text first and use text levels only as a guide.

A few concluding takeaways follow.

How Levels Help Students and Teachers

- They provide one way to consider if a book is one that a student may be able to read and comprehend.

- They provide a shorthand to allow students to peek at the book's complexity, which is often a hard thing for a child to judge by just holding a book in their hand.

- They can help teachers get to know their books, and children's literature in general, and what to expect of them.

- They can assist children in choosing books they can read from a selection of books they are interested in reading more quickly, so they spend more time reading.

- They help children find books that will present limited challenges so they can work on their reading goals.

- They help children select texts they are more likely to be able to read and comprehend, so they are less likely to abandon their books because they get to be too difficult.

How Levels Can Become Problematic

- If overemphasized, levels can cause a reader's identity to fade into the background, as they overidentify with just a letter or number.

- If overused, levels can eliminate choice, forcing students to only pick from a single level or bin.

- If levels are misunderstood, teachers could use them instead of their knowledge of their readers to lead their reading instruction.

- If levels are used inflexibly, teachers could misunderstand that there is variability to what a reader can read based on a number of reader factors (engagement, background knowledge, etc.).

Conducting Goal-Setting Conferences

Decades of research indicates that teachers play a crucial role in supporting student comprehension. Offering students ample time to read and reread and providing them with targeted strategies and feedback, ideally one-on-one or in small groups, fosters tremendous reading growth (Hattie 2008). After ensuring students have books they can and want to read, the next step toward this intentional, focused, individualized instruction is the goal-setting conference.

A goal-setting conference will give you the opportunity to sit with a child, encourage the reader to reflect on his or her reading process and progress, and work together to set a reading goal (Serravallo 2013, 2014, 2019). In a goal-setting conference, I try to guide the student toward choosing a goal that matches what their assessment(s) show. Giving students choices can help yield more engagement and ownership (Pink 2011). The teacher has an important role in using guiding questions and choosing proper artifacts to share with the student.

Read the sample transcript beginning on page 221 to get a sense of how a goal-setting conference might sound. You'll notice that I ask Carly to reflect on her responses to a whole-book assessment.

Children grow as readers and thinkers when they sense we really want to know them as readers and thinkers.

She read *Amber Brown Is Not a Crayon* by Paula Danziger and responded to a couple of prompts for each goal (Plot and Setting, Character, Vocabulary and Figurative Language, and Themes and Ideas). I ask her to reflect on how the reading went, which questions felt tricky for her, and which felt more doable. I am trying to get her to figure out what goal would make the most sense for her by acknowledging the areas where she needs the most help. I already know what I want her to notice because I've already evaluated her responses. You will notice my guiding language.

As you read the sample, notice how the following principles, which should guide all conferring, are met:

- **Keep it positive.** Children grow as readers and thinkers when they sense we really want to know them as readers and thinkers. Appreciate each student's successes and approximations. It is important to always begin by naming a child's strengths as a reader, as well as their most pressing needs.

- **Invite elaboration.** The conference, at its heart, is a conversation in which both parties have a role. Students' written comments provide wonderful opportunities for you to invite them to say more. But some children find it easier to show what they know verbally and to give insight into their comprehension by talking with you about it. Often, the more you can get the student to talk, the more you'll learn about them as a reader and a thinker.

- **Listen well.** Go into the conference not only with a specific goal in mind but also with open ears. Be open to what the student might suggest—or to what you might discover, which may be a skill that's even more pressing or compelling. Listening well also allows you to suggest a goal that relates to something the student says.

- **End with a tangible, attainable goal.** The best goals come from a careful analysis of an assessment and, when possible, from the student's own realization of their needs. Try your best to guide each student toward noticing what you notice. Be sure to wrap up the conference by articulating a specific goal (the *what*) and a strategy (the *how*). Leaving the student with tangible artifacts—such as a sticky note on which you've jotted goals or a great next-book idea—will always help your teaching stick.

Sample Goal-Setting Conference

Teacher: Hi, Carly. I just finished looking at what you wrote when you were reading *Amber Brown Is Not a Crayon*. I thought we could talk a bit about it.

Carly: Okay.

Teacher: First, I'm wondering what you thought about the book.

Carly: I liked it. I thought it was good because it teaches you a lesson.

Teacher: At the end of your response sheet, you describe that lesson in a really insightful way. Do you know what that means? It means you had a deep thought about the book. It's great that you let books teach you lessons. I'm also wondering what it was like to answer the questions.

Early on in the conference, name a strength a child has shown so they feel confident and are receptive to your subsequent suggestions. The tone of the conference needs to be conversational and friendly.

Carly: It was a little bit easy and a little bit hard.

Teacher: Can you tell me what you mean by that?

If you allow it, students will let you do all the talking in the conference. I try to offer children opportunities to elaborate whenever I can, to learn how they think about what they think their—metacognition.

Carly: Well, in the beginning, it felt a little bit hard, but then as I kept going I got more used to it, and then it was okay.

Teacher: That's interesting. I noticed that you had a little trouble with the first five questions. Those are all in the beginning. You're right. Do you notice anything about the types of questions those first five are? What they are asking you to do as a reader?

Carly: Well, this is about Amber, and this is about Amber and Justin.

Teacher: Yes, I see that, too. We can call those questions character questions because they are asking you about the characters in the book and their relationships. It seemed like questions about characters were trickier for you than questions about other aspects of the book.

Carly: Yeah. This one was kind of hard. And this one. And this (*points to character prompt*).

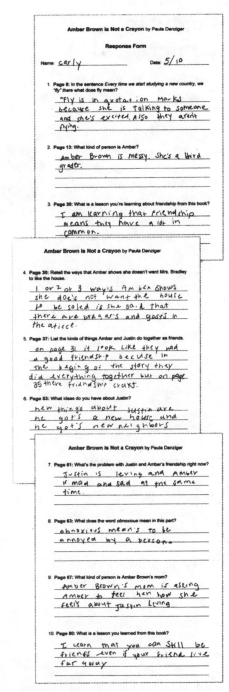

View Carly's responses up close at http://hein.pub/UTR.

Helpful Language to Use in Goal-Setting Conferences

- How did it feel to take this assessment?

- What did you notice about yourself as a reader when you took this assessment?

- Let's talk about some of the prompts that you felt strong responding to.

- Let's talk about some of the prompts that felt difficult to respond to.

- What do you think might be a good goal for you, based on what we've noticed?

- I'm going to offer you some options of strategies that might be helpful . . .

- So, can you say back to me how you're going to work on your goal this week?

- Let's plan to meet again by _____ to see how this is going for you.

Teacher: Let me tell you what I think about when I see your responses. Right here, for the question, "What kind of person is Amber?" you wrote down what Paula Danziger says right in the text, like that she's messy and that she's a third grader. Then, on page 53, when you were asked about Justin, you wrote down that his dad lives far away, which is true but is also a fact right from the text. These kinds of questions were trying to get you to express your own thoughts and ideas about the characters. Do you know what I mean by that?

Carly: Yeah. Like when it asks about Justin and Amber, I could have said that they're nice to each other because the author doesn't say that.

> • Although this isn't the most insightful answer, it does indicate that Carly is able to identify an idea and distinguish it from a text detail. This is encouraging because it means that what I'm about to teach her is within her Zone of Proximal Development (ZPD) (Vygotsky 1978).

Teacher: Yes, exactly. Something the author doesn't tell you would be your own idea.

Carly: Oh. Yeah, getting my own ideas about characters is hard for me sometimes.

Teacher: Would you like for this to be your goal for the next couple of weeks? We'll meet once every four days or so and talk about the characters in books you pick that are just right for you. You can try to tell me a bit about the ideas you have about those characters, not just what the author tells you.

> • Here, I'm clarifying the goal or what we'll work on. I haven't yet given her a strategy for working toward that goal.

Carly: That's a good idea because then I'll think more about the characters, and maybe the beginning of the book won't be so hard and I'll like it more.

Teacher: Yes! I want to give you a strategy that will help you with this. One of the things that helps me when I'm trying to think about characters is to pay close attention to the way they act, speak, and think. When the author gives me details about how a character acts, speaks, or thinks, I stop and wonder, "Hmmm. What kind of person would act, speak, or think like that?" Let's try this together on a book we both know—our read-aloud, *How to Be Cool in the Third Grade* by Betsy Duffey.

> • Now that we've decided on a goal, I'm offering her a strategy. Notice that the strategy is a step-by-step how-to. She can "take" these steps

*with her as she continues to read independently, in this book and
other books, and practice using them to think about the characters.*

Carly: Okay. So what part do I go to?

Teacher: Let's try it here. Reread the start of the book right here, where
Robbie is lying in bed thinking about the start of school.

- *As Carly reads the page, I start to record some notes on a note-
taking form. Specifically, I record the strategy that I introduced
to Carly, as well as the fact that she seemed to understand
the concept of an idea versus something in the text, but that
the way she conveyed the idea—"nice"—was very basic.*

Carly: Okay, I finished.

Teacher: Do you have an idea of your own? Something the author
didn't tell you?

Carly: Well, I think that Robbie wants to be cool, and he's having a hard
time falling asleep so probably he's kind of worried.

Teacher: Well, you're right, the author didn't come right out and say
that Robbie is worried. That's your own idea, and it describes how
Robbie is feeling in this scene. What about the *kind of person* he is? Can
you think of a trait to describe him?

- *Notice I honor her first try as an approximation toward what
I was going for. I named what Carly did and then redirected
her to try something slightly more sophisticated.*

Carly: Well, no. Um. Well, maybe he's worried about what other people
think. Like, he wants to be popular and not unpopular.

Teacher: Well, that's a little closer to a trait. What do you call someone
who cares about what others think?

Carly: Maybe self-conscious?

Teacher: That's a phrase that describes him!

Carly: Yeah.

Teacher: Okay, I'm going to leave you to practice this on your own for
a bit, and I'll check in with you at the end of our independent reading
time. I'm going to give you two things to help you. First, I wrote the
strategy on a sticky note. I'm going to give this to you to stick in your
book so you can remember the steps of the strategy. Second, I have

> When the author gives
> details about how a
> character acts, speaks,
> or thinks, stop and think,
> "Hmm... what kind of
> person would act/
> speak/think like that?"

A tangible artifact at the end
of a conference helps make
teaching stick.

Sample Character Traits

able	demanding	hopeless	restless
active	dependable	humorous	rich
adventurous	depressed	ignorant	rough
affectionate	determined	imaginative	rowdy
afraid	discouraged	impatient	rude
alert	dishonest	impolite	sad
ambitious	disrespectful	inconsiderate	safe
angry	doubtful	independent	satisfied
annoyed	dull	industrious	scared
anxious	dutiful	innocent	secretive
apologetic	eager	intelligent	selfish
arrogant	easygoing	jealous	serious
attentive	efficient	kindly	sharp
average	embarrassed	lazy	short
bad	encouraging	leader	shy
blue	energetic	lively	silly
bold	evil	lonely	skillful
bored	excited	loving	sly
bossy	expert	loyal	smart
brainy	fair	lucky	sneaky
brave	faithful	mature	sorry
bright	fearless	mean	spoiled
brilliant	fierce	messy	stingy
busy	foolish	miserable	strange
calm	fortunate	mysterious	strict
careful	foul	naughty	stubborn
careless	fresh	nervous	sweet
cautious	friendly	nice	talented
charming	frustrated	noisy	tall
cheerful	funny	obedient	thankful
childish	gentle	obnoxious	thoughtful
clever	giving	old	thoughtless
clumsy	glamorous	peaceful	tired
coarse	gloomy	picky	tolerant
concerned	good	pleasant	touchy
confident	graceful	polite	trusting
confused	grateful	poor	trustworthy
considerate	greedy	popular	unfriendly
cooperative	grouchy	positive	unhappy
courageous	grumpy	precise	upset
cowardly	guilty	proper	useful
cross	happy	proud	warm
cruel	harsh	quick	weak
curious	hateful	quiet	wicked
dangerous	healthy	rational	wise
daring	helpful	reliable	worried
dark	honest	religious	wrong
decisive	hopeful	responsible	young

readwritethink

Character trait lists can be easily found online. They can provide a helpful support for students working on inferring about characters. This one came from www.readwritethink.org.

Taking notes will help you remember what you taught, what you noticed as the student practiced the strategy, and ideas for follow-up teaching. Plus, students might take the teaching more seriously when they witness the teacher writing it down! Download goal-specific note-taking forms at http://hein.pub/UTR.

a list of character traits—words and phrases that describe characters. If you find yourself stuck for what words to use when describing a character, check this list. Can you say back to me what you're going to work on for the rest of independent reading?

I'm leaving Carly with some tangible artifacts to support her as she practices independently. I'm also having her say back the work we did together so that I'm sure she understands my expectations.

Carly: Yeah, I'm going to use this list if I have to, and I'm going to use this sticky to remember the strategy. I'm reading a different Amber Brown book, and when I'm reading it, I'm going to think about the characters. Should I write down my ideas?

Teacher: Yes, I think that's a good plan. That way when I check back, you'll have something to show me. Why don't you use sticky notes or your reading notebook—whatever you'd prefer?

Carly: Okay, I'll write on sticky notes.

At this point, I finish up my notes before moving on to another student for a conference. I'll touch base with Carly before the end of independent reading time, if only for a moment, to make sure she's on the right track and able to continue independently until our next conference in a few days.

Strengths	Teaching Opportunities
Carly 10/2 • understands difference between an idea and a detail from the text. • self-aware of need for reading goal around character.	• using character list to use more precise vocab. when stating ideas • revist – char. do/say/think leads to idea about kind of character.

Using a Variety of Reading Strategies

Content for Teaching Comprehension

The strategies you offer students must not only support their goals, but also align with the level of text the child is reading. Having a knowledge of text levels will help you craft and choose strategies that will work best for each individual student.

What Is a Reading Strategy?

My definition of "strategy" is a step-by-step how-to that a teacher may offer a student as a scaffold as they work toward a goal. In my definition, a strategy is never a word or short phrase but rather a series of phrases or sentences that break down the thinking work into a recipe of sorts (Afflerbach, Pearson, and Paris 2008; Serravallo 2015).

To craft strategies for my students, I find it helpful to think about my own process. Let me walk you through my thinking, using a

Whether you're working with students individually, in small groups, or as a whole class, it can be helpful to keep the level of text they are reading in mind as you choose and craft strategies to offer them.

nonfiction text and considering the strategies I might use to support a reader who is working to determine main idea.

Looking at a section in the text *Ants, Bees and Other Social Insects* by Kris Hirschmann, I notice a boldfaced topic sentence that reads, "All social insects use smell and sound to help them communicate" (12). This repeated feature helps to direct the reader to what the section is mostly about. Several plain-text sentences follow to support the statement.

To explain how I'd use this bolded topic sentence, I might say, "I read the bold heading. Then, I read the rest of the section. Then, I look back at the bold heading and ask myself, 'Does it seem like most of the facts in this section connect back to the heading?'"

Looking at the same spread, I also notice a lot of repeated words or synonyms. When taken together, these words could help me figure out what the page is mostly about. I see *smell*, *stinky*, *scent trail*, *chemical scent*, *smell* again; then *sound*, *squeak*, *sounds* again, *buzzing noise*, and *speak* (12–13). This collection of cohesive words definitely helps me realize the section is about how animals use smells and sounds. So, I could phrase this as a strategy in a step-by-step way by saying, "I look across the section for words that are the same or similar (synonyms). I think about how those repeated or similar words all relate back to the topic. I use the common words in a main idea statement."

In both examples, I'm trying to unpack a process for readers, to tell them more than *what to do* and instead offer them support with *how to do it*.

WHAT YOU MIGHT TEACH A READER TO DO (NOT A STRATEGY)	HOW A READER MIGHT DO IT (A STRATEGY)
Figure out the main idea	Read the bold heading. Then, read the rest of the section. Next, look back at the bolded heading and ask yourself, "Does it seem like most of the facts in this section connect back to the heading?"
Understand a vocabulary word	Read the sentence before the word, the sentence that contains the word, and the sentence that follows the word. Think about how the information relates to the word you're trying to figure out. Insert a synonym that makes sense in place of the word.
Study the photograph	Look at the photograph as a whole. Name what you see. Zoom in on parts of the photograph. Name what you see in each part. Explain what the photograph teaches you.

Articulating strategies is a way to make your teaching explicit and to offer children a scaffold they can use as they practice working on their goal during lessons and during independent reading. Notice that the phrasing of the strategies is general enough that students can apply the procedure to book after book, which will encourage transfer and repeated practice. Throughout this repeated practice, the strategy should eventually become automatic, meaning that the student will not need to apply conscious attention to the steps any longer, and the strategy can fade into the background. For 300 strategies, many of which align to the comprehension goals discussed in this book, see *The Reading Strategies Book* (Serravallo 2015).

Remember, the strategy is just a means to work toward a goal; after the student has demonstrated they are using the strategy with automaticity, conscious attention to the steps is no longer necessary. Most students will be working on a goal for several weeks, and during that time they should learn multiple strategies. (See web below.)

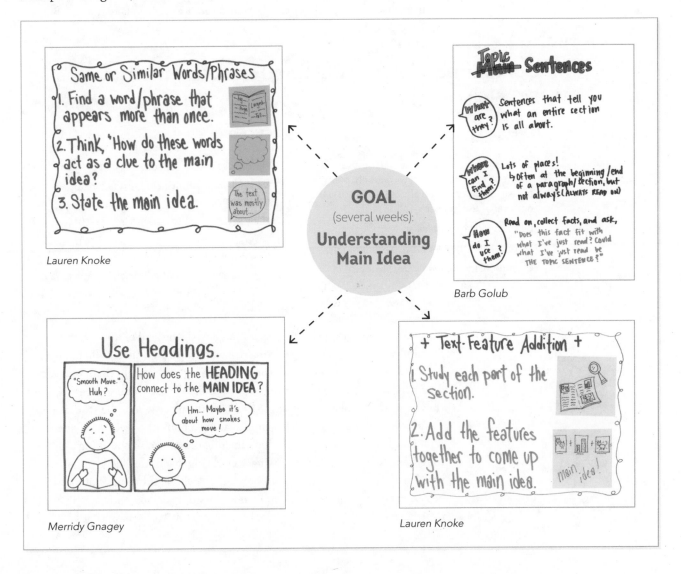

Lauren Knoke

Barb Golub

Merridy Gnagey

Lauren Knoke

Using Your Knowledge of Text Levels When Deciding Which Strategies to Teach

Although it's important to word a strategy in a way that will allow the reader to apply it from book to book to allow for repeated practice and transfer, a single strategy will not necessarily work for every book. It's important to consider the complexities, features, and characteristics of the level of text the student is reading to state the strategy in a way that will actually work in that text.

Let's practice applying what you know about text levels to this discussion of appropriate strategies for readers who are working on reading books in those levels. Let's start with fiction and consider two readers—one reading *Days with Frog and Toad* (Level K) (1979) and another reading *Because of Winn-Dixie* (Level R) (2000). Let's say their goal is the same: to understand Plot and Setting. Would the strategies we teach them be the same? First, let's review what we know about the plots and settings of Levels K and R, from pages 56 and 70.

Comparing Plot and Setting Text Characteristics at Levels K and R

LEVEL K	LEVEL R
• Episodic chapters, stories across several chapters, or single stories without chapter breaks. In any case, the plot is sequential with one event clearly leading to the next.	• Flashbacks and foreshadowing are common.
• Settings tend to be familiar.	• No single plot; often includes subplots or multiple plotlines.
• Setting shifts are supported by illustrations.	• Many settings will be unfamiliar to readers.
• Clear problem-solution story structure.	• Settings are not only background; they take on central importance to the plot.
	• Multiple problems that get resolved rather than solved.

Let's take one of the skills associated with the goal of understanding Plot and Setting: visualizing setting. If I were working with a child reading a book at Level K, I'd likely teach the child strategies that help them to use the illustration on the page, together with their background knowledge of when they've been to a place like that, to describe the place where the story is happening. Would that work with a child reading a book at Level R? Likely not. First of all, most Level R books don't include illustrations, so asking a child to refer to them would be confusing. Activating prior knowledge might be helpful, but not in the same way as for a child who is thinking about a time he's been to a place like that. For a student reading *Sadako and the Thousand Paper Cranes* (2004), who has never been to post–WWII Japan, that's impossible. However, you could suggest that the student carefully read the description of the setting and use any images they have seen in books or on TV that relate to the same time and place, to help them imagine the setting.

Let's take another Plot and Setting–related skill: retelling important events. For a child reading a book at Level K, because the plot is often centered on a main problem, I'd likely teach the student to anchor their retelling on the problem, identifying it, explaining how it becomes more challenging, and finally revealing how the problem is solved. The plots are sequential and one event clearly leads to the next, so this strategy would be helpful. Not so with the student reading a book at Level R, where they are likely to encounter plots and subplots, flashbacks, and foreshadowing. In this situation, a simple sequential retelling won't suffice. Instead, I might teach students reading texts at Level R to think of each chapter as having one main event. At the end of each chapter, they can say in a sentence what is the main thing that happened in that chapter. Then, they can put together all the events when retelling the entire book. For students working on making sense of more than one main plotline, I might invite them to keep two plot mountain graphic organizers in front of them as they read. Each time they come to a new, significant event, they could jot it down on the corresponding plot mountain. At the end of the book, they could think about how the events from each of the two plot mountains connect.

Please see the chart on pages 230–231 for more examples and explanations of how I consider text complexity when crafting or choosing strategies for readers.

Understanding the levels, or more likely level *ranges*, that will work best with each strategy can help you group your students to work with efficiency. I find that I tend to group children mostly by their goal (e.g., all students working on strategies for vocabulary in one group) rather than level (e.g., all students reading Level R books in one group). However, I do consider the level of text they are reading when forming the group because I want to be sure that the strategy I'm offering them makes sense with the books they're reading. For example, it's likely that I'd form a group of students working on the goal of Character with levels ranging from J to M or N to P because the complexity of characters in each of those level ranges is similar.

In sum, whether you're working with students individually, in small groups, or as a whole class, it can be helpful to keep the level of text they are reading in mind as you choose and craft strategies to offer them.

SAMPLE STRATEGIES ALIGNED TO LEVELS OF TEXT: **FICTION**

SAMPLE STRATEGY	WHAT TEXT LEVELS IS IT BEST FOR?	WHY?
Character: Look at a character's face in the picture. Notice how the character is feeling. Name the feeling.	J–O	At Levels P and above, frequent illustrations of characters inside the story are rare. At higher levels, students will need to infer character feelings based on descriptions in the text and will need to visualize the character's facial expressions rather than rely on an illustration.
Character: Think of what problems the character is dealing with internally, that can't be seen. Notice how the character feels in response to those problems, and what they are doing to solve the problems.	N–W	In levels up to M, characters tend to be dealing with a clear, *external* problem (e.g., a hat that won't fit, a kite that won't fly, solving the mystery of the missing key). Although characters do have feelings, their internal struggles aren't as developed as you'll find in books at Level N and above.
Themes and Ideas: Reread the last sentence or two in the story. Notice what the character learns. Think about what you can learn.	J–M	In texts at Levels J–M, the stories often are wrapped up with a brief lesson at the very end. With little inference required, a reader should be able to figure out a lesson. At higher levels, students will often need to read the final chapter and think about the main struggles of the character to infer a theme. Also, at higher levels, there are often multiple themes to consider.
Themes and Ideas: Notice when an object is repeated in the text. Think about what idea it might represent. Consider how it connects to something in the story—a character, setting, central problem, and so on.	Q–W	Concrete objects start to represent abstract ideas in Levels Q and above. Although a reader could infer a deeper symbolic meaning of Toad's hat in *Days with Frog and Toad,* I wouldn't teach it to a child reading a text at that level.

SAMPLE STRATEGIES ALIGNED TO LEVELS OF TEXT: **NONFICTION**

SAMPLE STRATEGY	WHAT TEXT LEVELS IS IT BEST FOR?	WHY?
Main Idea: Scan the table of contents, and notice the topics and subtopics the book will be covering. Think about what each section—as well as the whole book—is mostly about.	J–W	As long as the book has a table of contents, this will be helpful.
Main Idea: Point around the page, saying what each text feature is teaching you. Put all the information together to say what the page is mostly about.	M–W	Below Level M, readers are likely to read nonfiction texts that are set up with main text and a single illustration or photograph on the page. This isn't always true, and there are certainly texts at higher levels that follow the text-plus-photo layout (see, for example, most books by Seymour Simon).
Key Details: Notice when an author includes a fact meant to shock, amaze, or entertain you. Think, "Is this fact central to what the section is mostly about, or is it extra information meant to help engage me as a reader?"	M–W	In lower-level texts, most of the facts will fit cohesively with the main idea or main topic on the page. At higher levels, with busier pages, you will start to notice facts that feel more ancillary to the main idea, though they are related to the topic.
Vocabulary: Separate the unknown word into a prefix, root, and/or suffix. Analyze each part, thinking of words you know that have similar parts and what those parts mean. Put the information together to figure out that word.	R–W	It is unlikely that students will have knowledge of Greek and Latin roots, or will have explored cognates in word study, before they are in fourth grade. I recommend saving this strategy for students reading on a fourth-grade level, around Level R.

What Research Says About Comprehension Instruction

 A student's academic progress throughout secondary school is profoundly shaped by the extent to which they understand what they read (Sweet and Snow 2003).

 Teachers who emphasize higher-order thinking and strategic approaches to comprehension processes promote greater reading growth (Taylor, Pearson, Peterson, and Rodriguez 2003).

 Choice, interesting texts, and strategy instruction yield readers who are highly strategic and comprehend more deeply (Guthrie, Wigfield, Barbosa, et al. 2004).

 Small groups and individual conferring make a difference. Students who work on comprehension strategies with teacher-student ratios of 1:1 or 1:3 outperformed those in a 1:10 group (Linan-Thompson and Hickman-Davis 2002).

 Interventions that accelerate reading development typically spend most of their time (two-thirds) on reading and rereading, rather than skill practice in isolation (Allington 2011b).

Using a Variety of Structures

Methods for Teaching Comprehension

Conferring individually or working with students in small groups of up to three is the best way to get to know readers and provide them with customized feedback (Linan-Thompson and Hickman-Davis 2002). However, with a class of twenty-five-plus students, you must deliver instruction using a variety of teaching methods and work with students in a variety of whole-class, small-group, and individual instruction. As you support students' goals, consider options from the menu on page 234, which lists the teaching structures I rely on most.

As a teacher of reading, it is less the case that I am trying to get children to arrive at a specific answer and more that I am trying to coach children into ways of thinking about texts.

STRUCTURE	GROUP SIZE	ESPECIALLY GOOD FOR
Interactive Read-Alouds	Whole class or small group	• Showing students how to orchestrate many strategies • Providing a lot of support for a new learning goal • Providing opportunities for readers to deepen comprehension through conversation • Supporting thoughtful annotating and note-taking
Video-Alouds	Small group or whole class	• Engaging students in reading a nontraditional "text" • Introducing new strategies • Providing a lot of support for a new learning goal
Minilessons	Whole class	• Introducing a strategy and inviting students to try it • Reteaching a strategy that is challenging students
Guided Reading	Small group of three or four students	• Giving students experience with texts at their instructional level • Supporting students who are emerging bilinguals • Supporting students with a new genre or text type
Partnership and Book-Club Conferences	Two to four students	• Holding students accountable for ongoing work around their goal • Helping students and their peers share and work collaboratively toward goals • Supporting students with conversation skills alongside their comprehension goal(s)
Small-Group Strategy Lessons	Small groups of two or three students	• Providing guided practice for students so they can transfer skills to independent reading • Teaching students who have a common goal • Holding students accountable for ongoing work around their goal
Close Reading	Small group or whole class	• Introducing a challenging text in a supportive forum in which students can learn comprehension strategies they can use when they read independently • Supporting thoughtful annotating and note-taking • Encouraging careful rereading
Research-Compliment-Teach Conferences	One student	• Checking in with an individual student to monitor progress with a strategy, skill, and/or goal • Holding a student accountable for ongoing work • Reteaching strategies or offering new strategies that support the goal

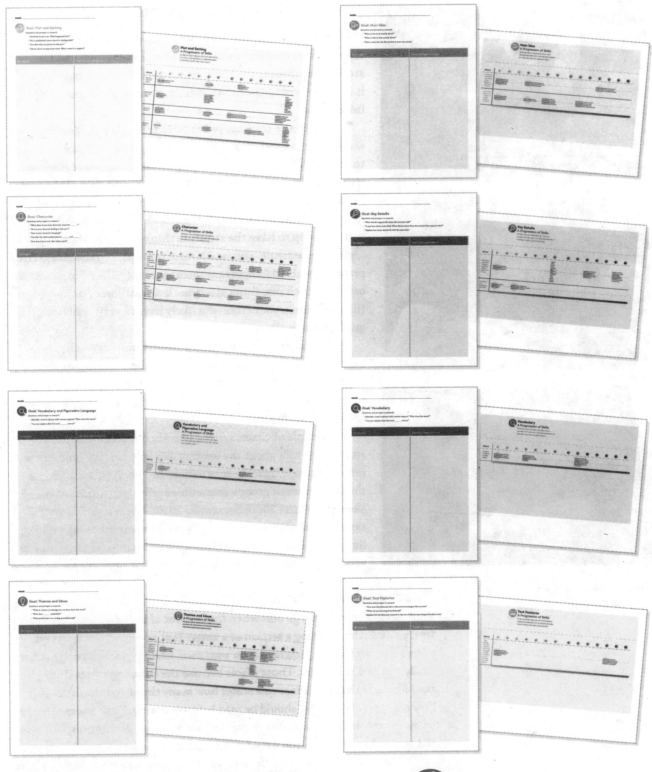

Note-taking forms that allow you to keep assessment questions and prompts, as well as the Progression of Skills handy as you teach are available for download at http://hein.pub/UTR.

Give readers a variety of ways to engage with text.

Interactive Read-Alouds

The interactive read-aloud provides an opportunity for you to share a text with the whole class or a small group and for students to discuss the piece. It is more than just "storytime"; it is true teaching time that, ideally, is carefully planned and intentional.

Before the reading, you will identify stopping points across the text and, during the reading, give students an opportunity to witness your thinking (via a think-aloud) or prompt them to stop and jot, turn and talk, or act out a part of the text. At these stopping points, you guide students in integrating many skills and strategies. For example, in a given read-aloud, you may stop to have the students think about character, determine a theme, and retell important parts of the story. This practice sends the important message that readers don't just do or think about one thing at a time. It also allows you to engage the students in your class who likely have a variety of goals in guided, whole-class practice.

Consider carving out about twenty minutes each day outside of reading workshop or independent reading time for a whole-class interactive read-aloud. You also may use the structure, in an abbreviated form, with a small group of readers for particular purposes.

A couple of times a week, provide opportunities for students to talk about the reading as a whole class (sometimes referred to as a "grand conversation" or "whole-class conversation") or in small groups (sometimes referred to as "read-aloud clubs") (Calkins 2000; Serravallo 2010). Meaningful conversation gives students a chance to work on their speaking and listening skills, to deepen their understandings of texts, and to engage in meaningful social interactions around books.

Read-Aloud Structure

Read-aloud lessons often go best when the amount of text read is finite. Therefore, you start by selecting a section of a longer text or one whole short text. After selecting the text, you read it on your own, finding places where you naturally respond as a reader. Those places become the stopping points during the read-aloud. No hard-and-fast rule states how many times you should stop or how many words or pages should be read before stopping. This process should be more organic. Such decisions should be based on your genuine responses to the text and on the goals you have for your group of readers.

There are a number of different types of prompts that encourage active thinking about and participation with the text.

Turn-and-Talk: Stop the reading and prompt students by thinking aloud briefly and asking a question. Students then turn and discuss their response with a partner. Students are often paired up at the start of the year and remain partners for a good portion of it.

Think-Aloud: Pause the reading and voice your thoughts about what's going on in the text. I try to make my think-alouds sound authentic, as if the thought just occurred to me in the moment of reading. The think-aloud provides a model for what students should be doing as they read.

Stop-and-Jot: This is like a turn-and-talk, except instead of talking with a partner, each reader jots their thinking in a reading notebook or on a sticky note.

Stop-and-Act: This is also like a turn-and-talk, except readers are prompted to act out a part of the text. Often the readers will assume the roles of characters and act out a part of the text to develop deeper understanding. They might even invent and act out their own scene inspired by the story and the characters' beliefs and behaviors.

Offering Guidance Through the Whole-Class Conversation

A couple of times a week, set aside some or all of your regularly scheduled read-aloud time for a whole-class conversation about the text read up to that point. You may need to guide these conversations heavily at first. You may need to ask students to sit in a circle, and you may have to coach them on their body language, the importance of facing the speaker, taking turns when talking, and gaining the floor respectfully. As time goes by, though, the need for such heavy guidance will fade, and students will embrace protocols naturally. They'll likely start initiating conversations, noticing when someone is trying to interject, and steering the conversation in new directions.

As you listen to your students talk, assess their comprehension work. Every word they say helps you gain insight into their thinking. Also, don't be afraid to stop the conversation to give students a strategy to use to continue or to deepen the discussion. You might also float around the outside of the circle, whispering into individual readers' ears, coaching and prompting them.

For more information about read-alouds:

The Art of Teaching Reading by Lucy Calkins

Talk About Understanding: Rethinking Classroom Talk to Enhance Comprehension by Ellin Oliver Keene

The Ultimate Read-Aloud Resource: Making Every Moment Intentional and Instructional With Best Friend Books by Lester Laminack

Comprehension Through Conversation by Maria Nichols

Teaching Talk: A Practical Guide to Fostering Student Thinking and Conversation by Kara Pranikoff

The Ramped-Up Read-Aloud: What to Notice as You Turn the Page by Maria Walther

Video-Alouds

The "video-aloud" is identical in purpose and form to the interactive read-aloud, except that students watch a video rather than listen to you read aloud a book or other text. Short clips—lasting no more than three to five minutes—are best because they allow for a lot of interaction with the "text" and don't require long stretches of passive viewing. I find that movie trailers work well because they often summarize a whole storyline in just a few minutes. Music videos that tell a story are good for the same reason. Taking excerpts from longer texts, such as your students' favorite TV shows or movies, is also a great option. For nonfiction texts, short documentaries like the Richard Attenborough series on the BBC are engaging and rich.

Video-Aloud Structure

The structure of a video-aloud is identical to an interactive read-aloud but with a different type of "text." Before you screen the video with your students, plan a number of stopping points to enable children to interact with the text and with one another. Consider noting time markers as you would page numbers in a book, and think about how you'll use turn-and-talk, stop-and-jot, think-aloud, and stop-and-act prompts to guide students' thinking. During and after the video, you can support student conversation about this audiovisual text.

For more information about supporting students with conversation:

The Art of Teaching Reading by Lucy Calkins

Minilessons for Literature Circles by Harvey "Smokey" Daniels and Nancy Steineke

Comprehension Through Conversation: The Power of Purposeful Talk in the Reading Workshop by Maria Nichols

Teaching Talk: A Practical Guide to Fostering Student Thinking and Conversation by Kara Pranikoff

The Reading Strategies Book: Your Everything Guide to Developing Skilled Readers by Jennifer Serravallo

Teaching Reading in Small Groups: Differentiated Instruction for Building Strategic, Independent Readers by Jennifer Serravallo

Minilessons

Minilessons are used consistently in reading workshop. Typically, at the beginning of workshop time, the entire class gathers for a brief lesson. During the lesson, you demonstrate a reading strategy that will help students handle a particular reading challenge and will lift the level of their work. The goal of each minilesson is not to give an assignment of the day but rather to offer students a strategy that will become a part of their ongoing reading repertoire. For this to happen, you should ground the lesson in the "why" or "when"—the context in which to use the skill or strategy. You should also give

students a brief opportunity to try the skill or strategy, assessing students' facility with it and making plans for follow-up instruction. Minilessons typically last around ten minutes (Calkins 2000; Calkins and Tolan 2010).

Minilesson Structure

You can find many structures for minilessons out there, but the one I find most helpful was developed by the Teachers College Reading and Writing Project and has been written about by Lucy Calkins (2000). This structure allows you to activate students' prior knowledge and incorporate today's strategy into their existing schema, to offer direct instruction and a brief opportunity for all learners to practice whatever it is you're teaching, and to provide a clear link to the readers' independent work.

Connect: Orient readers to the lesson. Ground the lesson in the larger context of a unit of study or a goal that the class has been working on for some time. You may offer an example of a student who has attempted the strategy or a brief anecdote or metaphor that relates to it.

Teach: Clearly and explicitly state the strategy and demonstrate it, using a text that is familiar to the whole class.

Actively Engage: Give all students an opportunity to practice the strategy, using a shared familiar text or students' independent reading books. You might do this by having them turn and talk to a partner. At other times, you might have them practice independently.

Link: Remind readers of the teaching point, and send them off to continue practicing independently.

For more information about minilessons:

The Art of Teaching Reading by Lucy Calkins

A Quick Guide to Making Your Teaching Stick, K-5 by Shanna Schwartz

Guided Reading

In a guided reading lesson, you work with a small group of students who are reading the same book at the same level and practice a strategy or strategies that you have determined they need, based on assessments (Fountas and Pinnell 2017b; Calkins 2017a; Richardson 2016). Provide support to students before, during, and after their reading of the text—a text that, typically, is just beyond their independent level of practice. The goal is to help students use and practice reading strategies in the guided reading text so that they can later apply them to their independent reading.

After you introduce a text and give students time to practice reading in a guided reading lesson, students can reread it during independent reading to increase fluency, accuracy, and comprehension. Over the course of the school year, students should be grouped and regrouped in a dynamic fashion, based on ongoing assessment and observation (Fountas and Pinnell 2017a). Each guided reading lesson usually lasts around twenty minutes.

Guided Reading Lesson Structure

Because the text used in a guided reading lesson will be slightly beyond what your students can read independently, a teacher's support is critical. Before the lesson begins, I introduce the book, keeping in mind, as suggested by Irene Fountas and Gay Su Pinnell, the possible supports and challenges within the text and the knowledge, experience, and background of the readers in the group (2017a). As students read aloud, listen in and interact with them to confirm they're applying the strategy well, redirect them if they're not, and/or teach them a new strategy. After the reading, discuss the text with the children and possibly offer an additional teaching point.

Book Introduction: Consider including one or more of the following: activating the readers' prior knowledge, frontloading main plot points, explaining challenging text elements, offering a question to focus the reading, and reviewing the meaning of hard-to-understand vocabulary or language.

Reading and Coaching: Have group members read silently and independently as you work with them, one by one. Typically, you have the child read aloud while assessing fluency and/or print strategies such as their use of meaning, syntax, or visual cues, accordingly. If a student is working on a comprehension goal, you may ask brief questions or prompt them to demonstrate thinking. Based on what you hear from each student, coach and prompt them to offer needed support. You may confirm or redirect what the child is doing or prompt them to try a new strategy.

Discussion and Teaching: After students have finished the entire text, and after you've had a chance to work with each group member individually at least once, engage all group members in a discussion of the text and/or encourage them to practice a new strategy.

Link to Independence: Suggest to students that they reread the guided reading book on their own to practice the strategy or strategies you offered during the lesson and to increase their accuracy, fluency, and comprehension.

A Note About Guided Reading with Chapter-Book Readers

When students start reading chapter books, I use guided reading only in rare instances. One instance is for students who are emerging bilinguals; they often benefit from guided reading because of the pre-teaching of vocabulary and language that can happen during the book introduction. Other times I might use chapter books for guided reading to introduce a new genre or to offer students discrete practice with a skill. In all cases, I select texts that are short.

If you want to support students as they read typical-length chapter books, you may instead choose to structure students in a book club and borrow aspects of a guided reading lesson, such as a short text introduction to support prior knowledge of content they'll encounter in the book, when you meet.

For more information about guided reading:

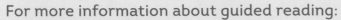

A Guide to the Reading Workshop: Primary Grades
by Lucy Calkins

Guided Reading: Responsive Teaching Across the Grades,
2nd edition by Irene Fountas and Gay Su Pinnell

The Next Step Forward in Guided Reading:
An Assess-Decide-Teach Framework for Supporting
Every Reader, Grades K–8 by Jan Richardson

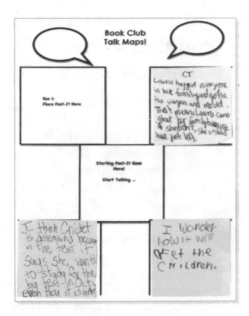

This "Talk Map" provides a concrete support for students during conversations. Tools such as this one can help them practice strategies for conversation you choose to teach.

Partnerships and Book-Club Conferences

Reading partnerships and book clubs, in which students read and talk about a common book, play an important role in the reading workshop. Allowing time for students to talk helps them rehearse and revise their ideas about books, practice with peers some behaviors they will use when reading independently, and develop communities around common texts. When children talk, their thinking becomes visible. So, during partnerships and book clubs, listen closely to ensure that your readers get the most out of the experiences—and then teach strategies to improve speaking and listening skills, and/or comprehension, as you see fit.

A partnership or book club is also a ready-made small group! After you teach individual readers a strategy, they can support one another over time as they continue to practice it in a variety of contexts, including partnerships and book clubs.

Structure of a Conference to Teach into Partnerships and Book Clubs

This type of conference—the kind that teaches into readers' talk—usually lasts about five minutes. Five minutes for each group of two to four students means you will be able to check in with and support many students in a short amount of time. When all students are partnered or grouped, working together independently, move around the classroom, stopping briefly at each partnership or group to assess, and then guide students toward deeper comprehension.

Research: Begin by listening in for comprehension and conversational skills that surface in the talk.

Decide: Select a strategy to teach—either comprehension- or conversation-based—and a method for teaching it.

Compliment: Reinforce the behavior or strategy you've noticed students doing or using, explain why it's helpful, and encourage them to continue doing or using it.

Teach: Offer students a new strategy to try. Explain the strategy in a step-by-step way.

Coach: Stick around to coach them as they try it briefly.

Link: After some practice, reiterate the strategy you coached the students to practice, and remind students to keep practicing.

For more information about conferring during conversation:

The Art of Teaching Reading by Lucy Calkins

Comprehension Through Conversation by Maria Nichols

Teaching Talk by Kara Pranikoff

A Teacher's Guide to Reading Conferences by Jennifer Serravallo

Teaching Reading in Small Groups by Jennifer Serravallo

Small-Group Strategy Lessons

For a small-group strategy lesson, you identify a few students who would benefit from the same instruction. If strategy lessons are formed wisely, they save time because you can meet with several children at once for under ten minutes, as opposed to individual children in conferences of about five minutes each. That kind of efficiency benefits you and the students, and it lets them know that there are others practicing the same strategy (Serravallo 2010; Calkins 2000).

Strategy-Lesson Structure

Typically, the strategy lesson starts with an explanation of why you've brought the children together. At this time you can also compliment students on some habit or behavior you've noticed that you want them to continue. From there, tell students clearly and explicitly what they should practice. Sometimes you will demonstrate the teaching point for the group and then have students try it in their own books, as you coach. Sometimes you will practice the

strategy together on a shared text before students try it on their own. Other times you will just have the children jump right into their books and try it. Keep in mind that most of the lesson time should be devoted to students' practice in their own books, as you guide them. All students should be working simultaneously as you move among them, prompting and coaching and supporting, like a circus plate-spinner who keeps all the plates in the air by not lingering too long with any one. This practice time is essential in helping students transfer previously taught strategies into their own reading (Serravallo 2010).

Connect: Tell students why you've brought them together, then name a common strength.

Teach: State the strategy they'll be practicing with you. If they need it, you might offer a brief demonstration, allow time for shared practice, or give an example or an explanation of the strategy.

Coach: Coach students one at a time as they practice the strategy using their own self-selected independent reading books. You may offer a shared text in addition to or instead of their own books.

Link: Invite students to continue working independently, applying and reapplying the strategy in a variety of texts.

For more information about strategy lessons:

The Art of Teaching Reading by Lucy Calkins

Teaching Reading in Small Groups: Differentiated Instruction for Building Strategic, Independent Readers by Jennifer Serravallo

A Teacher's Guide to Reading Conferences by Jennifer Serravallo

Close Reading

In a well-crafted close reading lesson, I guide students through a careful and deliberate examination of the text details. I explain strategies clearly and demonstrate how to use them while reading so that students may transfer them to their own reading as needed. The purposeful questions I ask will, ideally, help foster rigorous reading, high-level thinking, and deep engagement with the text, awakening and affirming in students an inquisitive stance as they read. This showcases the types of questions a student can ask themselves to arrive at deeper comprehension.

The approach I use during a lesson on close reading is not one you would want readers to follow every time they read. Reading would become slow, laborious, and tedious. Instead, encourage students to use it on texts that are particularly interesting, surprising, or even confusing. Have them slow down, analyze, and read with extreme care and caution.

Short, complex texts that are rich with possible layers of meaning are best for close reading lessons. Therefore, careful text selection is crucial. When conducting small-group or whole-class lessons, choose a self-contained text or an excerpt from a longer text that is around 800 words and on one or two pages. This length of text will allow students to read slowly and carefully and to revisit the text as necessary to comprehend it fully, without becoming bored. Before the lesson, come up with questions that will prompt deep discussion about the text—not questions that elicit "guess-what-I'm-thinking" answers. Expect and encourage conversation among students, not just between you and a student or students.

Questions to Elicit Deep Thinking During Close Reading Lessons

USE OPEN-ENDED QUESTIONS TO PROMPT DISCUSSION, SUCH AS:	AVOID QUESTIONS WITH A CLEAR, SINGLE ANSWER, SUCH AS:
• The story is set in ____. Why is that important? • The text says ____. What are your thoughts about the character? • Why would the author have chosen the word ____ here? • How does this author note add to what you've learned in this book? • What is the perspective of this author on this topic? How can you tell? • What real-world issue is showing up in this book?	• What are three things Mrs. Mackle likes to do? • What details prove that Herbie is a good friend? • Who is the author of this text? • List three things you learned from reading this text. • How many . . . ? • Who is . . . ? • What is . . . ? • Where is . . . ?

Close Reading Lesson Structure

Because the text used for a close reading lesson may be above the level at which some or most students in the class can read with independence, you play a crucial role. You must, for example, support students in determining where to stop and think and what to stop and think about, which allows students to understand and practice more than they would if attempting the work on their own. As mentioned earlier, questioning while reading and rereading is one of the most important hallmarks of the close reading lesson. What follows is a possible structure for the lesson (Beers and Probst 2012). You may notice that this is similar to an interactive read-aloud, with four important differences.

1. The text is highly visible to all.

2. The teacher plans many more stopping places.

3. The text is very short.

4. Rereading is very common.

Introduce a Technique, Tip, or Concept: As in a minilesson, if you tell students what they will be learning about before they practice it, they are more likely to remember it and reapply it to their independent reading. Therefore, explain to them that this lesson is less about *this text* than about *how you might approach any text*. In your introduction, in addition to that explanation, you can give an example or even do a very brief demonstration.

Apply: Read together from an enlarged copy of a text by displaying it using a digital projection system or transposing the text onto a chart. While you may be tempted to just give each student his or her own copy, try to resist— it can lead to disengagement or distraction, because some students read ahead or focus on a portion of the text other than the one being discussed. Model your thinking and pose questions to help students analyze the text. Alternate between partner turn-and-talk, small-group discussion, and whole-class discussion.

Review: Reinforce the tip(s) and technique(s) you applied so that students may transfer them to their independent reading.

For more information about close reading:

Notice & Note: Strategies for Close Reading
  by Kylene Beers and Robert E. Probst

Reading Nonfiction: Notice & Note Stances, Signposts, and Strategies by Kylene Beers and Robert E. Probst

Text Complexity: Raising Rigor in Reading
  by Doug Fisher, Nancy Frey, and Diane Lapp

Falling in Love with Close Reading: Lessons for Analyzing Text–and Life by Christopher Lehman and Kate Roberts

The Reader, the Text, the Poem: The Transactional Theory of the Literary Work by Louise Rosenblatt

Research-Compliment-Teach Conferences

A conference is a valuable teaching opportunity. During independent reading, when every child is reading self-selected books at their independent level, make your way around the classroom, briefly meeting each student. The goal is to reinforce skills that a reader has already acquired and to teach or reteach a strategy that will help the reader work toward their goal. Unlike in a goal-setting conference, in a research-compliment-teach conference you provide follow-up instruction for a goal that has already been established. The conference is not about teaching the meaning or content of a specific book; it is about supporting the reader with strategies as they work toward their goal. This type of reading conference tends to last about five minutes (Serravallo 2019).

Research-Compliment-Teach Conference Structure

Consider following a predictable structure to keep conferences short and explicit (Calkins 2000; Calkins 2017a; Calkins 2017b; Serravallo 2019). The following is a conference structure that has worked well for me to identify how students are doing with their goals, identify strengths, and teach a new strategy that builds on that strength.

Research: Ask questions about the child's reading, and/or observe and listen to the child read. Research with the student's goal in mind.

Decide: Considering the student's goal and what the child is able to do, decide on something to reinforce (which later becomes the compliment) and something to introduce (which becomes the strategy you teach).

Compliment: Explicitly name something the student is mastering. Try to express the strength as a procedure ("I notice you're thinking about the text and the features to come up with the main idea") rather than product ("That's a great idea!") so that it's replicable.

Teach: Name a strategy. If the student needs support, you may choose to demonstrate quickly. Try to keep this brief, so that you give ample time for the student to practice.

Coach: Provide feedback as the child tries the strategy. Take notes on what you observe.

Link: Repeat what you've done together, and promise to follow up soon.

For more information about individual conferences:

Conferring: The Keystone of Reader's Workshop
   by Patrick Allen

A Teacher's Guide to Reading Conferences
   by Jennifer Serravallo

The Art of Teaching Reading by Lucy Calkins

Conclusion

THE ALCHEMY OF READING

I n 1996, Irene Fountas and Gay Su Pinnell published their seminal *Guided Reading: Good First Teaching for All Children*. More than twenty years later, revisiting the book is an eye-opener. In some ways, it seems to me, we've come full circle. The authors write

A gradient of text is not a precise sequence of texts through which all children pass. . . . The teacher who recognizes the convenience of the gradient yet reminds herself of its limitations will be able to make cautious choices and test her decisions against children's behavior while reading each text. (1996, 113)

Clearly, the gradient is a tool; it is a guide—one consideration among many as you work to match your students with text that will help ensure their reading success.

Effective reading instruction may have more in common with alchemy than mechanics. In other words, teaching reading isn't a process of precise mechanization and getting all the right components to sync up just so. In every reading engagement, multiple variables come together. Certainly the reader-text match is important; so, too, are the teacher's depth of knowledge and ability to teach children.

Still, the more we become aware of all the individual elements—the goals and skills and the assessing, evaluating, and teaching dynamic—and do our best to thoughtfully consider them all as we bring them together in the service of our students, the more likely we are to develop students who can read, want to read, and do read—with confidence, skill, and delight. Reading is truly one of life's greatest pleasures. Let's never lose sight of that as we help our students discover their own magical independent reading journeys.

As Dick Allington (2005) once wrote, "In the end, no matter what procedure is used to attempt to put more appropriate books into the hands of students, it comes down to each kid and each book" (52). And that gets to the heart of our professional responsibility—to understand every text we use in our classrooms and every reader under our care.

Professional Resources

Afflerbach, P. 1990. "The Influence of Prior Knowledge and Text Genre on Readers' Prediction Strategies." *Journal of Literary Research* 22 (2).

Afflerbach, P., and P. Johnston. 1986. "What Do Expert Readers Do When the Main Idea Is Not Explicit?" In *Teaching Main Idea Comprehension*, edited by J. F. Baumann. Newark, DE: International Reading Association.

Afflerbach, P., P. D. Pearson, and S. G. Paris. 2008. "Clarifying Differences Between Reading Skills and Reading Strategies." *The Reading Teacher* (61) 5.

Allen, P. 2009. *Conferring: The Keystone of Reader's Workshop.* Portland, ME: Stenhouse.

Allington, R. L. 2000, 2005, 2011a. *What Really Matters for Struggling Readers: Designing Research-Based Programs* (1st, 2nd, and 3rd eds.). New York: Pearson.

———. 2011b. "Research on Reading/Learning Disability Interventions." In *What Research Has to Say About Reading Instruction*, 4th ed., edited by S. J. Samuels and A. E. Farstrup, 236–265. Newark, DE: International Reading Association.

Allington, R. L., and R. E. Gabriel. 2012. "Every Child, Every Day." *Educational Leadership* 69 (6).

Anderson, R. C., and P. D. Pearson. 1984. "A Schema-Theoretic View of Basic Processes in Reading." In *Handbook of Reading Research*, edited by P. D. Pearson. New York: Longman.

Atwell, N. 2007. *The Reading Zone: How to Help Kids Become Skilled, Passionate, Habitual, Critical Readers.* New York: Scholastic.

Baumann, J. F., and E. J. Kame'enui. 1991. "Research on Vocabulary Instruction: Ode to Voltaire." In *Handbook of Research on Teaching the English Language Arts*, edited by J. Flood, J. M. Jensen, D. Lapp, and J. R. Squire. New York: Macmillan.

Baumann, J. F., E. J. Kame'enui, and G. E. Ash. 2003. "Research on Vocabulary Instruction: Voltaire Redux." In *Handbook of Research on Teaching the English Language Arts*, edited by J. Flood, D. Lapp, J. R. Squire, and J. M. Jensen. Mahwah, NJ: Lawrence Erlbaum Associates.

Beaver, J. 2002. *Developmental Reading Assessment.* New York: Pearson.

Beaver, J., and M. Carter. 2006. *Developmental Reading Assessment*, Second Edition. New York: Pearson.

Beck, I. L., M. G. McKeown, and L. Kucan. 2002. *Bringing Words to Life: Robust Vocabulary Instruction.* New York: Guilford.

Becker, W. C. 1977. "Teaching Reading and Language to the Disadvantaged—What We Have Learned from Field Research." *Harvard Educational Review.* 47: 518–43.

Beers, K. 2002. *When Kids Can't Read: What Teachers Can Do.* Portsmouth, NH: Heinemann.

———. 2017. @KyleneBeers, Twitter, October 17, 2017.

Beers, K., and R. E. Probst. 2012. *Notice & Note: Strategies for Close Reading.* Portsmouth, NH: Heinemann.

———. 2016. *Reading Nonfiction: Notice & Note Stances, Signposts, and Strategies.* Portsmouth, NH: Heinemann.

Betts, E. A. 1946. *Foundations of Reading Instruction with Emphasis on Differentiated Guidance.* New York: American Book Company.

Bishop, R. S. 1990. "Mirrors, Windows, and Sliding Glass Doors." *Perspectives: Choosing and Using Books for the Classroom.* 6 (3) Summer.

Botelho, M. J., and M. K. Rudman. 2009. *Critical Multicultural Analysis of Children's Literature: Mirrors, Windows, and Doors.* London: Routledge.

Burroway, J. 2006. *Writing Fiction: A Guide to Narrative Craft.* New York: Longman.

Calkins, L. M. 2000. *The Art of Teaching Reading.* New York: Pearson.

———. 2017a. *A Guide to the Reading Workshop: Primary Grades.* Portsmouth, NH: Heinemann.

———. 2017b. *A Guide to the Reading Workshop: Intermediate Grades.* Portsmouth, NH: Heinemann.

Calkins, L. M., and M. Ehrenworth. 2017. *A Guide to the Reading Workshop: Middle School Grades.* Portsmouth, NH: Heinemann.

Calkins, L. M., and K. Tolan. 2010. *Following Characters into Meaning.* In *Units of Study for Teaching Reading, Grades 3–5* by L.M. Calkins and colleagues. Portsmouth, NH: Heinemann.

———. 2015. *Building a Reading Life.* In *Units of Study for Teaching Reading, Grade 3: A Workshop Curriculum* by L. M. Calkins and colleagues. Portsmouth, NH: Heinemann.

Cappellini, M. 2004. *Balancing Reading & Language Learning: A Resource for Teaching English Language Learners, K–5.* Portland, ME: Stenhouse.

Carretti, B., N. Caldarola, C. Tencati, and C. Cornoldi. 2014. "Improving Reading Comprehension in Reading and Listening Settings: The Effect of Two Training Programmes Focusing on Metacognition and Working Memory." *British Journal of Educational Psychology* 84 (2).

Carver, R. P. 1994. "Percentage of Unknown Vocabulary Words in Text as a Function of the Relative Difficulty of the Text: Implications for Instruction." *Journal of Reading Behavior* 26: 413–37.

Cazden, C. B. 1988. *Classroom Discourse: The Language of Teaching and Learning.* Portsmouth, NH: Heinemann.

Clay, M. 1994. *Reading Recovery: A Guidebook for Teachers in Training.* Portsmouth, NH: Heinemann.

———. 2000. *Running Records for Classroom Teachers.* Portsmouth, NH: Heinemann.

Coleman, D., and S. Pimental. 2012. "Revised Publisher's Criteria for the Common Core State Standards in English Language Arts and Literacy, Grades 3–12." www.corestandards.org/assets/Publishers_Criteria_ for_3-12.pdf.

Csikszentmihalyi, M. 1991. "Literacy and Intrinsic Motivation." In *Literacy*, edited by S. R. Graubard, 115–40. New York: Noonday.

Cullinan, B., and S. Fitzgerald. 1984–1985. "Background Information Bulletin on the Use of Readability Formula." *Reading Today* 2 (3).

Cummins, J. 2008. "BICS and CALP: Empirical and Theoretical Status of the Distinction." *Encyclopedia of Language and Education*, 2nd ed., edited by B. Street, and N. H. Hornberger, 71–83. New York: Springer Science + Business Media LLC.

Daniels, H. S., and S. K. Ahmed. 2014. *Upstanders: How to Engage Middle School Hearts and Minds with Inquiry.* Portsmouth, NH: Heinemann.

Daniels, H. S., and N. Steineke. 2004. *Minilessons for Literature Circles*. Portsmouth, NH: Heinemann.

Dale, E., and J. S. Chall. 1948. "A Formula for Predicting Readability." *Educational Research Bulletin* 27: 11–20, 37–54.

DeFord, D., and A. Klein. 2008. "Teacher Decision Making Is the Key to Choosing Among Leveled Books and Going Beyond." In *Beyond Leveled Books: Supporting Early and Transitional Readers in Grades K–5*, edited by K. Szymusiak, F. Sibberson, and L. Koch. Portland, ME: Stenhouse.

DeFord, D. E., C. A. Lyons, and G. S. Pinnell. 1991. *Bridges to Literacy: Learning from Reading Recovery*. Portsmouth, NH: Heinemann.

Derman-Sparks, L. "Guide for Selecting Anti-Bias Children's Books." https://socialjusticebooks.org/guide-for-selecting-anti-bias-childrens-books/.

Duffy, G. G., L. R. Roehler, E. Sivan, G. Rackliffe, C. Book, M. S. Meloth, and D. Bassiri. 1987. "Effects of Explaining the Reasoning Associated with Using Reading Strategies." *Reading Research Quarterly* 22: 347–68.

Duke, N. K., and V. S. Bennett-Armistead. 2003. *Reading and Writing Informational Texts in the Primary Grades*. New York: Scholastic.

Dzaldov, B. S, and S. Peterson. 2005. "Book Leveling and Readers." *The Reading Teacher* 53 (3): 222–29.

Ebe, A. 2011. "Culturally Relevant Texts and Reading Assessment for English Language Learners." *Reading Horizons* 50 (3).

Ernst-Slavit, G., and M. Mason. 2014. "Making Your First ELL Home Visit: A Guide for Classroom Teachers." ¡Colorín Colorado! www.colorincolorado.org/article/making-your-first-ell-home-visit-guide-classroom-teachers.

Fall, R., N. M. Webb, and N. Chudowsky. 2000. "Group Discussion and Large-Scale Language Arts Assessment: Effects on Students' Comprehension." *American Educational Research Journal* 37 (4): 911–41.

Fisher, D., N. Frey, and D. Lapp. 2012. *Text Complexity: Raising Rigor in Reading*. Newark, DE: International Reading Association.

Forster, E. M. 1927. *Aspects of the Novel*. London: Edward Arnold Publishers.

Fountas, I. C., and G. S. Pinnell. 1996. *Guided Reading: Good First Teaching for All Children*. Portsmouth, NH: Heinemann.

———. 1999. *Matching Books to Readers: Using Leveled Books in Guided Reading, K–3*. Portsmouth, NH: Heinemann.

———. 2005. *Leveled Books, K–8: Matching Texts to Readers for Effective Teaching*. Portsmouth, NH: Heinemann.

———. 2007a. *The Continuum of Literacy Learning, Grades 3–8: A Guide to Teaching*. Portsmouth, NH: Heinemann.

———. 2007b. *Benchmark Assessment System*. Portsmouth, NH: Heinemann.

———. 2010. *The Fountas & Pinnell Leveled Book List, K–8+: 2010–2012 Edition*. Portsmouth, NH: Heinemann.

———. 2016. "A Level is a Teacher's Tool, NOT a Child's Label." http://blog.fountasandpinnell.com/post/a-level-is-a-teacher-s-tool-not-a-child-s-label.

———. 2017a. *Guided Reading: Responsive Teaching Across the Grades*, 2nd ed. Portsmouth, NH: Heinemann.

———. 2017b. *The Fountas & Pinnell Literacy Continuum, Expanded Edition: A Tool for Assessment, Planning, and Teaching, PreK–8*. Portsmouth, NH: Heinemann.

Freeman, D., Y. Freeman, M. Soto, and M. Ebe. 2016. *ESL Teaching: Principles for Success*. Portsmouth, NH: Heinemann.

Freytag, G. 1894. *Technique of the Drama*. Chicago: S. C. Griggs & Company.

Gibbons, P. 1993. *Learning to Learn in a Second Language*. Portsmouth, NH: Heinemann.

———. 2014. *Scaffolding Language, Scaffolding Learning: Teaching English Language Learners in the Mainstream Classroom*, 2nd ed. Portsmouth, NH: Heinemann.

Glasswell, K., and M. P. Ford. 2010. "Teaching Flexibly with Leveled Texts: More Power for Your Reading Block." *The Reading Teacher* 64 (1): 57–60.

Goodman, Y., and G. Owocki. 2002. *Kidwatching: Documenting Children's Literacy Development*. Portsmouth, NH: Heinemann.

Goodman, Y. M., D. J. Watson, and C. Burke. 1987. *Reading Miscue Inventory: Alternative Procedures*. New York: R.C. Owen Publishers.

Goodman, Y. M., D. J. Watson, and C. L. Burke. 2005. *Reading Miscue Inventory: From Evaluation to Instruction*. Katonah, NY: Richard C. Owens Publishers, Inc.

Gordon, C. J., and P. D. Pearson. 1983. "The Effects of Instruction in Metacomprehension and Inferencing on Children's Comprehension Abilities" (Technical Report No. 227). Urbana, IL: University of Illinois Center for the Study of Reading

Gourley, J. W. 1984. "Discourse Structure: Expectations of Beginning Readers and Readability of Text." *Journal of Reading Behavior* 16: 169–88.

Graham, S., and M. Hebert. 2010. "Writing to Read: A Meta-Analysis of the Impact of Writing and Writing Instruction on Reading." *Harvard Educational Review* 81 (4): 710–44.

Guthrie, J. 2008. *Engaging Adolescents in Reading*. Thousand Oaks, CA: Corwin Press.

Guthrie, J., and N. Humenick. 2004. "Motivating Students to Read: Evidence for Classroom Practices That Increase Motivation and Achievement." In *The Voice of Evidence in Reading Research*, edited by P. McCardle and V. Chhabra. Baltimore: Paul Brookes.

Guthrie, J., K. McGough, L. Bennett, and M. E. Rice. 1996. "Concept-Oriented Reading Instruction: An Integrated Curriculum to Develop Motivations and Strategies for Reading." In *Developing Engaged Readers in School and Home Communities*, edited by L. Baker, P. Afflerbach, and D. Reinking, 165–90. Hillsdale, NJ: Erlbaum.

Guthrie, J., A. Wigfield, P. Barbosa, K. Perencevich, A. Taboada, M. Davis, N. Scafiddi, and S. Tonks. 2004. "Increasing Reading Comprehension and Engagement Through Concept-Oriented Reading Instruction." *Journal of Educational Psychology* 96 (3): 403–23.

Hammond, W. D., and D. Nessel. 2011. *The Comprehension Experience*. Portsmouth, NH: Heinemann.

Hansen, J. 1981. "The Effects of Interference Training and Practice on Young Children's Reading Comprehension." *Reading Research Quarterly* 16: 391–417.

Harris, A. J., and E. Sipay. 1990. *How to Increase Reading Ability*, 10th ed. White Plains, NY: Longman.

Harvey, S. 1997. *Nonfiction Matters: Reading, Writing, and Research in Grades 3–8*. Portland, ME: Stenhouse.

Harvey, S., and A. Goudvis. 2000. *Strategies That Work: Teaching Comprehension for Understanding and Engagement*. Portland, ME: Stenhouse.

Hattie, J. 2008. *Visible Learning: A Synthesis of Over 800 Meta-Analyses Relating to Achievement*. London: Routledge.

Heard, G. 2016. *Heart Maps: Helping Students Create and Craft Authentic Writing*. Portsmouth, NH: Heinemann.

Hiebert, E. H. 2011. "Using Multiple Sources of Information in Establishing Text Complexity." *Reading Research Report,* no. 11.03. Santa Cruz, CA: Text Project and University of California, Santa Cruz. http://textproject.org/library /reading-research-report/a-case-for-using-multiple-sources-of-information -in-establishing-text-complexity/.

Hiebert, E., and P. D. Pearson. 2014. "Qualitative Analysis of Text Complexity." *The Elementary School Journal* 115 (2).

Hu, H., and P. Nation. 2000. "Unknown Vocabulary Density and Reading Comprehension." *Reading in a Foreign Language* 13 (1): 403–30.

Hunter, P. 2012. *It's Not Complicated: What I Know for Sure About Helping Students of Color Become Successful Readers.* New York: Scholastic.

Ivey, G., and K. Broaddus. 2001. "Just Plain Reading: A Survey of What Makes Students Want to Read in Middle School Classrooms." *Reading Research Quarterly* 36: 350–77.

Jitendra, A. K., M. K. Hoppes, and Y. P. Xin. 2000. "Enhancing Main Idea Comprehension for Students with Learning Problems: The Role of a Summarization Strategy and Self-Monitoring Instruction." *The Journal of Special Education* 34: 127–39.

Keene, E. O. 2012. *Talk About Understanding: Rethinking Classroom Talk to Enhance Comprehension.* Portsmouth, NH: Heinemann.

Keene, E., and S. Zimmermann. 1997. *Mosaic of Thought: Teaching Comprehension in a Reader's Workshop.* Portsmouth, NH: Heinemann.

Kintsch, W. 2004. "The Construction-Integration Model of Text Comprehension and Its Implications for Instruction." In *Theoretical Models and Processes of Reading,* 5th ed., edited by R. Ruddell, and N. Unrau. Newark, DE: International Reading Association.

Kragler, S., and C. Nolley. 1996. "Student Choices: Book Selection Strategies of Fourth Graders." *Reading Horizons* 36 (4): 354–65.

Krashen, S. 2004. *The Power of Reading: Insights from the Research.* Portsmouth, NH: Heinemann.

Kuhn, D. 2007. "Is Direct Instruction an Answer to the Right Question?" *Educational Psychologist* 42 (2): 109–13.

Laminack, L. 2016. *The Ultimate Read-Aloud Resource.* New York: Scholastic.

Laufer, B. 1988. "What Percentage of Text-Lexis Is Essential for Comprehension?" In *Special Language: From Humans to Thinking Machines*, edited by C. Lauren and M. Nordman. Bristol, UK: Multilingual Matters.

Lehman, C. and K. Roberts. 2013. *Falling in Love with Close Reading: Lessons for Analyzing Text—and Life.* Portsmouth, NH: Heinemann.

Lifshitz, J. 2016. "Having Students Analyze Our Classroom Library To See How Diverse It Is." https://crawlingoutoftheclassroom.wordpress.com/2016/05 /07/having-students-analyze-our-classroom-library-to-see-how-diverse -it-is/.

Linan-Thompson, S., and P. Hickman-Davis. 2002. "Supplemental Reading Instruction for Students at Risk for Reading Disabilities: Improve Reading 30 Minutes at a Time." *Learning Disabilities: Research & Practice* 17 (4): 242–51.

Lynch-Brown, C., and C. M. Tomlinson. 1993. *Essentials of Children's Literature.* Boston: Pearson.

Miller, D. 2002. *Reading with Meaning: Teaching Comprehension in the Primary Grades.* Portland, ME: Stenhouse.

———. 2009. *The Book Whisperer: Awakening the Inner Reader in Every Child.* San Francisco: Jossey-Bass.

———. 2017. "On the Level." https://nerdybookclub.wordpress.com/2017/10/15/on-the-level-by-donalyn-miller/.

Miller, D., and B. Moss. 2013. *No More Independent Reading Without Support*. Portsmouth, NH: Heinemann.

Miller, G. A. 1999. "On Knowing a Word." *Annual Review of Psychology* 50: 1–19.

Mooney, M. E. 2004. *A Book Is a Present: Selecting Text for Intentional Teaching*. Katonah, NY: Richard C. Owens Publishers.

Moss, B., and T. A. Young. 2010. *Creating Lifelong Readers Through Independent Reading*. Newark, DE: International Reading Association.

Mulligan, T., and C. Landrigan. 2018. *It's All About the Books: How to Create Bookrooms and Classroom Libraries That Inspire Readers*. Portsmouth, NH: Heinemann.

Nagy, W. E., R. C. Anderson, and P. A. Herman, P. A. 1987. "Learning Word Meanings from Context During Normal Reading." *American Educational Research Journal* 24: 237–70.

National Governors Association Center for Best Practices, Council of Chief State School Officers. 2010. *Common Core State Standards*. Washington, DC: National Governors Association Center for Best Practices, Council of Chief State School Officers.

Nichols, Maria. 2006. *Comprehension Through Conversation: The Power of Purposeful Talk in the Reading Workshop*. Portsmouth, NH: Heinemann.

Paris, S. G., D. R. Cross, and M. Y. Lipson. 1984. "Informed Strategies for Learning: A Program to Improve Children's Reading Awareness and Comprehension." *Journal of Educational Psychology* 76: 1239–52.

Peterson, B. 1991, 2001. *Literary Pathways: Selecting Books to Support New Readers*. Portsmouth, NH: Heinemann.

Pink, D. H. 2011. *Drive: The Surprising Truth About What Motivates Us*. New York: Riverhead Books.

Pinnell, G. S., D. E. DeFord, and C. A. Lyons. 1988. *Reading Recovery: Early Intervention for At-Risk First Graders*. Arlington, VA: Education Research Services.

Pranikoff, K. 2017. *Teaching Talk: A Practical Guide to Fostering Student Thinking and Conversation*. Portsmouth, NH: Heinemann.

Rasinski, T. 2003. *The Fluent Reader: Oral Reading Strategies for Building Word Recognition, Fluency, and Comprehension*. NY: Scholastic.

Reis, S. M., D. B. McCoach, M. Coyne, F. J. Schreiber, R. D. Eckert, and E. J. Gubbins. 2007. "Using Planned Enrichment Strategies with Direct Instruction to Improve Reading Fluency, Comprehension, and Attitude Toward Reading: An Evidence-Based Study." *Elementary School Journal* 108 (1): 3–24.

Reutzel, D. R., and P. C. Fawson, 2002. *Your Classroom Library—Giving It More Teaching Power: Research-Based Strategies for Developing Better Readers and Writers*. New York: Scholastic.

Rhodes, L. K. 1979. "Comprehension and Predictability: An Analysis of Beginning Reading Materials." In *New Perspectives on Comprehension: Monographs in Language and Learning*, no. 3, edited by J. C. Harste and R. F. Carey.

Richardson, J. 2016. *The Next Step Forward in Guided Reading*. New York: Scholastic.

Ripp, P. 2017. "When We Make a Child a Level." https://pernillesripp.com/2017/08/28/when-we-make-a-child-a-level/.

Rosenblatt, L. 1978. *The Reader, the Text, the Poem: A Transactional Theory of the Literary Work*. Carbondale, IL: Southern Illinois University Press.

Rupley, W. H., J. W. Logan, and W. D. Nichols. 1998–1999. "Vocabulary Instruction in a Balanced Reading Program." *The Reading Teacher* 52 (4).

St. Catherine University. *Research on Diversity in Youth Literature*. https://sophia
.stkate.edu/rdyl.

Santman, D. 2005. *Shades of Meaning: Comprehension and Interpretation in Middle
School*. Portsmouth, NH: Heinemann.

Schwanenflugel, P., and N. F. Knapp. 2017. "Three Myths About 'Reading Levels'."
www.psychologytoday.com/us/blog/reading-minds/201702/three-myths
-about-reading-levels.

Schwartz, S. *A Quick Guide to Making Your Teaching Stick, K–5*. Portsmouth, NH:
Heinemann.

Sedita, J. 2005. "Effective Vocabulary Instruction." *Insights on Learning Disabilities*
2 (1): 33–45.

Serravallo, J. 2010. *Teaching Reading in Small Groups*. Portsmouth, NH: Heinemann.

———. 2013. *The Literacy Teacher's Playbook, Grades 3–6: Four Steps for Turning
Assessment Data into Goal-Directed Instruction*. Portsmouth, NH: Heinemann.

———. 2014. *The Literacy Teacher's Playbook, Grades K–2: Four Steps for Turning
Assessment Data into Goal-Directed Instruction*. Portsmouth, NH: Heinemann.

———. 2015. *The Reading Strategies Book: Your Everything Guide to Developing Skilled
Readers*. Portsmouth, NH: Heinemann.

———. 2019. *A Teacher's Guide to Reading Conferences, Grades K–8*. Portsmouth, NH:
Heinemann.

Sibberson, F., and K. Szymusiak. 2008. *Day-to-Day Assessment in the Reading
Workshop: Making Informed Instructional Decisions in Grades 3–6*. New York:
Scholastic.

Smith, N. B. 2002. *American Reading Instruction*. Newark, DE: International Reading
Association.

Souto-Manning, M., and J. Martell. 2016. *Reading, Writing, and Talk: Inclusive Teaching
Strategies for Diverse Learners, K–2*. New York: Teachers College Press.

Stanovich, K. E. 1986. "Matthew Effects in Reading: Some Consequences of
Individual Differences in the Acquisition of Literacy." *Reading Research
Quarterly* 21: 360–407.

Stewart, Melissa. 2018. "Understanding—and Teaching—the Five Kinds of
Nonfiction." www.slj.com/?detailStory=understanding-teaching-five-kinds
-nonfiction.

Sweet, A., and C. Snow. 2003. "Rethinking Reading Comprehension. Solving
Problems in the Teaching of Literacy." ERIC Document Reproduction Service
no. ED481439.

Szymusiak, K., and F. Sibberson. 2001. *Beyond Leveled Books: Supporting Transitional
Readers in Grades 2–5*. Portland, ME: Stenhouse.

Szymusiak, K., F. Sibberson, and L. Koch. 2008. *Beyond Leveled Books: Supporting
Early and Transitional Readers in Grades K–5*. Portland, ME: Stenhouse.

Tatum, A. 2009. *Reading for Their Life: (Re)Building the Textual Lineages of African
American Adolescent Males*. Portsmouth, NH: Heinemann.

Taylor, B., P. Pearson, D. Peterson, and M. Rodriguez. 2003. "Reading Growth in
High-Poverty Classrooms: The Influence of Teacher Practices That Encourage
Cognitive Engagement in Literacy Learning." *Elementary School Journal* 104
(1): 3–28.

Truss, L. 2006. *Eats, Shoots & Leaves: The Zero Tolerance Approach to Punctuation*.
New York: Avery.

Vosniadou, S., and A. Ortony. 1983. "The Influence of Analogy in Children's Acquisition of New Information from Text: An Exploratory Study" (Technical Report No. 281). Urbana, IL: University of Illinois Center for the Study of Reading.

Vygotsky, L. 1978. *Mind in Society: The Development of Higher Psychological Processes.* Cambridge, MA: Harvard University Press.

Walther, M. 2018. *The Ramped-Up Read-Aloud.* Thousand Oaks, CA: Corwin Press.

Wilde, S. 2000. *Miscue Analysis Made Easy: Building on Student Strengths.* Portsmouth, NH: Heinemann.

Wilhelm, J. D. 2001. *Strategic Reading: Guiding Students to Lifelong Literacy, 6–12.* Portsmouth, NH: Heinemann.

Worthy, J., and N. Roser. 2010. "Productive Sustained Reading in a Bilingual Class." In *Revisiting Silent Reading: New Directions for Teachers and Researchers*, edited by E. Hiebert and R. Reutzel. Newark, DE: International Reading Association.

Wu, Y., and S. J. Samuels. 2004. "How the Amount of Time Spent on Independent Reading Affects Reading Achievement." Paper presented at the annual convention of the International Reading Association, Reno, NV.

Zimmermann, S., and C. Hutchins. 2003. *7 Keys to Comprehension: How to Help Your Kids Read It and Get It!* New York: Harmony.

Children's Literature

Ada, A. F. 1995. *My Name Is Maria Isabel*. New York: Atheneum Books for Young Readers.

Adler, D. A. Cam Jansen series. New York: Puffin Books.

Aliki. 1986. *A Medieval Feast*. New York: HarperCollins.

Alvarez, J. 2001. *How Tia Lola Came to Stay*. New York: Yearling Books.

Ancona, G. 2014. *Capoeira: Game! Dance! Martial Art!* New York: Lee & Low Books.

Applegate, K. 2008. *Home of the Brave*. New York: Square Fish.

Arlon, P. 2018. *Farm*. New York: Scholastic.

Armstrong, W. H. 1969. *Sounder*. New York: Harper & Row.

Arnosky, J. 2008. *All About Manatees*. New York: Scholastic.

Ashley, Susan. 2004. *Bees*. New York: Gareth Stevens Publishing.

Avi. 1996. *The Barn*. New York: Avon Camelot.

———. 2012. *The True Confessions of Charlotte Doyle*. New York: Scholastic.

Baker, L. 1993. *Life in the Oceans: Animals, People, Plants*. New York: Cooper Square Press.

Ballard, R. 1993. *Finding the Titanic*. New York: Cartwheel Books.

Barrows, A. Ivy and Bean series. San Francisco: Chronicle Books.

———. 2007. *Ivy and Bean*. San Francisco: Chronicle Books.

Bateman, R. 1998. *Safari*. New York: Little, Brown and Company.

Behrens, J. 1982. *Gung Hay Fat Choy: Happy New Year*. New York: Children's Press.

Bell, S. *The Amazing Social Lives of African Elephants*. Troy, MI: Momentum.

Bennett, P. 2001. *The Natural World: Under the Ocean*. Hauppauge NY: Barron's Juveniles.

Berger, M. 2015. *Germs Make Me Sick!* New York: HarperCollins.

Berger, M., and G. Berger. *Howl! A Book About Wolves*. New York: Cartwheel Books.

Bernier-Grand, C. T. 2001. *In the Shade of the Níspero Tree*. New York: Yearling Books.

Blackstone, S. 2007. *Skip Through the Seasons*. Cambridge, MA: Barefoot Books.

Blume, J. 1972. *Tales of a Fourth Grade Nothing*. New York: Dutton.

———. 2014. *Freckle Juice*. New York: Atheneum Books for Young Readers.

Bourgeois, P. Franklin series. Toronto, ON: Kids Can Press.

Bowman, D. J. 2018. *The Navajo*. North Mankato, MN: Capstone Press.

Boyd, C. D. 1996. *Circle of Gold*. New York: Bantam Books

Bradley, K. B. 2016. *The War That Saved My Life*. New York: Puffin Books.

Brasch, N. 2004. *Dancing Around the World*. New York: Longman Books.

Brezenoff, S. 2010. Field Trip Mysteries series. North Mankato, MN: Stone Arch Books.

Bridwell, N. Clifford the Big Red Dog series. New York: Cartwheel Books.

Bulla, C. R. 1998. *The Paint Brush Kid*. New York: Random House Books for Young Readers.

Burke, M. B. 1999. *Think Like a Scientist*. Orlando, FL: Steck-Vaughn.

Butler, D. H. 2018. King & Kayla series. Atlanta: Peachtree Publishers.

Cahill, B. 2013. *Freedom of Speech and Expression*. Concord, MA: Red Chair Press.

Cameron, A. Gloria series. New York: Puffin Books.

———. 2001. *Gloria's Way*. New York: Puffin Books.

———. 2013. *The Stories Julian Tells*. New York: Tamarind.

Carlson, N. S. 1989. *The Family Under the Bridge*. New York: HarperCollins.

Carney, E. 2009. *Frogs!* Washington, DC: National Geographic Children's Books.

Carosella, M. 2011. *Founding Mothers: Women Who Shaped America*. Huntington Beach, CA: Teacher Created Materials.

Cella, C. 2012. *Earth Day (Let's Celebrate)*. North Mankato, MN: Capstone Press.

Cerullo, M. M. 2000. *The Truth About Great White Sharks*. San Francisco: Chronicle Books.

Chambers, V. 2001. *Quinceañera Means Sweet Fifteen*. Burbank, CA: Disney-Hyperion.

Cherry, L. 2000. *The Great Kapok Tree: A Tale of the Amazon Rain Forest*. Boston: HMH Books for Young Readers.

Chew, R. 2014. A Matter of Fact Magic series. New York: Random House Books for Young Readers.

Christopher, M. 2008. *The Olympics: Unforgettable Moments of the Games*. New York: Little, Brown Books for Young Readers.

Clapper, N. B. 2018. Let's Look at Countries series. North Mankato, MN: Capstone Press.

Cleary, B. Ramona series. New York: HarperCollins.

Clements, A. 2003. *The Jacket*. New York: Atheneum Books for Young Readers.

———. 2007. *Jake Drake, Bully Buster*. New York: Atheneum Books for Young Readers.

Coerr, E. 2004. *Sadako and the Thousand Paper Cranes*. New York: Puffin Books.

Cohn, J. 2012. *Hand to Paw: Protecting Animals*. Huntington Beach, CA: Teacher Created Materials.

Collard, S. B. 1999. *Animal Dazzlers: The Role of Brilliant Colors in Nature*. New York: Scholastic.

Collins, T. 2016. *Building the Great Wall of China*. North Mankato, MN: Capstone Press.

Creech, S. 2011. *Walk Two Moons*. New York: HarperCollins.

Crisp, M. 2003. *Everything Dog: What Kids Really Want to Know About Dogs*. New York: Cooper Square Publishing.

Cristaldi, K. 1992. *Baseball Ballerina*. New York: Random House Books for Young Readers.

Cromwell, S. 1997. *My First Book About the Internet*. New York: Troll Communications.

Crum, M. B. 2007. *The Power of the Wind*. Boston: Rigby.

Curtis, C. P. 1995. *The Watsons Go to Birmingham—1963*. New York: Random House.

Dahl, R. 1961. *James and the Giant Peach*. New York: Alfred E. Knopf.

———. 1964. *Charlie and the Chocolate Factory*. New York: Alfred E. Knopf.

———. 1966. *The Magic Finger*. New York: Harper & Row.

Danziger, P. Amber Brown series. New York: Puffin Books.

———. 2006. *Amber Brown Is Not a Crayon*. New York: Puffin Books.

Darling, K. 1996. *Arctic Babies*. New York: Walker & Company.

Davies, N. 2005. *One Tiny Turtle*. Somerville, MA: Candlewick Press.

———. 2009. *Extreme Animals: The Toughest Creatures on Earth*. Somerville, MA: Candlewick Press.

———. 2009. *What's Eating You? Parasites—the Inside Story*. Somerville, MA: Candlewick Press.

DeClements, B. 2008. *Nothing's Fair in Fifth Grade*. New York: Puffin Books.

DeGross, M. 1998. *Donavan's Word Jar*. New York: HarperTrophy.

dePaola, T. 1975. *The Cloud Book*. New York: Scholastic.

———. 1999. *26 Fairmount Avenue*. New York: G. P. Putnam's Sons.

DiCamillo, K. Bink and Gollie series. Somerville, MA: Candlewick Press.

———. 2000. *Because of Winn-Dixie*. Somerville, MA: Candlewick Press.

———. 2001. *The Tiger Rising*. Somerville, MA: Candlewick Press.

———. 2003. *The Tale of Despereaux*. Somerville, MA: Candlewick Press.

———. 2006. *The Miraculous Journey of Edward Tulane*. Somerville, MA: Candlewick Press.

Duffey, B. 1993. *How to Be Cool in the Third Grade*. New York: Scholastic.

Evans, L. 2008. *Tricks and Traps*. New York: Scholastic.

Fleischman, S. 2003. *The Whipping Boy*. New York: Greenwillow Books.

Fowler, A. 2001. *Antarctica*. New York: Children's Press.

———. 2010. *Inside an Ant Colony*. New York: Children's Press.

Freedman, R. 1989. *Lincoln: A Photobiography*. Boston: HMH Books for Young Readers.

———. 1995. *Immigrant Kids*. Glenview, IL: Scott Foresman.

Friedman, M. 2009. *Antarctica*. New York: Children's Press.

Friesinger, A. 1998. *Save the Manatee*. New York: Random House Books for Young Readers.

Funke, C. 2007. *Igraine the Brave*. Somerset, UK: Chicken House.

Ganeri, A. 2015. *Coming of Age Around the World*. North Mankato, MN: Heinemann-Raintree.

Gantos, J. 1998. *Joey Pigza Swallowed the Key*. New York: Farrar, Straus and Giroux.

Gardiner, J. R. 1980. *Stone Fox*. New York: Harper & Row.

George, J. C. 1959. *My Side of the Mountain*. New York: E. P. Dutton.

Gibbons, G. 1990. *Beacons of Light: Lighthouses*. New York: HarperCollins.

———. 1991. *From Seed to Plant*. New York: Holiday House.

———. 1997. *The Moon Book*. New York: Holiday House.

———. 2004. *Mummies, Pyramids, and Pharaohs: A Book About Ancient Egypt*. New York: Little, Brown Books for Young Readers.

Giff, P. R. 2004. *Pictures of Hollis Woods*. New York: Yearling Books.

Graham, I. 2009. *Planes, Rockets, and Other Flying Machines*. Brighton, UK: Book House.

Granfield, L. 2003. *America Votes: How Our President Is Elected*. Toronto, ON: Kids Can Press.

Green, D. 2009. *Astronomy: Out of this World!* New York: Kingfisher.

Greenfield, E. 1995. *Koya DeLaney and the Good Girl Blues*. New York: Scholastic.

Grimes, N. 2010. *Almost Zero*. New York: Puffin Books.

———. 2010. *Make Way for Dyamonde Daniel*. New York: Puffin Books.

———. 2011. *Planet Middle School*. New York: Bloomsbury Publishing.

———. 2016. *Garvey's Choice*. Honesdale, PA: WordSong.

Gutman, D. 2000. *Babe & Me*. New York: Scholastic.

Gutner, H. 2002. *The Chicago Fire*. New York: Scholastic.

Harvey, M. 1998. *Look What Came from Mexico*. New York: Scholastic.

Havill, J. 1986. *Jamaica's Find*. New York: Scholastic.

Hayden, K. 2001. *Horse Show*. St. Louis, MO: Turtleback Books.

Haydon, J. 2002. *15 Facts About Snakes*. Boston: Rigby.

Haywood, K. 2008. *Eagles: Endangered!* New Rochelle, NY: Benchmark Education.

Hesse, K. 1999. *Just Juice*. New York: Scholastic.

Hirschmann, K. 2004. *Ants, Bees, and Other Social Insects*. New York: Scholastic.

Holmes, J. A. 2011. *Have You Seen Duck?* New York: Scholastic.

Holmes, K. J. 1997. *Owls*. New York: Scholastic.

Hopping, L. J. 1994. *Tornadoes!* New York: Scholastic.

Horne, R., and T. Turner. 2008. *101 Things You Wish You'd Invented . . . and Some You Wish No One Had.* London, UK: Walker Children's Books.

Howe, J. Pinky and Rex series. New York: Scholastic.

———. 1979. *Bunnicula, Rabbit Tale of Mystery.* New York: Scholastic.

———. 1996. *Pinky and Rex and the Bully.* New York: Scholastic.

Hurwitz, J. Riverside Kids series. New York: HarperCollins.

———. 1981. *Baseball Fever.* New York: William Morrow and Company.

Jackson, D. M. 2014. *Extreme Scientists: Exploring Nature's Mysteries from Perilous Places.* Boston: HMH Books for Young Readers.

Jacobson, J. 2005. *Andy Shane and the Very Bossy Dolores Starbuckle.* New York: Scholastic.

Jenkins, S., and R. Page. 2008. *What Do You Do with a Tail Like This?* Boston: HMH Books for Young Readers.

Johnston, N. 1995. *Remember the Ladies: The First Women's Rights Convention.* New York: Scholastic.

Juarez, C. 2018. *Africa.* North Mankato, MN: Capstone Press.

Jules, J. Sofia Martinez series. North Mankato, MN: Picture Window Books.

Juster, N. 1961. *The Phantom Tollbooth.* New York: Random House.

Kadohata, C. 2013. *The Thing About Luck.* New York: Atheneum Books for Young Readers.

Kalman, B. 1987. *Forest Mammals.* St. Catharines, ON: Crabtree Publishing Company.

———. 1993. *Canada Celebrates Multiculturalism.* St. Catharines, ON: Crabtree Publishing Company.

Kamma, A. 2004. *If You Lived When There Was Slavery in America.* New York: Scholastic.

———. 2008. *If You Lived When Women Won Their Rights.* New York: Scholastic.

Kent D. 1993. *The Titanic.* New York: Children's Press.

King, S. 1999. *The Running Man.* New York: Signet.

Kinney, J. Diary of a Wimpy Kid series. New York: Scholastic.

Kirby, P. 1992. *Glorious Days, Dreadful Days: The Battle of Bunker Hill.* North Mankato, MN: Heinemann-Raintree.

Kirby, S. Captain Awesome series. New York: Little Simon.

Kline, S. Horrible Harry series. New York: Puffin Books.

———. 2017. *Horrible Harry and the Birthday Girl.* New York: Puffin Books.

Konigsburg, E. L. 1967. *From the Mixed-Up Files of Mrs. Basil E. Frankweiler.* New York: Atheneum Books for Young Readers.

Krishnaswami, U. 2011. *The Grand Plan to Fix Everything.* New York: Atheneum Books.

———. 2016. *Book Uncle and Me.* Toronto, ON: Groundwood Books.

Kroll, S. 1994. *Lewis & Clark: Explorers of the American West.* New York: Holiday House.

Kudlinski, K. V. 2005. *Boy, Were We Wrong About Dinosaurs!* New York: Scholastic.

Kunhardt, E. 1987. *Pompeii . . . Buried Alive!* New York: Scholastic.

Lai, T. 2011. *Inside Out and Back Again.* New York: HarperCollins.

Landau, E. 2003. *The Civil Rights Movement in America.* New York: Children's Press.

Lasky, K. 2000. *Interrupted Journey: Saving Endangered Sea Turtles.* New York: Scholastic.

Lattimore, E. F. Little Pear series. Boston: Houghton Mifflin Harcourt.

Lauber, P. 1986. *Volcano: The Eruption and Healing of Mount St. Helens.* New York: Simon and Schuster.

———. 1994. *Who Eats What? Food Chains and Food Webs.* New York: HarperCollins.

———. 1996. *Hurricanes: Earth's Mightiest Storms.* Boston: Houghton Mifflin.

Leaf, M. 1936. *The Story of Ferdinand*. New York: Viking Press.

Le Guin, U. K. 2003. *Catwings*. New York: Orchard Books.

L'Engle, M. 1962. *A Wrinkle in Time*. New York: Farrar, Straus and Giroux.

Lenihan, M. *Rescuing Stranded Whales*. New York: Pearson.

Levin, A. 2015. *Bears*. North Mankato, MN: Capstone Press.

Lewin, T. 2003. *Lost City: The Discovery of Machu Picchu*. New York: Puffin Books.

Lewis, C. S. 1950. *The Lion, the Witch, and the Wardrobe*. New York: Macmillan.

Lin, G. Ling & Ting series. New York: Little, Brown and Company.

———. 2007. *The Year of the Dog*. New York: Little, Brown and Company

———. 2009. *Where the Mountain Meets the Moon*. New York: Little, Brown Books for Young Readers.

Lindgren, A. 1950. *Pippi Longstocking*. New York: Viking Press.

Lobel, A. Frog and Toad Series. New York: HarperTrophy.

———. 1979. *Days with Frog and Toad*. New York: HarperTrophy.

Lombard, J. 2006. *Drita, My Homegirl*. New York: Scholastic.

Look, L. Alvin Ho series. New York: Yearling Books.

Lord, B. B. 1984. *In the Year of the Boar and Jackie Robinson*. New York: Harper Row & Publishers.

Lord, C. 2008. *Rules*. New York: Scholastic.

Lowry. L. 1989. *Number the Stars*. New York: Bantam Books.

———. 1993. *The Giver*. Boston: Houghton Mifflin.

MacLulich, C. 2005. *Insects*. New York: Scholastic.

Maloof, T. 2015. *Extreme Weather*. Huntington Beach, CA: Teacher Created Materials.

———. 2017. *Abolitionists: What We Need Is Action*. Huntington Beach, CA: Teacher Created Materials.

Manes, S. 1982. *Be a Perfect Person in Just Three Days!* New York: Scholastic.

Manushkin, F. Katie Woo series. North Mankato, MN: Picture Window Books.

Markle, S. 2008. *Animal Heroes: True Rescue Stories*. Minneapolis, MN: Millbrook Press.

Marsh, L. 2010. *Amazing Animal Journeys*. Washington, DC: National Geographic Readers.

Marshall, J. Fox series. New York: Penguin Young Readers.

Martin, A. M. 1988. *The Baby-Sitters Club*. New York: Scholastic.

Martin, P. A. F. 2003. *Manatees*. New York: Children's Press.

Marx, T. 2008. *Everglades Forever: Restoring America's Great Wetlands*. New York: Lee & Low Books.

McClosky, K. 2016. *The Real Poop on Pigeons*. New York: TOON Books.

McDaniel, M. 2011. *The Industrial Revolution*. New York: Children's Press.

McDonald, M. Judy Moody series. Somerville, MA: Candlewick Press.

———. 2010. *Judy Moody Saves the World!* Somerville, MA: Candlewick Press.

McKissack, P. 2006. *Abby Takes a Stand*. New York: Puffin Books.

McNeese, T. 2003. *The Challenger Disaster*. New York. Children's Press.

Meadows, D. 2009. *Trixie the Halloween Fairy*. New York: Scholastic.

Medearis, A. S. 1996. *The Spray-Paint Mystery*. New York: Scholastic.

Milton, J. 1994. *Big Cats*. New York: Penguin Young Readers.

Minarik, E. H. The Little Bear series. New York: HarperTrophy.

Mohr, N. 1999. *Felita*. New York: Puffin Books.

Montgomery, L. B. Milo and Jazz Mysteries series. Minneapolis, MN: Kane Press.

Morrison, Y. 2007. *Earth Matters*. New York: Scholastic.

Myers, W. D. 1992. *The Righteous Revenge of Artemis Bonner*. New York: HarperTrophy.

———. 2001. *Handbook for Boys*. New York: HarperTrophy.

Naidoo, B. 1986. *Journey to Jo'burg: A South African Story*. New York: HarperTrophy.

Naylor, P. R. 1991. *Shiloh*. New York: Bantam Books.

Nelson, K. 2011. *Heart and Soul: The Story of America and African Americans*. New York: HarperCollins.

Newman, S. 2010. *Ancient Greece*. New York: Scholastic.

Niz, E. S. Our Physical World series. North Mankato, MN: Capstone Press.

Noble, T. H. 1980. *The Day Jimmy's Boa Ate the Wash*. New York: Puffin Books.

Nuzzolo, D. 2008. *Bull Sharks*. North Mankato, MN: Capstone Press.

O'Brien, R. C. 1971. *Mrs. Frisby and the Rats of NIMH*. New York: Atheneum.

O'Dell, S. 2010. *Island of the Blue Dolphins*. Boston: HMH Books for Young Readers.

Omoth, T. 2017. *Cuban Immigrants: In Their Shoes*. Troy, MI: Momentum.

Orwell, G. 1950. *1984*. New York: Signet.

Osborn, M. P. Magic Tree House series. New York: Random House Books for Young Readers.

Otto, C. B. 2001. *Shadows*. New York: Scholastic.

Parish, P. Amelia Bedelia series. New York: HarperCollins.

Park, L. S. 2006. *Archer's Quest*. New York: Yearling Books.

Paterson, K. 1977. *Bridge to Terabithia*. New York: Thomas Y. Crowell Company.

———. 1978. *The Great Gilly Hopkins*. New York: Thomas Y. Crowell Company.

Paulsen, G. 2006. *Hatchet*. New York: Simon & Schuster Books for Young Readers.

Pennypacker, S. Clementine series. Burbank, CA: Disney-Hyperion.

———. Stuart series. New York: Scholastic.

———. 2005. *Stuart Goes to School*. New York: Scholastic.

———. 2008. *The Talented Clementine*. Burbank, CA: Disney-Hyperion.

Pfeffer, W. 2003. *Wiggling Worms at Work*. New York: HarperCollins.

———. 2016. *Sounds All Around*. New York: HarperCollins.

Philbrick, R. 1993. *Freak the Mighty*. New York: Scholastic.

Pilkey, D. Captain Underpants series. New York: Scholastic.

———. Ricky Ricotta's Mighty Robot series. New York: Scholastic.

Platt, R. 2008. *Moon Landing*. London: Walker Children's Books.

Preszler, J. 2006. *Diwali: Hindu Festival of Lights*. North Mankato, MN: Capstone Press.

Prior, J. O. 2014. *America's Natural Landmarks*. Huntington Beach, CA: Teacher Created Materials.

Prokos, A. 2007. *Guilty by a Hair! Real-Life DNA Matches*. New York: Children's Press.

Quinlan, S. E. 2009. *Puffins*. Minneapolis, MN: Lerner Publications.

Raatma, L. 2016. *Caring*. North Mankato, MN: Capstone Press.

Reed, J. 2002. *Penguins*. New York: Scholastic.

Ride, S. 1986. *To Space and Back*. New York: HarperCollins.

Riggs, K. 2011. *Amazing Animals: Elephants*. North Mankato, MN: Creative Paperbacks.

Riordan, R. 2006. *The Lightning Thief*. Burbank, CA: Disney-Hyperion.

Rissman, R. 2012. *Ants*. North Mankato, MN: Heinemann-Raintree.

Rivera, A. *Inclined Planes*. Rocky River, OH: Kaeden.

Robbins, K. 2006. *Pumpkins*. New York: Roaring Brook Press.

Roberts, C. 2017. *Refugees and Migrants*. Hauppauge, NY: Barron's Educational Series.

Robinson, F. 1999. *A Dinosaur Named Sue: The Find of the Century*. New York: Cartwheel Books.

———. 2000. *Fantastic Frogs!* New York: Cartwheel Books.

Rounds, G. 1995. *Sod Houses on the Great Plains*. New York: Holiday House.

Rowling, J. K. Harry Potter series. New York: Scholastic.

———. 1997. *Harry Potter and the Sorcerer's Stone*. New York: Scholastic.

Roy, R. A to Z Mysteries series. New York: Random House.

Ruffin, F. E. 2000. *Martin Luther King, Jr. and the March on Washington*. New York: Penguin Young Readers.

Rushby, P. 2000. *Different Homes Around the World*. Boston: Rigby.

Rustad, M. E. H. 2011. *Ants and Aphids Work Together*. North Mankato, MN: Capstone Press.

Ryan, P. M. 1999. *Amelia and Eleanor Go for a Ride*. New York: Scholastic.

———. 2005. *Becoming Naomi León*. New York: Scholastic.

Rylant, C. Henry and Mudge series. New York: Aladdin.

———. Mr. Putter and Tabby series. Boston: Harcourt Trade.

———. Poppleton series. New York: Scholastic.

———. 1995. *Gooseberry Park*. New York: Scholastic.

Sachar, L. Marvin Redpost series. New York: Random House.

———. 1987. *There's a Boy in the Girls' Bathroom*. New York: Alfred A. Knopf.

———. 1993. *Marvin Redpost: Why Pick on Me?* New York: Random House.

———. 1998. *Holes*. New York: Random House.

Scieszka, J. 1991. *The Time Warp Trio: Knights of the Kitchen Table*. New York: Penguin.

Scott, J. 2012. *Wild Wetlands*. New York: Scholastic.

Selsam, M. 1992. *How Kittens Grow*. New York: Scholastic.

Seuling, B. 2004. *Robert and the Triple Rotten Day*. New York: Scholastic.

Sharmat, M. W. Nate the Great series. New York: Yearling Books.

———. 1983. *Nate the Great and the Snowy Trail*. New York: Yearling Books.

Short, J., J. Green, and B. Bird. 1997. *Platypus*. New York: Mondo Publishing.

Sill, C. 2012. *About Habitats: Oceans*. Atlanta, GA: Peachtree Publishers.

Simon, S. 1997. *Lightning*. New York: HarperCollins.

———. 2004. *Cool Cars*. New York: Scholastic.

———. 2006. *Horses*. New York: HarperCollins.

———. 2008. *The Human Body*. New York: HarperCollins.

Smith, R. 1990. *Sea Otter Rescue: The Aftermath of an Oil Spill*. New York: Puffin Books.

Smith, R. K. 2006. *Chocolate Fever*. New York: Bantam Books.

Soto, G. 1991. *Taking Sides*. Boston: Harcourt Trade.

Speare, E. G. 1958. *The Witch of Blackbird Pond*. Boston: Houghton Mifflin.

Spinelli, J. 1991. *Fourth Grade Rats*. New York: Scholastic.

———. 1996. *Crash*. New York: Alfred A Knopf.

———. 1997. *Wringer*. New York: HarperTrophy.

———. 2002. *Loser*. New York: HarperCollins.

———. 2002. *Stargirl*. New York: Ember.

Stamper, J. B. 2002. *America's Symbols*. Riverside, NJ: Newbridge Communications.

Staniford, L. 2016. *Firefighters to the Rescue Around the World*. North Mankato, MN: Heinemann-Raintree.

Steele, P. 1993. *Factory Through the Ages*. Mahwah, NJ: Troll Communications.

Steinbeck, J. 1939. *The Grapes of Wrath*. New York: Viking Press.

Stewart, D. 2000. *You Wouldn't Want to Be an Egyptian Mummy! Disgusting Things You'd Rather Not Know*. New York: Franklin Watts.

Stewart, M. 2006. *Energy in Motion*. New York: Children's Press.

———. 2011. *Deadliest Animals*. Washington, DC: National Geographic Children's Books.

———. 2015. *Meteors*. Washington, DC: National Geographic Children's Books.

St. George, J. 2005. *So You Want to Be an Inventor?* New York: Puffin Books.

Stille, D. R. 2000. *Tropical Rain Forests*. New York: Children's Press.

Stilton, G. Geronimo Stilton series. New York: Scholastic.

Stockdale, S. 2008. *Fabulous Fishes*. Atlanta, GA: Peachtree Publishers.

Stone, L. M. 1985. *Endangered Animals*. New York: Scholastic.

Strom, L. 2007. *Caught with a Catch: Poaching in Africa*. New York: Children's Press.

Tafolla, C. 2010. *Fiesta Babies*. New York: Tricycle Press.

Takmar, M. 2004. *Busy Bees*. Boston: HMH Books for Young Readers.

Tayleur, K. 2014. David Mortimore Baxter series. North Mankato, MN: Stone Arch Books.

Taylor, M. D. 1976. *Roll of Thunder, Hear My Cry*. New York: Penguin Group.

———. 1987. *The Gold Cadillac*. New York: Puffin Books.

Taylor-Butler, C. 2008. *The Digestive System*. New York: Children's Press.

Temple, F. 1992. *Taste of Salt: A Story of Modern Haiti*. New York: HarperCollins.

Thaler, M. Black Lagoon Adventures series. New York: Scholastic.

Thiessen, M. 2016. *Extreme Wildlife: Smoke Jumpers, High-Tech Gear, Survival Tactics, and the Extraordinary Science of Fire*. Washington, DC: National Geographic Children's Books.

Thimmesh, C. 2002. *Girls Think of Everything: Stories of Ingenious Inventions by Women*. Boston: HMH Books for Young Readers.

Thomson, S. L. 2009. *Where Do Polar Bears Live?* New York: HarperCollins.

Trueit, T. S. 2003. *Earthquakes*. London: Franklin Watts.

Van Leeuwen, J. Oliver and Amanda series. New York: Penguin Young Readers.

various. Detecting Disasters series. Mendota Heights, MN: Focus Readers.

various. Explore the Biomes series. North Mankato, MN: Capstone Press.

various. One World, Many Countries series. North Mankato, MN: The Child's World, Inc.

various. Reading Expeditions series. Washington, DC: National Geographic School Publishers.

Walsh, M. 2012. *10 Things I Can Do to Help My World*. Somerville, MA: Candlewick.

Waters, J. 2002. *All Kinds of People: What Makes Us Different*. North Mankato, MN: Compass Point Books.

Waters, K. 2008. *Hurricanes and Tornadoes*. New York: Scholastic.

We Are What We Do. 2010. *31 Ways to Change the World*. Somerville, MA: Candlewick Press.

Weeks, S. 2008. *Oggie Cooder*. New York: Scholastic.

Weeks, S., and G. Varadarajan. 2016. *Save Me a Seat*. New York: Scholastic.

Weiss, E. 2009. *The Sense of Taste*. New York: Children's Press.

Werther, S. P. 2002. *The Donner Party*. New York: Children's Press.

White, E. B. 2006. *Charlotte's Web*. New York: HarperCollins.

Wirth, C. 2002. *At 1600 Pennsylvania Avenue*. New York: Scholastic.

Wood, L. 2010. *Bats*. New York: Scholastic.

Woodson, J. 1991. *Last Summer with Maizon*. New York: Puffin Books.

———. 2003. *Locomotion*. New York: Puffin Books.

Yang, G. L., and M. Holmes. 2015. *Secret Coders*. New York: First Second.

Yardi, R. 2016. *The Midnight War of Mateo Martinez*. Minneapolis, MN: Carolrhoda Books.

Yee, L. 2011. *Warp Speed*. New York: Scholastic.

Yee, W. H. 2008. *A Brand-New Day with Mouse and Mole*. New York: Sandpiper.

Yep, L. 1975. *Dragonwings*. New York: Harper & Row.

York, V. 2010. *Play Ball!* New York: Scholastic.

Zemser, A. B. 1998. *Beyond the Mango Tree*. New York: Greenwillow Books.

Ziefert, H. 2014. *You Can't Taste a Pickle with Your Ear: A Book About Your 5 Senses*. Maplewood, NJ: Blue Apple Books.

Index

C

M

N